ICE IN THEIR VEINS

Praise for *Ice in Their Veins*

"An enlightening deep dive into the rich history of women's hockey. From those who won gold medals, to the women who never had the chance, *Ice in Their Veins* brings to life the collaborative journey to play the game we love, and build a brighter future."

CAMMI GRANATO, Hockey Hall of Fame member, Assistant General Manager of the NHL's Vancouver Canucks, Olympic gold medalist

"While hockey is riddled with what seems like insurmountable roadblocks and steeped with disturbing cultural barriers, the real-life narratives shared in this book speak to the sheer courage of the women who persisted just because they *loved* the sport. Truths are revealed about gender inequality, the need to compete, the desire to be validated and how egotistical control can harm others. This compilation of well researched and widely unknown stories provides a better understanding of how the accumulated efforts of these brave hockey pioneers have created a pathway forward for *all* women."

BERNICE CARNEGIE, Co-founder, The Carnegie Initiative and the Herbert H. Carnegie Future Aces Foundation, international speaker, author, and storyteller

"Ian has gone into great detail as a historian of the game to set the record straight: women have always been a leading force in the growth of hockey globally. *Ice in Their Veins* is an important collection of stories from hockey's forgotten history, honoring many heroes who deserve praise for their generations of work growing our game so it could one day flourish."

ANGELA RUGGIERO, Hockey Hall of Fame member, Olympic gold medalist and World Champion, Founder of Sports Innovation Lab

"The definitive history of the women's game, interwoven with Kennedy's touching personal story. As with all of his writing, Ian brings passion, dedication, and incredible research to honor the trailblazers and underrated stars of women's hockey history."

RYAN KENNEDY, Editor in Chief, *The Hockey News*

"Kennedy hits the mark in delivering powerful and inspirational stories of overcoming obstacles and triumph of the history of women in hockey. You can feel the passion for the game in this book. *Ice in Their Veins* is a must-read and a book that will leave you inspired."

NATALIE DARWITZ, Hockey Hall of Fame member, Team USA World Champion, PWHL Walter Cup champion

ICE IN THEIR VEINS

Women's Relentless Pursuit of the Puck

IAN KENNEDY

TIDEWATER
PRESS

Published by Tidewater Press
New Westminster, BC, Canada
tidewaterpress.ca

978-1-990160-42-4 (print)
978-1-990160-43-1 (e-book)

LIBRARY AND ARCHIVES CANADA CATALOGUING IN PUBLICATION
Title: Ice in their veins : women's relentless pursuit of the puck / Ian Kennedy.
Names: Kennedy, Ian (Ian D.), author.
Description: Includes bibliographical references and index.
Identifiers: Canadiana (print) 20240471148 | Canadiana (ebook) 20240473795 | ISBN 9781990160424
(softcover) | ISBN 9781990160431 (EPUB)
Subjects: LCSH: Hockey for women—History. | LCSH: Women hockey players—History. | LCSH: Hockey—
Social aspects.
Classification: LCC GV848.6.W65 K46 2024 | DDC 796.962082—dc23

Cover illustration: Corwin Dickson

Canadä

Tidewater Press gratefully acknowledges the support of the Government of Canada.

PRINTED IN CANADA

To Ezra and Stephanie, the women who inspire me daily.
And to Mern, whose story started this all.

Contents

Author's Note

These stories are not mine. They belong to the women who fought for their space, forged new paths, and created, against unrelenting opposition, a future in hockey for generations of women and girls to come. I hope this text serves to preserve their history and provides even an ounce of the much-deserved and long-overdue credit they are owed. I also hope this book highlights the many barriers and misogynistic beliefs women and girls have faced and continue to face today—in sports and in society.

Today, we are still using the term "pioneer" to describe women in the sport. In many ways, this is true but, more often, it erases those who came before, whose stories lay concealed on dusty shelves or have been expunged altogether.

Unless otherwise indicated, quotes are drawn from firsthand interviews. Quotes from other publications have been reproduced exactly as printed in their original form, regardless of modern styles or usage.

I've placed myself in this story not only as part of the problem, but also as a non-conforming participant who was impacted by the harmful definitions of masculinity I was taught within hockey. The future of women's hockey has never been brighter, and as we continue to collaboratively build this future, it's important we recognize and honor the women and girls who played when they were told not to, who organized, fought, planned, and above all, loved this game. They were and are the foundation on which the current and future success of women's hockey stands.

No One Had Done It Before Us
FOREWORD BY GERALDINE HEANEY

They've kind of been forgotten about, the early women and early accomplishments in women's hockey.

I was born in Ireland in 1967. It was the year of Canada's Centennial, and as I now know, the first year of two of women's hockey's biggest tournaments—the Lipstick Tournament in Wallaceburg and the Canadettes Tournament in Brampton.

When we immigrated from Ireland to Canada, my dad came first to get settled. We didn't have relatives here, and it was a big decision for them just to leave, but they wanted to get out because of all of the troubles in Ireland at the time—just for a better life for us and themselves—so my dad came over first.

My parents had never heard of hockey or seen this game before. When my mom brought us over six months later—there were three of us at the time—we got settled into the house, and my dad, on Saturday night, would say, "Okay we've got to put the hockey game on, this is what they do in Canada, they watch *Hockey Night in Canada*." My mom looked at it and was like, "This is what they do here?"

My parents didn't know the game, none of us knew the game, but back then, everybody was out playing street hockey on the road. Eventually, my brothers started playing on the ice. I'd always be at the rink, and when they played on the road, I'd play with them. They toughened me up a lot. They didn't treat me any differently than the boys on the road. I usually got stuck in net at first. One street would play the other street. Eventually they'd see I was a girl, and they wouldn't like it when I was in net because they couldn't score. It was just what we did; it was what Canadians did.

But I was sick and tired of playing on the road, I wanted to play on the ice. I kept asking my dad, "Why can't I play?"

My parents never told me I couldn't play. That was one of the biggest things, because a lot of the parents at the time would say, "No, girls don't play hockey." I remember hearing that a lot. We used to go on school trips to the rink for pleasure skating, and I would go with my hockey skates. Everyone would say, "Why are you wearing boy skates?" They weren't hockey skates, they were boy's skates. I just hung out with the boys and played any sport. There was a lot being said behind the scenes, but I just ignored it and did my thing. For myself and all the girls in my generation, we really taught ourselves. We were out on outdoor rinks and figured it out ourselves. We had a neighbor—he was Italian and they had a bocce ball court with the boards and all. That court would become our ice rink. We couldn't wait until March break when we would play down there on the bocce ball court and we'd hit each other over the boards into the snowbanks. It was the best rink.

At the time, girls couldn't play hockey with the boys; they weren't allowed to. But my dad kept looking and looking for a place for me to play because I kept bugging him. Then he saw an advertisement in the newspaper and he found me a team.

I spent almost twenty years playing for the Toronto Aeros. It was the only place I saw women's hockey growing up. When I was out in the street, I'd always pretend I was Darryl Sittler, and watching the Olympics I would always think I'd love to go, but it crossed my mind that I'd do it in ice hockey. I know they always talk about the women's game and how it's taken so long to get where it is—it has, but I never thought I'd be around for it.

Growing up, we played everywhere, including traveling to the Lipstick Tournament in Wallaceburg. I remember always looking forward to that tournament as a kid.

In 1987, I was playing hockey at Seneca College and for the Aeros when, all of a sudden, my coach at Seneca started talking about a world championship. Of course, it wasn't sanctioned but I was just happy to get an opportunity to play. After one nation dropped out, they added Mississauga as Team Ontario, which was going to be the host team. They were allowed some pickups and Lee Trempe, my coach at Seneca who also coached Mississauga, picked me up to play in that tournament. Angela James was also on that Team Ontario roster.

It was amazing to see Team Canada, the national champion Hamilton Golden Hawks. I always looked up to that team. They'd win all the time with Cathy Phillips and Marian Coveny. We were only Team Ontario, and I wanted to be on that other team, just to wear the Team Canada jersey.

At that tournament though, I just thought, "Wow, what an opportunity to play other countries." I was still getting to play and it was the start of the growth of the women's game internationally. No one had done it before us.

It was Team Ontario and Canada in the final. Canada beat us 4-0, but I remember beating the USA 5–4 in the semis, which was probably an upset at the time. There were a lot of girls on that team who never got recognized for what they've done for the women's game.

Going into 1990, there was going to be an official Women's World Championship. The tryouts were open to anyone; they didn't have the people to go out and recruit in those times. They had regional tryouts, then they cut it down to provincial tryouts. There were sacrifices we had to make—we paid to go there and took the time off work.

I wasn't even a Canadian citizen at the time. I'd been there all my life; I just wasn't born in Canada. I had to rush and get my citizenship. It happened just in time, and I got to play. Angela was on the team, Cathy Phillips, Vicky Sunohara, Shirley Cameron played, and we won gold.

I believe everything is about timing. After that first World Championship, we made it to the first Olympics in 1998, a lot of firsts. In 2002, I was part of the Canadian team that won gold at the Salt Lake City Olympic Games.

Years later, it was timing and a former teammate that brought me back to women's hockey. In 2022, my daughter was going off to university. My son was still playing hockey, but I'd decided to step away from coaching his AAA team to let him go off on his own. When Angela James called, I started laughing, saying, "I was thinking about taking a year off." Then she told me about this opportunity, and it was one I couldn't turn down. It just seemed like the right time and right fit.

I became the new head coach for the Premier Hockey Federation's Toronto Six. In my first season, we accomplished more firsts. We were the first team to ever pay a woman six figures to play professional hockey. When the season ended, we were the first Canadian team ever to win an Isobel Cup. Everything we'd worked for since I started playing was becoming a reality. Of course, things changed, and now a new league, a new chapter in women's hockey has begun with the PWHL. It's an exciting time for women in professional hockey, and more firsts and accomplishments will follow for years to come.

The opportunity just to see where the women's game has come since I started playing, it's incredible. I got to win Olympic and World Championship gold medals, and I had the honor to be one of the first women, alongside Angela and Cammi Granato, to be inducted into the IIHF Hall of Fame, and to be the third woman ever inducted into the Hockey Hall of Fame in 2013.

When we came to Canada, hockey was new, but the whole family fell in love with the game.

Women and girls were told hockey wasn't for them, that we weren't welcome. But we played anyway and we found ways. The truth is, hockey has always been a game for women, and it always will be.

Introduction

I grew up in a small town bisected by the Sydenham River that, each winter, would be covered with boots and skates. Bordering the acres of farmland were drainage ditches and creeks that became frozen paths, creating outdoor rinks. I started playing hockey when I was six. At the same time, my sister enrolled in figure skating. As I got older, I often attended power skating lessons at Wallaceburg Memorial Arena before school, even after I moved to play AAA with the Chatham-Kent Cyclones. I spent hours lying on my stomach on our living room floor organizing and reading the backs of hockey cards, flipping pages of *The Hockey News* magazine, and devouring any information about the sport I could. Each Christmas, I'd receive hockey almanacs and stats books, fables of hockey history. In Grade 6, I stepped on stage at my elementary school and delivered my speech about the Stanley Cup. I was obsessed and wanted to know as much about this game as possible.

Those hours and days spent pouring over hockey history, however, never involved women. The first woman I saw represented was Manon Rheaume who, in 1992 (when I was eight years old), played a period of preseason hockey with the NHL's Tampa Bay Lightning.

Decades later, I stumbled across a newspaper article about the first unofficial international women's hockey tournament. Attached was a photo of Marian Coveny. The article said she was Team Canada's first-ever captain. When I delved deeper, I was shocked to learn Coveny and I had something in common: we were both from Wallaceburg, a town of roughly 10,000 people approximately an hour east of Detroit and three hours southwest of Toronto.

I asked my parents about Coveny. They remembered her and her athletic prowess; she and my mom shared classes in high school. But neither knew of her historic role in Canadian hockey history. From that moment on, I was hooked. I tried to learn as much as I could about this woman who, had she been a man, would have had her name on signs entering our town and an arena named after her. Soon, I found myself captivated by the untold stories of many other women in hockey.

To uncover Coveny's accomplishments, I spent afternoons donning white gloves and sifting through stacks of old newspapers in our small-town museum. Her stories, and the stories of women like her, remain buried on shelves and on microfiche in library cabinets. They're often only snippets, footnotes below men's hockey stories, almost always lacking detail, and usually written in a way that diminishes, mocks, or dismisses the achievements of these women.

As I continued to read old copies of our local newspapers, I found they were filled with stories about the town's junior team, the Wallaceburg Lakers, which I'd eventually go on to captain. But, around Valentine's Day each year, men's hockey would give way to pages of coverage dedicated to an annual women's hockey event, dubbed the Lipstick Tournament. As I'd come to learn, the Lipstick Tournament was significant in the growth of women's hockey in North America, serving as a meeting ground and catalyst for the rebirth of competitive women's hockey in Canada and the United States. It was even considered the North American women's hockey championship. I'd been oblivious to the existence of women's hockey until I was a teenager, as well as to the Lipstick Tournament in my own hometown. It was a blind spot I set out to rectify, and I planned to start with Canada's first captain.

When I took to the internet, I quickly found Coveny's name, but not in the anticipated places. There were almost no news articles and even less information about her hockey career aside from the 1987 World Women's Hockey Tournament. Instead, I found her name on Caring Bridge, a website designed for individuals with medical conditions, typically those battling terminal illnesses, to communicate their story with friends and family. I looked at the names commenting and built up the confidence to reach out. I found Coveny's contact and set up an interview. Battling Stage 4 pancreatic cancer, communication was difficult, so I conducted the interview through her wife, Deb. Next, I reached out to her former Canadian teammates, Pat White and Sharon Sanderson, team manager Jackie Hughes, and Ontario Women's Hockey Association (OWHA) president Fran Rider. They all praised Coveny as an unheralded hero.

I typed the story and submitted it to *The Hockey News*. It was a dream come true for me to be published in this magazine, a publication I'd read and collected since I was a child. The issue was scheduled to come out in late January 2022. The holidays passed and the new year came, then, on January 6, my phone buzzed with a notification from Caring Bridge that Marian Coveny had passed away at age sixty-seven, only weeks before her story was set to reintroduce her to the hockey world. She never read it, but her wife would, her friends would, and her family would. It was read at her funeral, part of her eulogy. She received some of the recognition she so deserved.

Coveny's time should have been decades before. She should have been a household name in hockey, but women weren't supposed to succeed. At least that's what I'd been told, that "hockey is a man's game." And I believed it. I don't anymore, and haven't for a long time, but for much of my life I believed women like Coveny had no place in hockey. I believed women had a role in this world that did not involve professional sport. That space was mine; it was for men like me. I'm embarrassed to write those words, but they're true.

I grew up loving hockey, absorbing any form of the game I could, whether it was my own on-ice play, books, hockey cards, attending games as a fan, watching it on television, road hockey in our shed, or mini-sticks on the kitchen floor. I didn't know women played hockey, and to be completely honest, if someone had asked, I'd almost certainly have told them that women didn't belong in hockey.

Or perhaps that's a misrepresentation. Over time, moving through AAA hockey to Junior, I began to struggle. I lived in a world of cognitive dissonance. I loved playing the game, and in my final few seasons, once I'd moved to a new city to play, I loved my teammates. But overall, I fell out of love with the game for what it had done to me as a person; for the inner turmoil it caused as I tried desperately to fit into a world I felt completely uncomfortable in. The culture did something to me. It hurt me. It made me complicit. My hockey world was one where the primary focus of teams was the conquest of women, plus an endless cycle of drugs and alcohol. There was hazing, sometimes severe and sexual. There was fighting. We were taught what it meant to be masculine in hockey by unethical and vile men who preached the necessity of indoctrinating new generations with misogynist ideas. If you cried, if you failed, if you did not throw your body into harm's way, if you did not take every opportunity to exploit a woman, you were a "pussy," and you were told to stop "playing like a girl." You were told that if you excelled, if you rose through the ranks, that women were your reward and that rules did not apply.

At home, at church, at work, and in school, I was taught the hierarchy of gender. I was taught that, as a man, I was to be a leader, a protector, a provider, stoic and reliable, aggressive in what I wanted, unrelenting and brave. I was taught to rule with authority because of the sex a doctor assigned to me at birth. In hockey, I viewed women as secondary, as a group who could take the leftovers. Writing these words makes me sad. And I realize I'm still on a very long journey where I regularly fail to live in opposition to these ideas.

In Canada there is a Good Samaritan Act that protects bystanders who attempt to help. But I didn't help. I was afraid to help because I knew it would end my playing career and I would be ostracized. I'd be an outcast in the hockey world. So I lived for the freedom of being on the ice and dreaded the times in locker rooms, on bus rides, and at team parties. I developed anxiety and eventually, I recognize now, I started living with depression.

Over the decades that preceded stepping into a dream role with *The Hockey News*, I'd lost my love for hockey except for the skill, the skating, the feeling of scoring a goal. Ironically, it was women's hockey that helped bring back my love of the game. When I was twenty-four, I started coaching high school girls' hockey and, for the first time, saw the passion women and girls had for the game firsthand. I also saw the inequities, things I'd received readily that weren't available to these women. I came from a privileged experience, one where I'd never considered if my equipment would fit my body, if I could find a stick with the right flex, if my team would have ice time, or a league to play in. I saw my idols, the Steve Yzermans of the world, lift Stanley Cups, and sign multi-million-dollar contracts. I dreamed openly about a future that could involve professional hockey. As a coach, I quickly realized we chose our ice times after the boys' team had scheduled their games and practices. When I joined a new team as head coach, we had to share jerseys with a boys' team, but the boys' captains chose their jerseys first, so the captains of the girls' team had to settle for whatever number the boy had chosen. When it came time to travel, the boys' team got a new bus and a trailer for their equipment. We jammed our equipment in beside us in a bus without heat.

This time, I wasn't prepared to sit and watch. I demanded our team got our own jerseys, and we did. Buses and ice time were soon divided equally, and with those tiny changes came monumental leaps in the way our women's team viewed themselves. Through my coaching, something else changed too. From the hurt and scars inflicted on me by trying to conform to the masculinity that hockey had defined for me as a youth, something blossomed. I fell in love with the game again.

When I started writing critically about the sport, whether it was for *The Hockey News*, *Yahoo Sports*, *The Guardian*, *The Globe and Mail*, or *Toronto Star*, and making television and radio appearances with TSN, Sportsnet, CBC, CTV, and other networks, I found myself talking about, and writing about this harmful culture, sharing my experiences and embracing the outsider role I'd feared as a player.

I came to realize, however, even in that discomfort, that I was still a man in hockey, and that fact alone gave me more access and opportunity, even while challenging every aspect of the game, than women who were far more knowledgeable and accomplished than I was. Growing up, I'd felt like an outsider on the inside, but through the process of writing about Marian Coveny and interviewing her teammates and other pioneering women in the game, something else happened. I was welcomed in. I found myself writing about women's hockey and devouring every aspect of the game just as I had as a kid. Of course, I'd known about Hayley Wickenheiser and Cammi Granato. I'd watched women's hockey every four years at the Olympics, cheering Canada on for gold. But this was different. My love for the welcoming and passionate world of women's hockey replaced the sour taste of men's hockey. Women's hockey has had its own issues, but most of those were created at the hands of people like me, men who thought they owned a game, who gatekept, who demeaned, who openly discriminated.

In this story, the women involved certainly had ice in their veins, rising against all adversity. I, on the other hand, played freely, never questioning why women were kept from the sport. I conformed and laughed at the sexist jokes. I learned many of them. I saw teammates having sex; I heard them bragging about it with coaches and players. I drank until I blacked out. I laughed when players were forced to wear dresses with strings tied to the front, older veterans holding the string to lift those dresses at a party, exposing their genitals. I feared my turn playing Twister in my jock strap on a lubricated mat in the middle of a circle while veterans threw drinks at us and mocked. The game hurt me, and in turn, I played my role in hurting others, in excluding others. Until I was twenty-four, I never considered my role. And when I did, I felt waves of guilt.

Today, I don't watch much men's hockey, but I love the women's game. I spend my days happily writing about the past and present, and doing what I can to promote the sport, so that the cycle ends with this generation. So that little girls, and little boys, see themselves in the sport, and know that women can play professional hockey, that women belong in sport, and that there is a history of women who fought for their place, and a history of men who fought to hold them back. Without knowing this history, by pretending that women haven't played this game for as long as men, we risk perpetuating the same stereotypes and the same harm I was taught. Decades later, I'm still not there. I'm not the husband, or dad I want to be. I'm not always the advocate or ally others need. And when I place myself in this story, as I have, I know that my life has contributed to the problem.

CHAPTER 1

Lady-in-Waiting

During my second year at Western University, I took a course called Social Foundations of Sport. The old white man slated to be our professor, who smelled remarkably of cheap liquor, walked in the first day, steadied himself behind the lectern, stared out at the room of kinesiology students and stated emphatically that women's sports were not real. Real sports were played by the best athletes in the world, who were men. His purpose, I think, was to be provocative, to unleash the debate that followed. But to the friends around me, many of whom played on Western's women's sports teams, this was more than a debate—it was life.

Years later, I recalled that incident as I made space for my daughter. A bead of sweat eluded my toque, running down my nose. It was below freezing, but shoveling a rectangular space on the frozen pond in the rare winter sunlight made me sweat. I bordered our makeshift rink with knee-high walls of snow while my daughter sat patiently on a stool, her boots kicking rhythmically as if she were treading water. My wife sat beside her on her own stool, tying her skates. When I finished, I tied my daughter's skates and snapped on the bright pink helmet she'd chosen at the local sports store. I tucked her mittens into her snowsuit and watched as she stood precariously, taking cautious steps forward. She took my wife's hand and soon the familiar sound of blades holding to outdoor ice rose into the crisp air.

I sat on the stool and watched as they cut patterns this way and that, laughter muffled by scarves and snow, their voices reaching me sporadically. As they turned back, I could see their smiles. I pulled my phone from my pocket, removing my gloves to snap a photograph.

In 1891, another daughter was photographed skating on a similar outdoor rink. The photograph of Isobel Stanley taken by a writer for the *Ottawa Citizen* was the first of a woman playing hockey. Since then, women's access to the game has come, gone and returned, finally triumphing over more than a century of barriers constructed by men.

•

Women have been skating for centuries. In 1395, a Dutch teenager named Lydwina went skating with friends. "The little party fastened on their skates, intending to commence the holiday trip by way of the canal, on which was situated the home of Lydwina's family. Barely was this accomplished when, in the hurry to start, one of the girls pushed against Lydwina, causing her to fall with such violence on a rough piece of ice that a rib on her right side was severely fractured."[1] Lydwina never really recovered from this injury, her condition possibly exacerbated by multiple sclerosis. After her death in 1433, she became the patron saint of ice skaters and the chronically ill.

In 1687, the Princess of Orange (who would become Queen Mary, wife of William III) took up skating. A French count remarked that it was "a very extraordinary thing to see the Princess of Orange, with very short petticoats, and those tucked up to her waist, and with iron pattins on her feet, learning to slide, sometimes on one foot, sometimes on the other."[2]

On Turtle Island, as North America is known to some Indigenous peoples, "Shinny, a hockey-like ball game played on a field or on ice in winter, was often considered a women's game."[3] Skating as a pastime for aristocratic women migrated to Canada with the arrival of Lady Dufferin who arrived in Canada when her husband was appointed the third Governor General. Lord and Lady Dufferin, described as a "keen skater herself,"[4] built the first skating rink at Rideau Hall, the official residence of Canada's Governors General in Ottawa, in 1872.

Lady Dufferin was succeeded at Rideau Hall by Princess Louise Caroline Alberta, Duchess of Argyll, the namesake of Lake Louise and the province of Alberta. The fourth daughter of Queen Victoria, she arrived in Canada in 1878 when her husband was appointed Governor General. An early feminist, Princess Louise advocated for education and suffrage for women and participated in winter pastimes that included skating.

Another member of her household, Marie Evelyn Moreton, also enjoyed tobogganing and skating. Evelyn, as she was known, was the daughter of Princess Louise's lady-in-waiting and would return to Rideau Hall in 1921 as the wife of the twelfth Governor General, Baron (later Viscount) Julian

Byng. In her memoirs, she recalled that "Julian and I tried to skate—with woeful results, for I never got beyond the stage of pushing a chair round the rink, whilst enduring torment from aching shins, and he got far enough to plod round unsupported . . ."[5]

While her on-ice skills were limited, Lady Byng developed a passion for watching hockey. "But if plays were denied me, there was ice hockey, and woe betide any member of the staff who tried to make engagements for a Saturday during the hockey season, when I went regularly to 'root' for the 'Senators,' with such fine players as Gerrard, Nighbor, the Bouchers, Clancy and Denneny, to name a few in those long-past days, who gave me many happy evenings during our five years at Rideau Hall. The only blemish to that sport was the childish mentality among a section of the crowd which would vent its annoyance, on umpires or players, by showering the rink with rubbish, stopping the game and also—when coins were thrown— endangering players."[6]

It was her disapproval of the violence of hockey, both on and off the ice, that led to her honor her favorite player, Ottawa Senators forward Frank Nighbor, by donating the Lady Byng Trophy to the National Hockey League in 1925. The trophy has since been awarded annually "to the player adjudged to have exhibited the best type of sportsmanship and gentlemanly conduct combined with a high standard of playing ability."[7]

Lady Byng's trophy was not the first, or the most important, to come from Rideau Hall. That honor belongs to Lord Stanley of Preston who, in 1892, announced that he had "for some time past been thinking that it would be a good thing if there were a challenge cup which should be held from year to year by the champion hockey team in the Dominion. Considering the general interest which the matches now elicit, and the importance of having the game played fairly and under rules generally recognized, I am willing to give a cup which shall be held from year to year by the winning team."[8] Originally known as the Dominion Hockey Challenge Cup, that silver bowl would become the Stanley Cup, the oldest trophy in North American professional team sport.

Lord Frederick Stanley's passion for hockey began in 1888 when, as the newly appointed sixth Governor General of Canada, he and his wife, Lady Constance Villiers, began hosting skating parties on Rideau Hall's outdoor rink. The following year, Stanley took his family to the Winter Carnival in Montreal, where they witnessed their first game of organized hockey between the Montreal Victorias and Montreal Amateur Athletic Association. The Stanleys instantly fell in love with the sport. As Montreal's English-language newspaper *The Gazette* reported at the time, "His Excellency expressed . . . his great delight with the game of hockey and the expertness of the players."[9]

Following that game, the outdoor rink at Rideau Hall became a hub of activity. Their only living daughter, fourteen-year-old Isobel, took up the sport and, according to hockey historian Brian MacFarlane, "There is firm evidence that he [Lord Stanley] and Lady Stanley played a significant role in the development and growth of women's hockey—simply by creating an environment in which the game could be enjoyed in a casual manner by men and women alike."[10]

According to historian Jennifer Conway, the participation of men and women together was significant. "That was very unusual for nobility—higher-class workers—to be doing," she said in a March 12, 2016, interview with *The New York Times*. Lady Isobel's role was equally important. "What she did was really, really pioneering for the sport, in a bunch of ways." On March 8, 1889, in a newly constructed indoor arena, Rideau Skating Hall, Isobel's Government House team defeated the Rideau Ladies in what many contend was the first recorded women's hockey game.[11]

Beginning in the late 1800s, women began playing hockey across Canada and in parts of the United States. In New York, the "fad" of speed skating in hockey skates soon turned to hockey among women who "appeared in yellow gowns trimmed with black in fantastic designs." As the *Buffalo Courier Express* wrote in 1894, "Women's hockey clubs have been formed in many places and the game is quite as suitable for the gentler sex as it is for men."[12]

The game spread across the Midwest. In Nebraska, "so popular has the hockey skate become among the women members of one of the aristocratic clubs that not long ago a regular hockey team was organized among the smart set, and frequent practice is indulged in . . . These women practice their hockey game 'between sessions,' and not even a sheriff could get into the structure during the sacred hours devoted to their play."[13]

In Canada, women's hockey in the 1800s often involved university teams.

In 1872, New Brunswick's Mount Allison University became the first school in Canada to admit women; three years later, Grace Annie Lockhart graduated to become the first woman in the British Empire to receive a degree. Ontario's Queen's University admitted three women to study medicine in 1880 and Montreal's McGill University opened its doors to women in 1884.

Once admitted, women participated in all aspects of university life and began playing hockey immediately. Teams were formed in the late 1800s at the University of Toronto, Queen's in Kingston, McGill in Montreal, and even as far west as Mount Royal University and Calgary Collegiate Institute; more joined in the opening decades of the 1900s.

At McGill in the winter of 1894, women "were granted four hours of ice time per week on the indoor rink providing three men were on duty to guard the entrances. No male students were allowed to become involved and the players had to be comfortably and warmly dressed." The same year, women at Queen's University organized a hockey team called the Love-me-Littles, "the name reflecting the lack of acceptance by men at the university of a women's hockey team."[14]

As the *Queen's College Journal* noted in February of 1895, the women not only played against other women's teams, but challenged the men's hockey team for equal footing. "The members of the Love-Me-Little (girls) hockey team of Queen's College are thinking of challenging the Varsity Hockey Club to a friendly game. It was understood that their enthusiastic practise was held with a view to a match with Divinity Hall, but the Archbishop and the two Patriarchs, thinking of the disastrous follies of their own youth, sternly reprimanded the ambitious sports of the flock, and sent them to bed with a warning never to think of it again."[15]

The founding of the Rossland Winter Carnival in 1900 marked the birthplace of organized women's hockey in British Columbia. That year, the Rossland Ladies, wearing ankle-length dresses, beat Nelson 4-0 to become the first Carnival champions, and the champions of British Columbia. In 1911, organizers of the Rossland tournament decreed that the event was the "Ladies Championship of the World." The tournament continued for seventeen years, until play was stopped by the epidemic of Spanish influenza.

In the United States, Constance Applebee introduced field hockey for women when she arrived from England to take a summer course at

Harvard University in 1901. She put on a demonstration for classmates at Harvard and, seeing the interest, embarked on a trip to more than a half dozen colleges in the Northeast to showcase the sport and help establish the game. Three years later, she was hired as the athletic director at one of those schools, Bryn Mawr College. The sport of hockey became entrenched in America, gradually migrating from the grassy fields of summertime to the frozen ponds and rinks of winter.

A similar evolution was taking place in Australia. In 1904, a refrigeration executive named Henry Newman Reid opened the first Glaciarium in Adelaide. It was followed by the Melbourne Glaciarium in 1906, and the Sydney Glaciarium in 1907. An exhibition of field hockey on ice was held at the Adelaide facility in 1907. The following year, an exhibition game of women's ice hockey was staged at the Melbourne Glaciarium to entertain several hundred officers and men of the American Fleet visiting for a week.

H. Newman Reid's only daughter, Mireylees, would later play ice hockey in New South Wales. In a March 9,1950 interview with *The Sydney Morning Herald*, she said, "I grew up skating. I was carried over the ice before I could walk, and put on it as soon as I could."

As women struggled for equality, sports evolved from a pastime of the privileged to a path to autonomy, clearly evidenced by cycling. Sports historian M. Ann Hall maintains that, with spinning spokes powered by the legs of women covered in bloomers, bicycles in the 1890s became "the embodiment of the New Woman, the one leaving behind the fragile stereotype of her earlier, domestic sister and marching determinedly towards more education, work, service and suffrage."[16]

The bicycle made women more mobile, threatening existing social structures. As *The San Francisco Call* put it, "It really doesn't matter much where this one individual young lady is going on her wheel. It may be that she's going to the park on pleasure bent, or to the store for a dozen hairpins, or to call on a sick friend at the other side of town, or to get a doily pattern off somebody, or a recipe for removing tan and freckles. Let that be as it may. What the interested public wishes to know is, Where are all the women on wheels going? Is there a grand rendezvous somewhere toward which they are all headed and where they will some time hold a meet that will cause this wobbly old world to wake up and readjust itself?"[17]

Women forming athletic clubs and competing in physically strenuous activities challenged Victorian notions of femininity. While it was acceptable for women to labor in private, as domestic mothers and wives, it was not acceptable to do so publicly. "No one denied the muscular effort involved in carrying a child and giving birth; it was public athletic performance by women and girls that was condemned as immodest, selfish, and attention-seeking, the trinity of bad-girl behaviors. And athletic risks undertaken in prime childbearing years were seen as foolhardy." Sports like tennis, croquet, golf, horseback riding, and fancy skating were seen as "more socially acceptable because they required elaborate outfits, stamping an assurance of femininity onto competitors in costume."[18]

Hockey, with its speed and physicality, was particularly alarming, and both media and spectators began paying special attention to ensuring decorum, genteel presentation, and the purity of those playing. By 1897, rinks were banning spectators from watching the hoydenish displays of women in hockey. As *The Gazette* explained, fans were not permitted as "this activity was unladylike and highly injurious to a woman's sensitive constitution."[19]

•

Today, as a member of the Professional Hockey Writers Association, I regularly come across the names of these forgotten women in hockey. In 2023, I wrote a story about the Premier Hockey Federation's championship game, where the Toronto Six triumphed in overtime over the Minnesota Whitecaps. I watched the postgame celebration as women lifted and kissed the trophy that had been awarded each season since 2016, beginning with the National Women's Hockey League champions. Their trophy was named after a teenage girl, the youngest Stanley daughter, who left behind a photograph and a love for the sport. The inscription reads: "The Lady Isobel Gathorne-Hardy Cup 1875–1963. This Cup shall be awarded annually to the greatest professional women's hockey team in North America. All who pursue this Cup, pursue a dream; a dream born with Isobel, that shall never die."

CHAPTER 2

A League of Their Own

Beneath the stands at the Woodstock District Community Complex, my heart was in my throat. Standing at the door to our dressing room, down by a goal heading into the third period of a potentially series-deciding playoff game, my voice caught. I was addressing our Junior team, the Woodstock Navy Vets, as captain. I spent my final two seasons of eligibility with this team while attending Western University in nearby London.

I remember telling my teammates that, for many of them, this was just another period of playoff hockey. Win or lose, they'd return to this room the following fall for a new season. For me, however, this was it. If we lost, it would mark the end of my Junior hockey career. I held back tears as I spoke, but twenty minutes later, after the final buzzer, I returned to the dressing room and sat in my stall, head in hands with a towel draped over my hair, sobbing. Seated next to me, my defense partner also cried, likely recognizing that his time would come. We'd spent our lives being told not to cry. Boys don't cry. Men don't cry. But once a year, an exception was made for this moment, for the loss of identity, of friends, of a group you'd been told was your family. And for the game we loved.

Growing up in the 1990s, sitting in front of our generational babysitter, the television, I remember hearing, "There's no crying in baseball." The phrase was immortalized in the 1992 film, *A League of Their Own*, about the All-American Girls Professional Baseball League (AAGPBL). The league was founded in 1943 by Major League Baseball executives anxious to capture the imagination of sports fans while millions of American men fought in World War II. This "lipstick league" was marketed as a novelty that juxtaposed femininity with athleticism. As league president and Baseball Hall of Famer Max Carey stated, "Femininity is the keynote of our league; no pants-wearing, tough-talking female softballer will play on any of our four teams."[1] Players were required to wear skirts and attend charm school where they learned how to apply make-up and behave appropriately in social settings. For owners intent on keeping stadiums filled, the league was a success, drawing upwards of 900,000 fans at its peak. It never occurred to me that a similar league for women may have existed in hockey.

•

Although it is the best known, the AAGPBL was not the first all-women's sports league. The Eastern Ladies Hockey League (ELHL), founded in Montreal in 1915, also kept arenas full and fans entertained while men were at war. Working-class women were thrust into jobs in factories and stores where they ably replaced men fighting overseas, and women from all social groups now found hockey a viable option. "Ice hockey was no longer a game played primarily by women in universities or from the more bourgeois sectors of society, because thousands of working-class girls took up the sport with enormous enthusiasm. It had a wide following among factory workers, department store clerks, secretaries and the like, especially in small towns, and slowly they began to organize themselves into leagues and organizations."[2]

The ELHL drew thousands of spectators to many games and produced bona fide stars. Edith Anderson was called a "phenom" by the *Ottawa Citizen*[3] and Eva Ault was nicknamed "Queen of the Ice."[4] But it was Albertine Lapensée who shone most brightly as the first superstar of women's hockey. Hailed by fans and newspapers as "the lady hockey marvel,"[5] she was indisputably "the world's premiere women's hockeyist."[6]

Albertine Lapensée was born in Cornwall, Ontario, on August 10, 1898. The fifth of seven children, she grew up skating on local ponds with her three older brothers. At age seventeen, she joined the Cornwall Victorias of the ELHL for the 1915–16 season and was an immediate sensation. Fans packed arenas to see her play. As *The Ottawa Journal* wrote, "She was the attraction that resulted in most of the spectators being present. Everyone wanted to see her perform."[7] Paced by Lapensée, "a tempestuous and controversial teenage superstar who might be the greatest female player of all time," the Victorias were nearly unstoppable. She led the Victorias to an undefeated season, winning forty-five games and tying one against the team of Anderson and Ault, the Ottawa Alerts. The papers called her the "Miracle Maid" and "Star of

Stars," helping her celebrity quickly rise as "thousands of fans flock[ed] to her every appearance."[8]

Lapensée's talent was undeniable. "She skates, shoots, back checks, and blocks with the ability of any amateur playing the game," *The Ottawa Journal* asserted.[9] Her shot was so powerful that one opponent, Montreal Westerns' netminder Corinne Hardman, started wearing a baseball catcher's mask at practice in preparation. Had she worn it during a game, Hardman would have been the first in hockey history to do so, usurping Queen's University's Elizabeth Graham, who donned a fencing mask in action in 1926. Three years later, Clint Benedict briefly wore a primitive leather mask in National Hockey Association (NHA) action with the Montreal Wanderers while recovering from a broken nose, long before Jacques Plante popularized the mask among NHL goalies in 1959.

Another Canadian woman was instrumental in developing the game in the United States. Kathleen Howard's husband, Tom, was a renowned hockey player who won a Stanley Cup with the Winnipeg Victorias in 1896. Three seasons later, Howard moved to New York where he retired from play following the 1905–06 season but continued coaching at Yale, Columbia, and with various youth programs. In 1916, Kathleen, herself "a hockey player of more than passing ability,"[10] formed a women's St. Nicholas club that would complement the existing men's team.

The St. Nicholas Blues' top player was Elsie Muller who, like her Canadian counterparts, grew up skating outdoors on the Hudson River and later at Lake Placid. Muller would go on to represent the United States in speed skating at the 1932 Winter Olympics. Captaining St. Nicholas, Muller "proved herself to be among the very best women ice hockey players of her era."[11]

At the time, New York City was in "the throes of skating madness" that extended to hockey. "The craze has clutched the old as well as the young; the girls and matrons just as it has the youths and papas. And the girls—well, they aren't content merely to skate this season. They want to play hockey, a game regarded by many as far more strenuous than football. Their wants are being filled."[12]

Kathleen Howard maintained, "There is no reason why a woman who can skate well should not develop into a hockey player. Hockey on ice is no more dangerous than field hockey, and throughout England, Canada, and some sections of the United States, field hockey is a very popular sport with women . . . Once they master the knack of skating while carrying a stick, they soon pick up the finer points of the game."[13]

In addition to New York, teams formed in Boston, Pittsburgh, and Cleveland, in pockets of Minnesota and Wisconsin, and even in California. In Boston, the Boston Girls' Hockey Club was led by Ruth Denesha, whose brother Harry, a player for the New York Athletic Club, coached the team. In Pittsburgh, three teams—the Polar Maids, Arctic Girls, and Winter Garden Girls—played at the city's Winter Garden weekly. An inaugural series between the Polar Maids and Winter Garden Girls was well received and attendance continued to grow. "Since the introduction of girls' hockey, considerable interest has been aroused among the local followers of the winter sport and each succeeding game finds a larger crowd."[14]

While there were no regional or national leagues, teams occasionally traveled between cities. In 1916, the Cornwall Victorias and Ottawa Alerts played a three-game series in front of packed crowds at Cleveland's Elysium Arena that was the de facto Canadian championship, despite being played in the United States. Cornwall won all three games, with Lapensée collecting fifteen of her team's eighteen goals. The Alerts would return to the USA the following year to play a three-game series against the Pittsburgh Polar Maids. Also in 1917, Kathleen Howard's St. Nicholas Blues traveled to Boston to face the Boston Girls' Hockey Club.

Despite their enthusiasm, American players generally acknowledged the superior skills of their Canadian counterparts. In a 1917 article published in *The Buffalo Commercial*, reporter Amy Lyman-Phillips wrote that "almost from infancy Canadian girls are taught to skate," and that "Canadian girls have no rivals in skating, the world over." She described a group of Americans who had traveled to Quebec, saying the Americans "gasped as two teams of girl hockey players met in conflict upon the glassy surface in a game as swift as the falling of a shooting star. Forged lightning over plate glass is not faster than the tireless lassies who belabored the puck with all the science and speed of a seasoned hockey player." Lyman-Phillips was convinced that it would not take long for the excitement of the sport and the belief that women could play hockey to spread to every corner of North America. "Not long hence their portraits will be flashed upon a thousand screens from

Tampa to Toronto, from Halifax to Portland, and the prowess of the fair Canadian hockey player will be published abroad, following a discreet silence of years upon the subject of women and hockey. Most men said, 'It can't be done! It's too swift and too dangerous for girls;' but the girls quietly gathered their forces in Canada and showed them that no sport exists at which the Canadian girl may not be proficient if she takes into her head to do so. And so it is that hockey is added to her accomplishments."[15]

Players like Lapensée, Anderson, and Ault even sparked speculation that the National Hockey Association (NHA), the predecessor of the NHL, would begin to "draft the best of the women players."[16] Lapensée in particular drew envy from both men and women. *The Ottawa Journal* maintained that she could "shoot as good as any forward in the NHA,"[17] and *The Montreal Star* observed, "There are a good number of boys in Cornwall who wish they were as adept with the stick and as clever on skates as Miss Lapensée. If they were they could be commanding good salaries in one or other of the big league teams."[18]

Regular comparison to the top men's players of the day soon sparked rumors that, given her dominance, Lapensée must be a man. The more she scored, the more people entertained this notion, which *The Montreal Star* stated was "gaining currency on account of her being so superior to any other lady player and her agility on the steel blades."[19] Unable to defeat her, opponents "and their supporters" claimed "she really was a boy in girls' clothing."[20]

During a game against the Montreal Westerns, an opponent pulled the toque from her head, hoping to show the presumed shortness of her hair. Instead, the action "caused (her hair) to fall in long braids down over her shoulders." Similarly, in a game against the Ottawa Alerts, the Ottawa team brought Lapensée to their dressing room to ascertain her womanhood and "settle the matter." At the end of the 1915–16 season, an investigation by *The Montreal Star* found that although Lapensée's "style resembles that of the average male professional to such an extent that it is little wonder that people unacquainted with the girl are led to believe from her play that she is a boy," the claims were false. Moreover, the paper stated, Lapensée's ability "only goes to show what degree of perfection young ladies can acquire in athletics if they are inclined that way and practice diligently."[21]

Throughout the 1916–17 season, Lapensée continued to draw crowds by the thousands whenever she stepped on the ice—without any compensation. Like the generations of women who would follow, her fight for equality failed. Lapensée realized how much money promoters were making and asked to be paid. When she was refused, she walked away from the game, at age eighteen, following the 1917 season,

Lapensée moved to New York, perhaps "drawn by the wonderful stories told her of the United States Metropolis."[22] Some believed this included the ability to freely express a more masculine gender. Whether it was to avoid constant gender policing, protest the lack of pay equity, or escape media scrutiny, Lapensée left Cornwall and, without their star, the Victorias folded.

At the time, *The Montreal Star* observed, presciently, that "Montreal may never see Miss Albertine Lapensée, the lady hockey marvel, again."[23] The only subsequent mention surfaced in American newspapers a month later claiming that Lapensée, "by far the speediest skater and most nimble player among the fair devotees of the Dominion's national winter sport"[24] might continue playing with St. Nicholas Rink. That rumor proved unfounded and Lapensée largely disappeared from the public record. A profile of the family published in the *Cornwall Standard Freeholder* on March 18, 1940, refers to her as Mrs. Albert Schmidt of New York but there is no other record of her life after hockey, including when she died.

•

As soldiers returned from World War I, men's hockey again became the focus for promoters and media, although women continued to form leagues and push for professional status. In fact, "the 1920s was a time when women began experimenting and competing seriously in new sports, at the same time consolidating their hold on others. Nothing seemed to hold them back. There was a growing public enchantment with these new stars of the athletic world and the sports press obliged by reporting their exploits and, for the most part, treating them seriously."[25]

Established teams like the Ottawa Alerts and Cornwall Victorias spawned powerhouse Prairie teams including the Calgary Regents and Edmonton Monarchs. Formed in 1914 as the Edmonton Victorias, and the only team to be coached by a woman, the Monarchs were "the team that has kept ladies' hockey before the public for the last decade or more. They are composed of a collection of real athletes, and a splendid type of young womanhood, who play the game for the delight and pleasure that they get out of having mastered the fastest game played."[26]

In British Columbia, the Rossland Ladies were undefeated for more than fifteen years. A rival team, the Nelson Ladies Club, featured three sisters: Dora, Cynda, and Myrtle Patrick, whose brother, Lester, coached the team in 1911. Also that year, he and his brother, Frank, formed a men's league, the Pacific Coast Hockey Association (PCHA), hoping to eventually compete for the prestigious Stanley Cup. Ten years later, the brothers saw a business opportunity and announced the PCHA would host an international tournament featuring the Vancouver Amazons (owned by Frank), the Victoria Kewpies, and Seattle Vamps. The Amazons went undefeated in the series to become women's hockey's first international champions. "The mainstay of the Vancouver team" was Kathleen Carson, who would "rain shots" on opponents' nets.[27] She eventually married the team's manager, Guy Patrick, brother to Frank and Lester.

The women's games were played during intermission and following men's PCHA contests. As fans had paid admission, all athletes were deemed professional and were banned from future amateur competition in any sport, even though only the men were paid. As president of British Columbia's Amateur Athletic Union, George Warren, explained, "I am sorry to have to take the action, but the rules say that no amateur can play on the same ice as professionals, where a gate is charged, so I have had to act accordingly."[28] This determination made the PCHA, alongside the ELHL, the first professional hockey league for women.

Beginning in 1917, top western Canadian teams met annually at the Banff Winter Carnival to contest the Alpine Cup. The Calgary Regents were the inaugural winners and, except for a loss to the Edmonton Monarchs the following year, reigned supreme until 1921. In 1922, the Vancouver Amazons defeated the reigning champions. As reported in *The Province*, Kathleen Carson "secured the puck, went straight down the ice, broke through the defense, and by a neatly placed shot scored the tying goal amidst great cheering from the spectators."[29] Carson went on to score the winning goal in overtime.

The following year, the Amazons lost the title to the upstart Fernie Swastikas. When the Swastikas returned home, the mayor of Fernie ordered all businesses to close for one hour, and all schools to close for the day, so that residents could celebrate their victory. "The train was met by a crowd numbering up in the thousands and when the girls stepped from the train they were given three hearty cheers, to which the girls replied with their club yell."[30] Team captain Dahlia Schagel addressed the large crowd that formed following a parade through the town. The Swastikas were the last team from British Columbia to hoist the cup.

•

The Banff Carnival "was an important space for women's teams from Western Canada to gather and compete," and "offered some legitimacy for women's skillful and physical on-ice performance."[31] However, both the tournament and the participating teams were run by men who continued to present the women's game as a novelty. Across North America, the focus was on spectacle instead of skill, with newspapers highlighting the appearance and personal characteristics of women on the rosters. In a typical example, *The Boston Globe* of December 26, 1920, described the Back Bay Hockey Club as "a team of rosy cheeked, fluffy haired girls."

Women's teams always traveled with older women serving as chaperones to ensure the moral purity of the players, a practice that began in the Victorian era. While rosters were only sporadically documented, and most often replaced first names with "Miss" or, in the case of a married woman, the name of her husband, chaperones were frequently named in news reports, signaling the importance of their role.

Media and promoters maintained that women's hockey avoided "many of the unsavory aspects of men's hockey (for example, fighting) that might threaten female character"[32] when, in actuality, the women's game was physical, in most cases featuring full bodychecking and, at times, fighting. As the gap between socially acceptable behavior and on-ice performance grew, there was an "emerging argument that competitive sports threatened women and girls' morals."[33] According to historian Andrew C. Holman, "Women hockey players succeeded when they cast aside traditional strictures that declared them physically unfit to play such an aggressive and dangerous game. But at the same time they were blunted when they would not or could not play ice hockey in the ways that men had 'branded' the game and sold it to growing audiences."[34]

Men's hockey, simply called "hockey," was presented as the real version of the sport; the women's game, primarily called "ladies' hockey," was seen as an imitation whose participants were expected to conform to social norms: its participants mild-mannered, docile, and seeking the approval of men. In a bid for independence, Canada's first provincial governing body, the Ladies Ontario Hockey Association (LOHA), was formed in 1922. The following year, the new Women's Intercollegiate Athletic Union began organizing women's hockey at the university level in Canada.

Both organizations struggled with recognition. "Plagued by a lack of acceptance in the broader hockey community, limited access to resources and inconsistent membership numbers, the LOHA spent the majority of its nineteen-year existence challenging traditional notions of appropriate feminine sport practices."[35] The idea that hockey would make women too "competitive, masculine, and unbecoming"[36] continued to grow until, in 1923, the Canadian Amateur Hockey Association (CAHA) voted to exclude the newly formed LOHA. As president W.A. Fry explained, "While the participation of women and girls in many competitive sports, such as tennis, swimming, skating and field and track events is growing, my belief is that hockey, for various reasons, should be an exception," leading him "to vote with the majority not to give them official recognition. In my opinion there is all the necessary scope for them in games where the personal contact element is not a factor."[37]

In response, Alexandrine Gibb, an athlete who participated in tennis, basketball, softball, and track and field, began advocating for a governing body focused solely on women's sport. An exceptional organizer and fierce advocate, she established the Ladies' Ontario Basketball Association in 1919 and partnered with fellow athlete Myrtle Cook to form the Toronto Ladies Athletic Club in 1923. It was here she coined the phrase "girls' sport run by girls" that would become a rallying cry for women across the country. In 1925, Gibb became the catalyst for the creation of the Women's Amateur Athletic Federation (WAAF) that "offered women the chance to control, organize, and develop women's competitive sport formally." Specifically, the WAAF opened doors for working-class women, who Gibb recognized had historically been shut out of athletic participation.

The WAAF's first president, Janet Allen, was also president of the LOHA and called upon men to support women's hockey. "I believe that if the men interested in hockey in the different centers were to try to interest the girls in their own towns in the game and would assist them in every way possible, our Association would be the better for it." [38]

Such support was not forthcoming. Undeterred, women continued to play hockey, determined to build on the foundation laid by Albertine Lapensée and her contemporaries. As journalist Bruce Yaccato observed, "If anyone should be classed in a league of their own, surely it should be the trail-blazing young women of Montreal. . . To say they're unsung is a sadly huge understatement."[39]

CHAPTER 3

No Man's Land

In the spring of 1937, as political tensions rose throughout Europe, my grandmother Katie, along with her parents and three siblings, left their Slovak village and traveled to the shores of the Atlantic Ocean where they boarded a ship for Canada. When they arrived, her family settled in the southern Ontario town of Wallaceburg.

Years later, she would bring her husband, John, a drink while he sat in front of their black-and-white television watching *Hockey Night in Canada*. She would listen to the game from the kitchen while she baked and canned vegetables from her garden. As they aged, John got a television in his bedroom, and the volume of the games increased as his hearing failed. Long before I took up the game, hockey provided an opportunity for them to integrate into popular culture, to immerse themselves into something deemed quintessentially Canadian.

A World War and many years earlier, George Ranscombe and Ada Amato had done the same thing, crossing the Atlantic Ocean with their seven children and settling in the southern Ontario region of Waterloo. Their youngest child, Hilda, was born in Canada in 1913. As it would for my grandparents, hockey became an important part of their new life.

Hilda could skate as soon as she could stand. She learned on Cressman Pond near her family home and later played alongside her siblings on the Grand River. According to NHL veteran Carl Liscombe, "Hilda was just as good as any boy, and better than most, myself included. When we picked teams, she was always the first one chosen."[1] By the 1930s, Hilda Ranscombe would be regarded as the best women's hockey player on the planet.

Decades later, in 1968, "an attractive, athletic-looking brunette"[2] stepped on the ice at Wallaceburg Memorial Arena, less than two kilometers from my grandmother's house. Then fifty-five years old and working at a real estate agency, Hilda Ranscombe was the special guest of the second annual Wallaceburg Lipstick Tournament.

•

Women athletes became front-page news when, for the first time, they were allowed to compete in athletics as part of the 1928 Olympics. Canada was represented by The Matchless Six: Jean Thompson, Ethel Catherwood, Fanny "Bobbie" Rosenfeld, Ethel Smith, Jane Bell and Myrtle Cook. Both Rosenfeld and Cook were former hockey players who would go on to promote the sport tirelessly.

Born in 1902, Myrtle Cook earned a spot on Canada's national track and field roster at age fifteen but would wait more than a decade to prove herself on the world stage. A month before the 1928 summer games in Amsterdam, she set a new world record of 12.0 seconds in the 100-meter dash. She was favored to win Olympic gold but was disqualified after false-starting twice. She did, however, help Canada win gold in the 4x100-meter relay.

Another member of the relay team was Toronto's Fanny Rosenfeld, nicknamed Bobbie because of her short hair. A multi-sport athlete, Rosenfeld, in addition to track and field, excelled at basketball, softball, and hockey. On the ice, she played from the early 1920s into the 1930s, primarily for the Toronto Ladies and Toronto Pats. Rosenfeld captained the Pats to the 1929 Ontario title, later starring in a 2-0 win over the Quebec champions, Montreal's Northern Electric, in what Alexandrine Gibb, writing in the *Toronto Star*, dubbed "a mythical Canadian girls' hockey championship."[3]

Gibb managed the Canadian women's Olympic team and simultaneously began writing a regular column, "No Man's Land of Sport," for the *Toronto Daily Star*. In 1930, while vacationing near Preston (now Cambridge), Ontario, she was approached by "a group of girls [who] came to ask me what I would advise them to do in order to get an athletic club on its way."[4] Hilda Ranscombe and her older sister, Nellie, and sisters Helen and Marm Schmuck, were playing softball for the Preston Rivulettes and wanted advice on how to keep the team together during the winter months. On Gibb's recommendation, the Rivulettes formed a hockey team and joined the LOHA in search of regular competition.

From the moment they stepped on the ice, the Rivulettes were nearly unbeatable. Between 1931 and 1940, the team won ten Ontario championships and were Dominion champions four times. Preston played 350 games, losing only twice. In comparison, the record for the longest unbeaten streak in the National Hockey League (twenty-five wins and ten ties) belongs to the 1979–80 Philadelphia Flyers. In women's hockey, the 2012 University of Minnesota Golden Gophers set an NCAA hockey record with sixty-two consecutive wins, including a perfect 41-0-0 season in 2012–13. Both achievements pale in comparison to Preston's.

The Rivulettes' dominance inspired fear in their opponents—"the cry from centres throughout Ontario . . . claimed that the Preston power had become too potent to cope with."[5] In a game that included full bodychecking and occasional fights, the Rivulettes were not only the most skilled, but also the toughest team in Canada. While Hilda Ranscombe was "without a doubt the best female hockey player in the world,"[6] one of the most physical was her teammate, Helen Schmuck. Like Albertine Lapensée before her, Schmuck's dominance occasioned gender policing. Following a February 1931 game against the LOHA champions, the Port Dover Sailorettes, the *Galt Evening Reporter* noted that "management of the Port Dover club wanted to have Conservator Helen Schmuck disrobe. They thought she was a boy."[7] Five years later, gender policing became front-page news when American sprinter Helen Stephens was required to undergo a medical examination to retain the gold medal she won at the 1936 Olympics.

Despite Preston's success, and their ability to draw thousands of fans to Galt Arena, the team had difficulty acquiring ice time. Arenas in the 1930s were for men's hockey; women were relegated to outdoor rinks, and late-night time slots men did not want. "Girls' hockey teams have to take the ice left-overs," Alexandrine Gibb complained. "From bantams to seniors, the boys get the preference in rinks throughout the province and when the boys' teams have completed their schedules . . . taken their defeats and victories . . . then the girls get the opportunity to take the ice."[8]

Myrtle Cook, who had moved to Montreal and began writing a sports column, "In the Women's Sportlight," for *The Montreal Star*, raised the same issue. "Montreal teams hung up their sticks two years ago when it became almost impossible to wiggle a sheet of frozen water out of the local ice palace owners," she wrote in 1933. "The girls had the alternative of playing their league games on outdoor rinks in various parts of the city. This did not appeal to the players who like their hockey under the big tent the same as their brothers. They voted to suspend operations pending more favorable times." That winter, the women of Montreal tried again, forming the six-team Montreal and District Ladies' Hockey League on the understanding that "if they make good via the gate" the men in charge of the Ice Palace would "permit them to call the place home-sweet-home for the balance of the season."[9]

The resurgence of hockey in Quebec, the dominance of the Preston Rivulettes and the durability of the Alpine Cup created momentum for a national championship that would include all provinces. In 1933, the Dominion Women's Amateur Hockey Association was established to lay out common rules, determine playoff formats, govern national competition and encourage participation from all provinces. "The success of the Association will depend on the co-operation and unanimity of purpose of those interested in the development of the game as Canada's premier winter sport for girls and young women," explained Mrs. F. Wyatt, the DWAHA's first president.[10]

That year, the Banff Winter Carnival would determine British Columbia's senior amateur women's provincial title and the senior amateur women's Alberta–British Columbia title. The inter-provincial champion would face teams from Manitoba and Saskatchewan for the western Canada senior amateur women's hockey championship. The western Canadian champion would go on to face the eastern champion in the Dominion championship.

At the Banff Winter Carnival, the veteran Edmonton Monarchs faced off against the upstart Edmonton Rustlers, who had previously competed at the intermediate level. Described as a "fast-skating and stick-handling aggregation who revel in tough going" who would "provide the ever-increasing following of ladies' hockey with some spectacular playing, which will be a revelation to all followers of hockey on seeing their first ladies' game,"[11] the Rustlers upset the Monarchs and won the right to face the Ontario champion Preston Rivulettes for the inaugural Dominion championship. Lady Bessborough, wife of the current Governor General, donated a cup to mark the occasion.

The Rustlers opened the two-game total point series in front of two thousand fans, winning 3-2 in a game where "both teams went out to win from the first bell. Skating was fast and checking hard and the bid for supremacy was earnest."[12] As she had all season, the spectacular Hazel Case paced the Rustlers. Case's hockey career was brief, but her sporting career was prolific: she won multiple Alberta golf titles and went on to win two Canadian national curling championships, skipping Team Alberta to titles in 1966 and 1968. The 1968 national championship team was a family affair that included Hazel Case and her three daughters Gail, Jackie, and June. She is a member of the Edmonton Sports Hall of Fame, Alberta Sports Hall of Fame, and Canadian Curling Hall of Fame.

The Rustlers handed the Rivulettes the only two losses in team history. "In Edmonton, the atmosphere was so different and we went with nine players and three were sick," Hilda Ranscombe recalled years later. "Myself, all I did on the ice was cough. The girls played good hockey but we only had one spare." Hometown bias may also have been a factor. Following their 2–1 loss in the second game, the referee, future NHL president Clarence Campbell reportedly came into Preston's dressing room and said, "Sorry girls, I couldn't let you win."[13]

The following season, 1934, teams from Quebec were looking forward to competing for an eastern Canadian championship and the right to play Ontario's champion for a spot in the Dominion final. To make it that far, however, the Quebec champions would need to defeat one of the longest running powerhouses in women's hockey, the Summerside Crystal Sisters from Prince Edward Island.

The Crystal Sisters were founded in the 1925–26 season alongside the Abegweit Sisters and Charlottetown Red Macs in a Prince Edward Island women's league. The following season it became a four-team league with the Montague Imperial Sisters contending annually for the island title. Captained by Irene Linkletter and starring her sister Zilpha, Ella Gay, and Ruth Campbell, the Crystal Sisters "soon proved that no team in the Maritimes was their equal, going on tours throughout the region where they rarely conceded a goal, let alone losing a game."[14]

A driving force behind women's empowerment in the Maritimes, the Crystal Sisters' accomplishments included beating a men's team. "The

Crystal Sisters undertook to show the so called sterner sex that they can hold their own in the sphere of sport as well as business, not to mention the domestic circle. The Giddy-unites, one of Summerside's crack teams, showed great pluck and determination to uphold the age old title of Lord and Master, but they were beaten by their fair opponents . . . The men, attired in pink silk bloomers to give them more freedom fought hard but the ladies showed superior skill in passing the puck and keeping out the Giddy-unites goals . . . The Crystal Sisters received a rousing reception from the crowd on their hard won victory and their vanquished foes, although rather crestfallen, gallantly cheered with the audience and admitted that they were outdone, at least on the ice, by the superior sex."[15]

The Montreal Maroons, winners of the Montreal and District Ladies' Hockey League in 1934, faced the Crystal Sisters for the right to play the Preston Rivulettes for a spot in the Dominion final against the Edmonton Rustlers. While the Montreal team included local star Simone Cauchon, touted as "probably greatest woman hockey player in Canada,"[16] *The Montreal Star* noted that "the Crystal Sisters team has a reputation for winning games down east that is not bettered by any other team in sport except the Edmonton Grads basketball squad. A record of continuous victories throughout eight years of their history, has placed the Crystal Sisters in the top spot in women's hockey east of Quebec. They have played over a hundred games and as one Maritime writer describes it, 'have never stubbed a toe.'"[17]

The score was tied 2–2 after regulation and remained so after thirty minutes of overtime. Unlike today's hockey, the teams did not continue to a shootout or additional overtimes to find a winner and "long after midnight officials of both clubs tried to reach an agreement for a replay. Maroons offered to play on Wednesday afternoon at the Forum but the Maritime champions decided they would default, explaining they were unable to finance any further progress in the series."[18]

Following the forfeit by the Crystal Sisters, the Preston Rivulettes, reigning Ontario champions, traveled to Montreal to face the Maroons. They won the game but were also forced to default as they lacked funds to travel west to play the Edmonton Rustlers for the Dominion title.

In 1935, Preston finally captured the Lady Bessborough Cup to claim their first Dominion title by sweeping the Winnipeg Eatons. The following year the team defaulted to the Winnipeg Rangers, unable to afford the journey west. The Winnipeg Rangers offered Preston fifty percent of the gate revenue but could not promise to cover expenses. With improved funding, Preston reclaimed the title in 1937, 1938 and 1939, defeating the Winnipeg Eatons and Winnipeg Olympics.

Financial constraints plagued all women's teams, largely due to the ongoing lack of support from their male counterparts. In 1927, four years after the CAHA had voted to exclude the LOHA, Bobbie Rosenfeld pleaded her case to the Ontario Hockey Association, saying, "All that is necessary is that someone should go out and say: 'We are interested in ladies' hockey.'"[19]

Not only were women denied financial support, they were prohibited from attracting private sponsors. Teams that accepted sponsorship were deemed professional and ineligible to play in national competitions. Les Canadiennes, one of the original teams in the Montreal and District Ladies' Hockey League, had quickly withdrawn when they were not permitted to have sponsor names on their jerseys. The CAHA agreed that these players could not be carded as eligible amateurs because they would "certainly rule that two different crests could not be worn at the same time" and that there would be "no sympathy for clubs which would use women players as advertising mediums."[20]

In 1937, as the Depression exacerbated their financial woes, Myrtle Cook and Bobbie Rosenfeld, then treasurer of the Dominion Women's Amateur Hockey Association, again brought their case to the CAHA, where they made a "plea for a small grant to help them complete Bessborough Cup finals next season." Looking for only a few hundred dollars to ensure a national title could be played for, the request was "met with scant support. The answer was no! The C.A.H.A. reported $34,000 bank balance!" Cook articulated the women's frustration in her column. "Women fans helped swell this C.A.H.A. balance when they supported amateur hockey faithfully all year—a little reciprocity on the part of the men's governing body would not have hurt anyone and might have done a lot of good for the game among the ladies . . . Voices of the C.A.H.A. men in attendance at the last Dominion Women's Amateur Hockey Association meeting indicated they would meet with sympathy from the men's body in their plea for a grant.

Wonder where these voices were when treasurer Fanny Rosenfeld pleaded well the cause of women."[21]

•

Women were also embracing hockey internationally. In Australia, teams from Sydney and New South Wales began playing for the Gower Cup, donated by the father of the Victoria Ladies Ice Hockey Club's captain, Keira Gower, in 1922. By August 4, 1924, *The Argus* newspaper declared that women's hockey had become a regular event. "These games are annual fixtures. Three tests are played and the team winning the majority of them receives, in the women's competition, custody for one year of the Gower Cup." The following year, Sydney's *The Sun* newspaper reported a "clamorous crowd" chanting "Come on, Vic" in support of the Melbourne side. "Long-drawn-out and shrill, the shout went round the Glaciarium last night for the encouragement of the six determined little figures who bore the letter V. in gold on their black uniforms."[22] By 1930, teams such as the Kookaburras and the Bohemians had also been formed.

Women were also playing hockey in Europe. The All England Women's Ice Hockey Association was established in 1930. The Manchester Merlins, London Lambs, London Lionesses, Queens Club, and Sussex Ladies all played for the Sheridan Cup, awarded to the top team in England. French teams included Edelweiss Chamonix, Droit au But, Flèches Noires, Club des sports d'hiver de Paris, and Gros Caillou Sportif.

As in Canada, England, and France each had their own stars. Connie Willan, captain of the Manchester Merlins, was "easily the fastest skater on the rink, and a magnificent hockey player as well."[23] The Merlins' goalie, Winifred Brown, was also a pilot and, in 1930, became the first woman to win the King's Cup Air Race. Zizi Du Manoir, a famed alpine and cross-country skier, was one of France's stars, as was Droit au But captain Jacqueline Mautin, who was "a true female tenor of the ice hockey . . . a dribbling virtuoso and much faster than her opponents."[24]

Throughout the 1930s, England and France competed for the Lady Greer Cup in front of large crowds. In a 1931 game in Paris, Mautin scored five goals in a 6–0 victory over the Sussex Ladies in front of an estimated 10,000 fans. England continued to develop teams domestically to improve their international results. In the spring of 1935, France and England played to a scoreless draw in front of a reported 9,000 fans at Empire Pool, now known as Wembley Arena. According to *The Daily Telegraph*, "The French girls, in the past, have generally been considerably better players than ours, but coaching and practice have greatly improved the English women, and there was nothing ladylike about this match. Fouls and other offenses against the rules were numerous . . . [T]he crowd, though they laughed at times at the obvious mistakes, were stirred to excitement by the pluck and fighting spirit of these young women. To see a girl charged headlong into the fence with a resounding crash, scramble at once to her feet and fly off in pursuit of her opponent, thrilled the crowd and brought roars of applause. The hardest knocks were accepted with stoical indifference by girls whose grandmothers would have fainted at the sight of them."[25]

In the USA, hockey for women struggled to recover from the slump in interest that followed World War I, despite pockets of success. In 1930, the University of Minnesota began hosting an annual women's hockey tournament for students and, in 1933, Eveleth, Minnesota, began "seeking recognition as one of the few towns in the country boasting a girls' puck league."[26] Kathleen Howard's St. Nicholas Blues survived, playing a pair of exhibition games against the Montreal Royals, formerly the Montreal Maroons, in August of 1934. By 1938, sisters Morice and Jean Sherwood were working to form an eight-team league in New York, with similar leagues cropping up in Atlantic City and Philadelphia.

In December 1939, the Montreal Royals and Toronto Ladies went on a US tour, hoping to spark interest in the sport and potentially launch cross-border competition. Their first stop was Providence, Rhode Island, where Providence "fans went overboard for the Canucks, cheering long and loud as the girls waged a 4-3 battle," according to Myrtle Cook. "Dispatches quote the gladiators as having uncorked some fancy stickhandling, stiff body checking, not to mention a threatened free-for-all!"[27]

After Toronto beat Montreal in Springfield, Massachusetts, the tour proceeded to Philadelphia. Toronto shut out Montreal and goalie "little Germain Blais pleased a crowd of 6,000 in Philadelphia Arena."[28] The final tour stops took place in Cleveland and Pittsburgh. Montreal won 3–1 in Cleveland, with center Dorothy (Dolly) Moore scoring a hat trick.

For women playing hockey, the stiffest opposition often came from public opinion. According to sports historian Carly Adams, "By being aggressive, tough, and occasionally violent . . . women were actively resisting prevailing notions of acceptable feminine behavior." Media of the time both responded and contributed to this stereotype. "Journalists commented explicitly on the appearance of female athletes and on personal information such as their marital status to assure the reader that sports were not stripping women of their feminine attributes . . . [U]nlike other sportswomen of the time, female hockey players did not showcase their femininities, thus posing a direct threat to the established male hockey culture."[29]

In the August 1938 edition of *Maclean's*, Elmer Ferguson, a long-time columnist and editor with *The Montreal Star*, wrote an article entitled "I Don't Like Amazon Athletes" in which he claimed he didn't "want to see the girls kept in the kitchen. Because, in the first place, men are far better cooks than women." Women had a place in sport as long as it was as "a girl whose physical perfection was enhanced by a clinging one-piece bathing suit," or a woman "of sheer glittering glory, of golden hair that blazes beneath the dazzle of the lights, of white skirt and trunks and shoes, and tightfitting bodice." He drew the line at "those violent, face-straining, face-dirtying, body-bouncing, sweaty, graceless, stumbling, struggling, wrenching, racking, jarring and floundering sports." Ferguson called women's hockey "a spectacle" that "reaches the lower levels of competitive athletic entertainment after you've watched the grace and speed and certainty and skill with which males perform." He believed, "In all truth, the girls in hockey skate in such rickety fashion, bobble along so uncertainly, that a good strong breeze will pretty nearly blow them off their stumbling feet, and body-checks are just so much wasted effort." No man would want a woman who wore "that peculiarly bewildered and distressed look which girl athletes under strain always possess, that strain which so ill becomes them." He could not see how "the more robust forms of athletics," including "struggling weakly and gracelessly around armed with hockey sticks . . . are going to enhance any feminine charms, or those charms which I always did associate with femininity."

In describing women who excelled in hockey as the "big, masculine, flat-chested, leather-limbed and horselike-looking stars of the game," Ferguson was echoing long-time *Vancouver Sun* editor Andy Lytle, who had called women's athletes "leathery-limbed, flat-chested girls" in 1933.[30] Despite his misogyny, Ferguson is so revered in hockey circles that, in 1984, the Hockey Hall of Fame created the Elmer Ferguson Award, awarded annually to a hockey journalist. To date, only a single woman, Helene Elliott in 2005, has been a recipient.

Bobbie Rosenfeld responded to Lytle's article in *Chatelaine*, maintaining that women athletes were "paragons of feminine physique, beauty and health." She called Lytle's claim that hockey was harmful "plain, ordinary, everyday tommyrot."[31]

Similarly, Olympian Roxy Atkins, who served as the LOHA's president following Rosenfeld, wrote a rebuttal article to Ferguson's, published by *Maclean's* on September 15, 1938. In "Elmer, You're Goofy," she pointed out that Ferguson "uses the same words and ideas that have been used by all those who have carried the banner inscribed, 'I hate women's sports,'" masking his intent to subjugate women with talk of beauty. "Sport is not responsible for whether or not she was pretty according to the Fergusonian standard," Atkins wrote of an athlete Ferguson belittled in his original article. "But I'll tell you what sport did for her. It gave her the chance to hear the shouts and cheers of the thousands; it enabled her to see her name in headlines across the very pages prepared by those who scoffed; it gave her 'a place in the sun' that most humans cherish and few attain."

In closing, Atkins focused in on the issue at hand—it was not beauty that concerned Ferguson, rather it was the idea that women would have a level playing field with men. "Mr. Ferguson, and I say this with all the femininity and grace I can command, 'Girls are human beings. They want an equal chance with men to go places, to see the world, to parade before crowds, to win medals and cups, to hear the cheers of the spectators. They want a chance to play, to develop physically, to cultivate the spirit of sportsmanship, to meet nice people, to have an interest beyond the home and the office.'"

Lytle and Ferguson were not alone. "The male press and promoters treated women's hockey with ambivalence . . . North American sportswriters portrayed women's hockey as 'other'—a different game. Male writers could not see it as a part of the modern brand. Reportage was brief, cursory, unserious, and often condescending."[32]

Famed sports mogul Walter Brown, who operated the Boston Garden, owned the NHL's Boston Bruins, served as president of the International Ice

Hockey Federation (IIHF), and is honored in the Hockey Hall of Fame, also did not believe in the women's game. Recalling the 1939 tour, Myrtle Cook explained that "Walter Brown . . . does not think much of girls' hockey . . . We asked him if he thought of booking a couple of Canadian teams for his ice. He exploded, 'Women's hockey! I should say not. They wouldn't draw.' Before a few more seasons roll around, the Bostonian may have to plate those hasty words. Women's hockey is improving each year. Crowds turned out elsewhere in America to watch Canadian teams . . . Some day (and we hope in ours) Canucks will be playing hockey with British teams—with French teams—with U.S. teams. The girls have caught up with the boys before in sport. Hockey should be no exception in the crowd drawing business."[33]

In different circumstances, Cook's optimism would have been justified. In Canada, Alexandrine Gibb's goal of a "girls' sport run by girls" had largely been realized. Despite financial hardship, the game had survived and a national organization had been created to increase participation. Led by Gibb and Cook, journalists were starting to acknowledge the talent on display, and the game was gaining popularity domestically and internationally. The best team in the world, the Preston Rivulettes, was planning a European tour to increase support for including women's hockey in the Olympics.

But by the time the Montreal Royals and Toronto Ladies were touring the United States, World War II was already underway. The conflict "reset priorities for the whole hockey world, male and female; for women, the war delivered a near-knockout blow."[34] It also killed women's sports journalism. After the death of her editor in 1936, Alexandrine Gibb faced stiff opposition from his replacement, Andy Lytle; the war provided a pretext to have her reassigned to covering women's war work. Myrtle Cook assisted with the training of military recruits, including coaching the Canadian Armed Forces track and field team. By the time the war ended, women's hockey was forgotten. Public interest waned, teams failed to re-form, and leagues were dead.

Gibb never returned to sports writing, and although Myrtle Cook continued to write "In the Women's Sportlight," "there was a paucity of press interest in women and girls on ice."[35]

Hilda Ranscombe, however, stayed on the ice. In 1946, still the star from a decade prior, she skated with the Galt Junior A Red Wings, a feeder team

39

for the NHL's Detroit Red Wings that included three future NHL players. One of them was Terry Sawchuk, who would go on to win the Vezina Trophy as the NHL's top goaltender four times.

Mary McGuire, a member of the 1938 Stratford Aces who faced the Rivulettes on multiple occasions, was there. "I can remember seeing Hilda, smooth as smooth, coming around her net carrying the puck, and skating through the whole team. I forget why this was set up—probably because everyone knew Hilda was the best female hockey player anywhere and they wanted to see how she would fare against a men's team—though it wasn't a real game . . . Hilda skated around them all and ended by scoring on Terry Sawchuk," she recalled. "I was there and I saw it. I knew many of the Galt Red Wings players. The crowd roared. They saw the greatest female hockey player score on the boy who would become the game's greatest goaltender."[36]

Hilda Ranscombe was inducted into the Canadian Sports Hall of Fame in 2015. The Preston Rivulettes followed in October of 2022, thanks in part to the advocacy of Carly Adams, who pointed out that "exclusion from halls of fame is just one way women's accomplishments are overlooked . . . The Rivulettes are inspirations for Canadians of all ages—their experiences are those of legends."[37]

CHAPTER 4

Put a Ring on It

Each week, my father took me to hockey practice. On the ice, the coaches would line us up parallel to the boards, with the last player in line making his way through the "gauntlet." As he skated between each teammate and the boards, the rest of us hit him as hard as possible, restricting his forward movement. When, or if, he reached the end, he would take his place, ready to exact his revenge on the next victim. After taking and receiving several dozen hits, we would line up on the goal line and complete "suicides": skating to the blue line and back, the red line and back, the far blue line and back, all the way down and back. Our exhaustion was revered, and a bloody nose—should our helmets slide up accidentally—was a war wound to be proud of. If anyone cried, they were shamed.

Afterward, after we had taken off our gear, my teammates and I would clamp our helmets on again and clench our fists inside our hockey gloves, preparing for a round of locker-room boxing or, as we called it, "helmets and gloves." It was a barbaric display of toxic masculinity at an age when our voices had yet to crack, and when a lone armpit hair could draw admiration from many. It was what boys were meant to do, or so we believed. We were taught to be tough, to not show emotion unless it was to celebrate victory or mourn defeat, to play through pain, and to never relent against our opponents. We were little soldiers heading out to "battle" in the corners, along the boards, and to take a hit for our team.

To train us for this combat, our coaches turned a blind eye to the hazy-eyed prepubescent youth leaving the dressing room, still seeing stars and hiding a week of headaches consistent with an undiagnosed concussion. Our masculinity and compliance were built, formed, and distorted until there was no other way to be. When we'd jump over the boards for a line brawl, our coaches would point and scream profanities at the opposing bench, saliva dripping from their frothing mouths. Should we fail, at any point, to fight, hit, or sacrifice, if we cried, if we didn't bury it all deep inside, the message would be clear—it was unacceptable to "play like girls."

•

Organized hockey for women disappeared during World War II and remained dormant. When a thirst for a return to the ice began in the 1950s, intensifying in the 1960s, a new version of the sport was introduced, one that was gentler, more socially acceptable for men and fathers watching their daughters, the type of game they believed girls should be playing. To satisfy a patriarchal society, men developed ringette as a sport they viewed as more acceptable and that would protect the bodies of women and girls.

"Like maple syrup and poutine, ringette is unmistakably Canadian," Ringette Canada's website proclaims. Ringette was invented in North Bay, Ontario, in 1963 by a man named Sam Jacks who, along with co-founder Mirl "Red" McCarthy, adapted the rules and strategies of hockey, sawing off the blades of hockey sticks but duplicating the skates, gloves, helmets, and padding. The game would be played on a hockey ice surface, utilizing hockey nets and hockey's blue lines, but ringette prohibited body contact in order to address concerns that hockey was too rough and could damage girls' reproductive organs. The game also set out to eliminate the need for costly gear and transformed the dangerous puck into a harmless rubber ring.

Limiting physicality was a primary goal not unique to ringette. According to former gender studies professor Iris Young, "Girls and women are not given the opportunity to use their full bodily capacities in free and open engagement with the world, nor are they encouraged as much as boys are to develop specific bodily skills."[1] As a result, women are often unsure of the true extent of their physical abilities.

Ringette provided space for women and girls to compete in sport while, perhaps unintentionally, enforcing anti-feminist ideas. As hockey writer Michael McKinley states, "Sam Jacks's invention was both a solution and a problem, for while it offered girls a chance to taste something of the game on ice, it was predicated on the notion that girls didn't want to play hockey the way boys did."[2] Girls who wanted to play hockey often faced "subtle and overt forms of discouragement" that implied an "impact on personal appearance and attractiveness" or subsequently, the "butch/masculine connotations associated with girls who play 'boys' sports." [3] Rooted in homophobia, this notion sought to deter women from entering the sport for fear of slurs and harassment.

Ringette was promoted heavily within Canada, and soon internationally. Canada's first provincial governing body, the Ontario Ringette Association, was formed in 1969, followed by Ringette Canada in 1974. The next year, the game was showcased on *Hockey Night in Canada*. After Sam Jacks' death in 1975, his wife, Agnes, continued to champion the sport. To encourage participation, she focused less on competition than on playing the game in a refined, peaceful way. Famously, she ended many of her speeches to young girls and their families with the same message: stay out of the penalty box.

Ringette was introduced to Finland in 1979, with a national association forming in 1983. In 1986, Canada founded the International Ringette Federation. Thousands of girls substituted pucks for rings, encouraged by parents who wanted their daughters to play a game they perceived as safer, while freeing up roster spots on hockey teams that their sons coveted. One of them was Jayna Hefford.

Jayna Hefford loved hockey. Beginning at age four, she grew up skating with her older brother on the backyard rink her father made each winter in Kingston, Ontario. She watched *Hockey Night in Canada* religiously; every four years she would watch men's hockey and women's figure skating during the Olympics.

When she was old enough to play, her parents signed her up for an on-ice sport of her own. "I never asked them why they put me in ringette, but I have to assume it was just because that's what parents did at that time, they put the girls in ringette and the boys in hockey," says Hefford. "My parents put me into ringette and I didn't know what the difference was, I don't think. I remember, after my first game, saying to them 'this isn't hockey.' It was different, the rules were different. It just wasn't what I envisioned."

Having watched players like Wayne Gretzky, Marcel Dionne, Denis Savard and Paul Coffey carry and pass the puck freely, Hefford was frustrated that she couldn't carry the ring over the blue line. "I remember that being really weird. I was like 'wait a second, I can't go to that part of the ice or I can't skate the ring across the line?' That made no sense to me," she explains.

"When you grow up watching hockey and playing hockey, the best part is you can get the puck and skate. You can pass the puck, not because you have to, just when it's a good opportunity to advance it."

Hefford also remembers a teammate scoring a goal. When team members celebrated, they were given a penalty for raising their sticks in the air, as hockey players often do. "I remember leaving that game at six years old and just understanding that this wasn't hockey, and what I wanted to play was hockey."

Hefford feels lucky to never have been pressured to stay in a sport she didn't enjoy. "I was pretty direct with my parents. Immediately they switched me onto a boys' hockey team. They never discouraged me from playing hockey or never ever said I wouldn't be able to play in the NHL," she recalls. "That just wasn't the way they raised me. But they probably thought that's what people did with their girls, put them in ringette. They learned pretty fast that's not what I wanted to do." Hefford never looked back, winning four Olympic gold medals and an Olympic silver, along with seven World Championship gold medals; she was later inducted into the Hockey Hall of Fame.

Ringette organizers continued to position the sport as a safer, more "feminine" option while hockey organizers like Fran Rider focused on providing opportunities for women and girls to enter sport in any capacity. "To us, if a girl wanted to play ringette and that was her choice, so be it," she explains. "But if she wanted to play hockey and had to play ringette instead, that wasn't right."

Women who preferred hockey began creating their own leagues, free from verbal abuse, where competitiveness would be seen as part of the game, not as an affront to masculinity. As one Manitoba organizer recalled, "when the girls showed any aggression on ice, it was taken the wrong way. It seemed like it was okay for the boys to go after pucks aggressively, but girls couldn't. The better girls were singled out by the players, parents, and coaches of the boys' teams and were called all sorts of names—'bitch' was a favourite. That's the main reason we formed the female league."[4]

In 1963, the Brampton Canadettes Girls' Hockey Association became the first in the world created specifically for girls and women. Four years later, the association hosted its first tournament. The Canadettes soon joined with other Toronto area teams—Don Mills, Lambton, and Burlington—to form the Central Ontario Women's Hockey League (COWHL). From the late 1960s through the 1990s, the COWHL was the top women's hockey league in the world, providing the majority of the players for Canada's inaugural Olympic roster.

Setting out to emphasize the autonomy of the "girls' sport run by girls" model, organizers inadvertently reinforced stereotypes typical of the pre-war years by including a gender marker that signaled which version of the sport was "real," a problem that persists. Men's hockey has the World Championship while all official International Ice Hockey Federation (IIHF) communications refer to the Women's World Championship.

Ringette, on the other hand, opted for the French suffix of "ette" that traditionally denotes an item as small, an imitation, and primarily feminine. It was a girls' sport played by girls but run by men. Most officials, organizers and coaches were men who had never played the game. "As much as the ringette athletes valued their sport experience, and enjoyed the fact that it was a predominantly female environment, the male presence in the position of power and authority inhibited their own aspirations . . . Where women aren't visible as effective leaders, where they don't have a significant say in their activities, there is neither true equality of opportunity, nor access."[5]

From the 1960s to the 1980s, hockey and ringette were at war. "[W]omen's and girls' hockey was challenged by more than want of perennial leagues and governing bodies, by more than a lingering chauvinism. It was compromised from within, by the emergence of ringette, a game designed expressly for girls . . . The game's growth enthused Canadians who believed that girls could excel in and control a segregated version of the game, their game. But the rise of ringette almost certainly slowed the revival of women's hockey by siphoning away a good many of its most able prospects."[6]

It was no coincidence that the first World Ringette Championships were held in 1990, just over a month before the first Women's World Hockey Championship, in the same city: Ottawa.

Canada, Finland, and the USA sent eight teams to compete for ringette's Sam Jacks Trophy. The lopsided result, in which Team USA did not score a single goal, became an issue for hockey's world championship organizers. "Unfortunately for the event organizers, the Ottawa media had just experienced another women's first 'world' championship, staged by Ringette Canada, in the Ottawa suburb of Gloucester, six weeks before the women's hockey event," wrote Patrick Alexander Reid of the 1990 Women's World Championship. They worried "that the members of the sports media would ignore the significance" of the tournament, and "they were concerned the event would likely only gain marginal media attention."[7]

One of the players at the 1990 Ringette World Championship was twenty-year-old Judy Diduck, who began playing ringette in Sherwood Park, Alberta, in 1979. Growing up, she'd skated and played street hockey with her brothers, including Gerald, a future first-round draft pick of the NHL's New York Islanders. "Everyone says I skate like a boy. We used to go public skating when I was little and that's where I learned to skate. I always wore boy's skates," she said. "I can't even skate in figure skates."[8]

Like many girls of her generation, Diduck wanted to play hockey but wasn't given the opportunity. "I tried [to play hockey] at ten and they wouldn't let me so I went to ringette and started playing," she recalled. "[Hockey] wasn't available so I didn't really think about it. At ten years old, it's not like you push the system too much and, back then, the system wasn't as flexible as it is now. I was more than happy playing ringette. It wasn't like it was the end of the world."[9]

Diduck became a ringette star, scoring twenty goals and four assists in only seven games at the 1987 national championships. In accordance with a long-standing practice that continues to this day, her achievements were validated by comparing them to men. "Diduck would probably cringe at the comparison but the 16-year-old Sherwood Park youngster could be described as kind of the Gretzky of ringette," Ron Lajoie wrote in 1983.[10] Even her mother compared her to men's hockey players, calling her "the Guy Lafleur of ringette."[11] One of the greatest ringette players in Canadian history, she was inducted into the Ringette Hall of Fame in 2009.

When she turned nineteen, a high-school friend convinced Diduck to join a hockey team, the Edmonton Chimos. "At that point, I didn't know there was so much ladies' hockey around Edmonton. I'd always loved hockey. We always played as kids in the basement shooting pucks or tennis balls or whatever and put the old pillows on the shins and we played street hockey out on the outdoor rinks. You know, kind of the typical story of a lot of Canadian kids."[12]

As the 1990 Ringette World Championship approached, Diduck was skating six days a week, playing both ringette and hockey. At times, the juggling act worked perfectly; other times she'd have to drop one sport for the other. Diduck started favoring hockey, declining a spot at the 1988 ringette national championships because of a conflict with her hockey schedule.

At the 1990 Ringette World Championships, Diduck helped Team Alberta win the first world title. With gold around her neck from the sport she'd spent many years dominating, Diduck felt it was time to allow her love for hockey to finally flourish. "It's such a tough choice. But I don't know how much more ringette I'll be playing, especially now that we've won," she explained. "But going out with gold is probably the best way to do it."[13]

After winning gold in February of 1990, Diduck changed sports permanently the following month when she stepped on the ice for the first IIHF World Championships of women's hockey. She wasn't alone. In fact, the popularity of ringette saw a rapid reversal in the 1990s. A trio of gold medals in hockey at the 1990, 1992, and 1994 World Championships, combined with the possibility that women's hockey would become an Olympic sport, tipped the scales. "Some girls try both," the *Edmonton Journal* observed. "But if they decide to jump from one to another, it's always ringette to hockey." "Unfortunately for ringette we're seeing more and more of that. We're seeing whole ringette associations switching over," Glynis Peters, the CAHA's manager of women's hockey observed in 1995.[14]

For Judy Diduck, the 1998 Winter Olympics would be her last international competition and the culmination of her hockey career. When her twenty-year-old teammate, Jayna Hefford, stepped on the ice, she represented a new generation of women's hockey players.

•

When I first stepped behind the bench to coach a women's team, the hurt inflicted by my own coaches still resided somewhere in my head, repressed deep inside. Whenever a player would yell, "Come on boys," I'd reassure my players that they were strong, powerful women, and that was fine. "Come on girls" held the same power on our bench, and on our ice. They didn't need to act like boys. When they cried, we consoled. It's an emotional game at times; it was okay to be hurt, to have your feelings hurt.

I told my teams time and time again that we were there to play hockey, that girls could be tough, they could play physical. In my first year, I lobbied to change the league rules; the equivalent level of boys' hockey played periods of 12–15–15 minutes instead of our 12–12–12. This difference implied that these athletes were delicate, that their bodies were incapable of six additional minutes. The rule changed, and our coaches preached over and over that they should be proud to be strong women in the sport. Day by day, we tried to chip away at the idea that men owned the game, made the terms of the game, or defined how women could play. More than once they watched me calmly—and sometimes less calmly—explain to a referee that what they had just called was not against the rules, that body contact was legal, and that the reason our opponent fell was because our players were stronger.

Over the five seasons I coached the same group of players, two graduated to NCAA Division I hockey, one also spending time with the Canadian U-18 national team. Five more played in different university or college leagues. Three chose NCAA scholarships for track and field over college hockey. Others gave up the game, completed their education, and are now in successful careers. Few saw a future in hockey, as there was no professional league paying a living wage.

Our players were athletes, hockey players, and more importantly, people. They were women and girls doing what they wanted, empowered to play sports they loved, and to make their own choices, without being told what it meant to play "girls'" sports—and certainly not considering any sport a man's domain.

CHAPTER 5

Applying Concealer

In church, I learned that God was a man. And I was taught that God had power over all things. It wasn't a difficult leap to see God and David and Moses and Paul as men who controlled all things in heaven and on earth. Before I learned about extinction, I learned animals were given to us by God for our use. Before I learned about climate change, I learned we were the rulers, that man had "dominion over the fish of the sea, and over the fowl of the air, and over the cattle, and over all the earth, and over every creeping thing that creepeth upon the earth." Whenever I walked into an arena, there were men. Men driving the Zamboni, men on the benches, men on the ice, all free to be themselves.

Women in hockey often needed to disguise their gender, camouflaging their identity from these men who claimed dominion over the ice. When they stepped onto the rink, they felt extra pressure to showcase their skill—to prove they were "real" hockey players, even when they were as good or better than the boys and men around them.

Today, many like to pretend that the struggle to keep women and girls out of hockey never occurred, that men never told women they did not belong. The Hockey Hall of Fame now houses exhibits intended to recognize the achievements of women and athletes of color, including a jersey and tournament patches donated by Bev Beaver, whose career was one for the ages. While traces of her story are now on display for all to see, during her playing days, Beaver, an Indigenous woman, was a hockey star hidden in plain sight.

•

In the 1950s, there was a pond near the old mill on Ontario's Six Nations of the Grand River where hockey players would congregate. With her toque pulled low and wearing her brothers' old clothes, Bev Beaver would step onto the ice and join the fray. As long as no one found out she was a girl, Bev could play.

Beaver was happy outdoors, growing vegetables, feeding their cows and pigs, and playing hide and seek. In warm weather, she and her siblings played baseball in the field behind their house; in the winter, they skated. When the temperature dropped, her brothers would build a dam in a low-lying area of their yard to create a larger ice surface. For years, her biggest competition was her cousin, Ed Staats, a goalie. "He'd get me to come in and shoot on him and I couldn't stop, so I would run into him and knock him down," Beaver recalls. "He said, 'I have to teach you how to turn because I'm tired of you running into me,' so he more or less helped me out with skating and taught me how to turn." Beaver spent hours at her cousins', not just working on her skating, but watching the Toronto Maple Leafs, as she didn't have a television at home.

Playing organized hockey seemed like an impossibility until Ed Staats' father, her uncle Hilton, asked her to join a team of Six Nations boys he was putting together. "I would always dress like a boy. I didn't want them to think I was a girl," Beaver explains. "I thought they might not want me to play. From my experiences with guys thinking girls couldn't do things like boys could, I would just disguise myself so they'd let me join in."

Her first official games came at the grimmest of locations, the Mohawk Institute, Canada's first residential school, nicknamed "Mush Hole" for the worm-infested mush they fed the students. The school was a site of abuse and trauma for many children from Six Nations and other First Nations from across Ontario. Bev's mother, Norma Henhawk, had been one of them.

Her mother rarely spoke of her time there so, when Beaver skated onto the outdoor rink at the Mohawk Institute as a preteen, she "didn't think much about it. We weren't told much about the residential school. My mother didn't say too much about the bad experiences, other than they were punished for speaking their language. She just said she was there for a while, her and her brother and sister."

At residential schools, including the Mohawk Institute, hockey was often used as a tool of assimilation. It was seen as a pathway to make children feel more Canadian, continuing the cultural genocide that, in addition to the loss of language, included family separation, loss of ceremonies and spiritual practices, and the death of thousands of Indigenous children. Luckily for Beaver, she escaped that fate but remembers seeing children her age who had been taken to the Mohawk Institute within Six Nations and the surrounding communities. "The Mush Hole kids, the kids who would come from Mohawk, they'd be dressed in their uniform, and that was strange. We knew that was where they were from. I sort of felt sorry for them because they had to be dressed like that and march around, be in line, they couldn't have fun like the rest of us."

Soon after those first games, Beaver's skills started attracting attention, and she was recruited to play for another Six Nations Peewee team. "I was going to their practices and a few exhibition games. Then they took me to a big tournament. I was all dressed and on the bench ready to play, but at the last minute the coach decided not to use me because he was afraid that if they found out I was a girl he might get disqualified from the tournament, which they eventually won. That was the closest I got to actually playing in an organized boys' game, other than exhibition."

Luckily, there would soon be a girls' team on Six Nations, formed in 1963. "The coach of the boys' Peewee team, his name was Oliver Smith. He had a daughter named Sarah, and she organized a women's hockey team for Six Nations and that's how I got started playing organized hockey with women."

Beaver was an offensive and physical force at a time when bodychecking was still allowed. She soon became a scoring phenomenon. Playing games locally in Hagersville, Brantford, and Burlington, Beaver would often record five, six, or seven points in a game, almost single-handedly defeating opponents and leading her team to tournament wins. When winter turned to summer, Beaver would take off her skates and step onto the diamond, transforming into one of Ontario's most feared pitchers with the Oshweken Mohawks fastball team. In 1967, she was awarded the regional Tom Longboat Award as the top Indigenous athlete in Southwestern Ontario.

The same year, Beaver left her Six Nations team to play for Burlington in the new Central Ontario Women's Hockey League, where she won the league scoring title in 1967 and 1972, was second in league scoring in the intervening years and was a five-time MVP. Beaver's prowess both on the field and ice earned her the national Tom Longboat Award in 1980 as Canada's top Indigenous athlete.

The following year, at the age of thirty-four, she decided to hang up her skates, but the draw of competition was too great. Two years later, Beaver was called back to play for Burlington, who needed a boost to get to the national championship. After two years off the ice, she managed sixteen points in fourteen games. At the provincial championships, she scored to defeat the reigning national champions from Agincourt, earning game MVP honors. She continued playing hockey until the early 1990s, ending her career playing with her daughter, Pamela, on the Brantford Lady Blues Senior B team.

Beaver was still playing in 1990 when the first Women's World Championship took place, but her prime years had passed. "It would have been fantastic if I'd been able to play for Team Canada, or in the Olympics," Beaver says. "It would have been nice to be recognized on a bigger scale and play against teams from other countries." She also regrets the lack of opportunity off the ice. "Modern day women's hockey is really recognized now on the sports channels, and some women are hockey broadcasters. That would have been nice for some of our older players, but at the time that wasn't possible."

Despite her incredible career and success, when Beaver sits down in front of her television to watch a hockey game, whether it be the Toronto Maple Leafs, or a women's game featuring Team Canada, she still wonders, "what if." What if she had been born in a time when women were welcomed in hockey?

•

While Bev Beaver was disguising herself on the ponds, Abigail Hoffman was registering for hockey in Toronto in the mid-1950s. She'd grown up near High Park playing on an outdoor rink across the street. At dinnertime, she wouldn't waste time taking her skates off, walking across her home's terrazzo floors to the table, eating quickly, and returning to the ice. When Hoffman turned nine, her father, Samuel, took his daughter to register for a newly formed league. "While I was inquiring about a girls' team, Abi wandered off into the crowd and handed in her birth certificate without telling me," he later recalled. "A few days later I received a call from the league saying Abby could play."[1] His "son," Ab, had been placed on the St. Catherines Teepees, a Toronto-based team nicknamed for a local Junior A club. "We didn't have the heart to tell him the boy was a girl and spoil her chances of playing," said Hoffman's mother, Dorothy Medhurst.[2]

The Windsor Star described Ab as a "rough, tough defenceman," quickly recognized as one of the best defenders in the league. Hoffman, dressed like the boys on her team and with her hair chopped short, fit in. On the ice, she was skilled and physical. When no one asked, Hoffman simply continued to play.

Three months after joining the league, Hoffman was named to the Little Toronto Hockey League's All-Star team. When she submitted her birth certificate again, league officials were surprised to see the word "female." Ab Hoffman was Abigail. "It completely knocked the wind out of me. No one noticed her birth certificate earlier because it was the last thing we expected," said Earl Graham, chairman of the Little Toronto Hockey League. "We thought she was a boy because she looked like a boy," explained Al Grossi, manager of Hoffman's team. "She had short hair and with hockey equipment we couldn't see any difference." Despite their surprise, both the league and team were on Abby's side. "I sure was fooled. I don't know what to say but we sure want Ab to stay with the team," said a ten-year-old teammate at the time.[3]

There was no rule that prohibited girls, so the league decided to allow Hoffman to play at the first Timmy Tyke Tournament, as well as at the Toronto Hockey League's year-end jamboree. Ralph Butler, league executive, said, "We hope she will continue playing and are making plans to have a special dressing room for her at all future games."[4]

Hoffman's story was widely reported in Canada and the US. Montreal Canadiens General Manager Frank Selke sent Hoffman a team windbreaker and a letter of support. "I have heard of your participation in hockey and feel that such devotion to Canada's principal game deserves a little reward," Selke's letter read. "I brought up five little girls myself and appreciate all their good qualities and I hope, in spite of all the newspaper publicity you now receive, that you will always remain as sweet as you are."[5]

Governing bodies in Canada and Ontario, however, were not prepared to welcome women to this men's sport. After the 1955–56 season, Hoffman was no longer eligible to play. Her parents filed suit in Ontario Supreme Court, which eventually upheld the league's decision. Unable to play on a boys' team, Abby hoped to play in a new league for girls that the Little Toronto Hockey League created in response to interest generated by her story—a hockey school for girls held in March of 1956 had attracted more than a hundred girls. Despite this initial promise, the league struggled to get off the ground. "Some of the men in the THL didn't want it, I think. Thought it would cost too much to rent the ice," Hoffman stated in a December 1956 radio interview with the CBC's Ed Fitkin.

When, in 1958, three girls registered for one of Ontario's largest youth tournaments, organizers reacted with alarm. "We decided it had gone far enough," tournament chairman Bruce Erskine told the Canadian Press. "No more girls . . . we're afraid they might get hurt."[6] As anticipated, later that year the Ontario Minor Hockey Association (OMHA) added a "no-girls" clause to their constitution.

Abby Hoffman's hockey career was officially over. Describing the case years later, a writer for the *Vancouver Sun* put it this way: "The body-checks were a robust part of her disguise. Her haircut was another. She wore it short, in the crew-cut fashion of Grade Three males." But, once discovered, "solemn to the rights of their sex, the officials ruled hockey out for hoydens."[7]

Similar prohibitions were introduced in other sports deemed too masculine. In 1959, the Boxing and Wrestling Commission banned girls, sure that "ladies' wrestling will add nothing to the general benefit or enjoyment of the citizens at large."[8]

Canadian sports organizations began formally banning girls from participating in hockey just as the United States began loosening its restrictions. Girls had long been prohibited from American school sports until, in 1957, "the long-entrenched official position statement of the Division for Girls and Women in Sport (DGWS) was amended to state that intercollegiate programs 'may' exist."[9]

Except for a brief return while attending Humberside Collegiate in 1963, Hoffman's hockey dreams were done. Instead, she started participating in track and field, becoming the Canadian record holder in the 800-meter event. In 1976, two decades after being turned away from hockey, Abigail Hoffman, dressed in the red and white of Canada, led the host nation onto the track at the Olympic Stadium in Montreal. A four-time Olympian, she was the first woman to serve as Canada's flagbearer. She would go on to become the first woman elected to the Canadian Olympic Committee's executive committee.

In 1981, Abby Hoffman was appointed Canada's new Director General of Sport, the first woman in the role. As she explained to the *Toronto Star*, "It is a bizarre notion that people sit here and run things from coast to coast. It's an absurd exercise." Instead, "Our role is to instill motivation and energy into the system." She began building systems that would ensure athletes like her could train properly, balance their careers, and see support from their government. She also encouraged sports organizations to find ways to keep athletes in sport longer and the corporate sector to invest in sponsorship. "The problem in Canada is that athletes see a conflict between career and sport. They don't feel they can combine both, but if corporations would co-operate, they could."[10]

Women's hockey was an immediate beneficiary. In 1982, the CAHA operated the first Canadian National Women's Hockey Championship with a significant corporate sponsor. The event was officially known as the Shoppers Drug Mart Women's Hockey Nationals, later becoming the Esso Women's Hockey Nationals.

That first season, a powerhouse team from Ontario, the Agincourt Canadians, defeated the Edmonton Chimos to earn the inaugural title. The following season, 1982–83, the Burlington Ladies defeated the Chimos. No longer hiding who she was, Bev Beaver lifted the Abby Hoffman Cup as a national champion.

CHAPTER 6

Be My Sweetheart

I was fifteen when I met Eric Harvey. He wore glasses, had stiffly gelled hair, and always wore a team tracksuit with a fanny pack full of the essentials—bandages, gauze and scissors—the telltale sign of an athletic trainer. Harv, as we affectionately called him, was there for every game, every practice, every event. He loved the sport, and he would do anything for the players on our team. When I left AAA hockey, Harv followed me to Junior in our mutual hometown of Wallaceburg. He'd tape my wrists before games and help me through shoulder injuries over the coming seasons. When hockey season ended, he would move on to lacrosse. Harv gave me my first hockey nickname—"Chugga"—because it took me a while to get going, but when I did I could hit like a train. I've never met anyone so dedicated to athletes.

I'd met Eric's mom, a perpetual volunteer and fan, many times, but I'd never had a full conversation with Grace Harvey until I saw a newspaper photo of a much younger woman named Grace Small, holding a hockey stick with a lipstick kiss on the blade. The accompanying article talked about how Grace had worked to form the first women's hockey team in Wallaceburg, Ontario, and how that team went on to host Ontario's first women's hockey tournament, the Lipstick Tournament.

•

Sitting in the cold stands of Wallaceburg Memorial Arena, her friends nestled beside her for warmth, Grace watched her brother fly down the wing. He was easy to spot. One of the smallest players on the ice, he danced around opponents, scoring at will with the Wallaceburg Hornets. Wayne would go on to star as a First Team All-American for Brown University, then play for Carleton University in Canada before embarking on an almost decade-long professional career in Switzerland.

"A bunch of us girls would go to the games and we got talking and said if the guys can play hockey, why can't the girls?" Small recalls. "We were just as good. Maybe we didn't play as well, but we were just as important."

In 1965, Small marched into the office of Harold Ribson, the town's recreation director and manager of the arena. "I approached him and said, 'if we can get some girls together, can we have some ice time?' He kind of snickered and said, 'If you can get some girls together, I will give you ice time.' So I proceeded. We went and talked to this one and that one and, sure enough, we got enough girls together to form a team. We called ourselves the Wallaceburg Hornettes because of the Hornets being the male counterpart."

As word of the new team spread throughout the halls of Wallaceburg District Secondary School, more girls were recruited, and the team was born. In 1966, impressed by the passion he saw on the ice, Ribson decided to host an unofficial one-day exhibition, inviting teams from Ontario, including Bev Beaver's Indigenous team from Six Nations of the Grand River, and nearby Michigan, home to three more women's teams. For US teams that didn't have leagues to play in, largely in Massachusetts and Michigan, tournaments provided the only opportunity to face serious competition.

The positive response was enough for Ribson to decide that the exhibition should become an annual tournament. He approached Jack Lacey, president of local manufacturer Wally Enterprises. Founded in 1946, Wally Enterprises started out with a workforce of women with their hair tied in bandanas bent over lathes making corn cob pipes to be shipped across North America. Twenty years later, the company had recently been sold to Hillerich and Bradsby and were now manufacturing hockey sticks. Named by the staff at Wally Enterprises, the inaugural Lipstick Tournament would be held near Valentine's Day, 1967.

"Wally Enterprises gave us pink sticks, all of our sticks were pink," Small recalls. "Because it was the centennial year, they decided that would be the first celebration we had. They had me endorse the little hockey stick—they had painted lips on the stick—I supposedly endorsed it with a kiss."

Billed as the North American Girls Hockey Championship Tournament, the Lipstick Tournament was the first annually contested women's hockey tournament played in Ontario, and the first standalone tournament in Canada. Unlike events in Banff and Rossland, which had been held in conjunction with carnivals, hockey would be its sole focus. Organizers sought to ensure the success of the event by inviting Detroit Red Wings General Manager Jack Adams, for whom the NHL's Coach of the Year award is named, and Vezina Trophy-winning goalie Johnny Mowers. Also in attendance was the crew from *Hockey Night in Canada*, who played a preliminary exhibition game against the hometown Hornettes, losing 6–2.

The tournament was a huge success, not only on the ice, but in the stands. "There were a lot of people during that first Lipstick Tournament, the arena filled up," recalls Small. "There was a lot of excitement, a lot of friendliness, a lot of camaraderie. We were excited to be part of something new, we were excited to be on the ice to play."

The quality of play impressed onlookers. The final game in particular, won by the Humberside Dairy Queens in a 2–1 decision over the Don Mills Satan's Angels, elicited "the opinion that the two teams would be capable of defeating a few of the men's teams competing in the area."[1] The most valuable player, the Lipstick Tournament Sweetheart, was given a heart-shaped, engraved locket; Miss Valentine received a bouquet of roses.

After their first tournament, the women on the Hornettes realized their skates were not suited to hockey. "We played with figure skates because we didn't put boys' skates on," says Grace Small. At the time, "hockey skates" were definitely boys' skates, while girls only wore figure skates.

Shirley Huff, an Indigenous woman from neighboring Walpole Island First Nation who played for Wallaceburg, was frustrated. "One thing about hockey, we had to use figure skates to play, and I was always tripping and falling all over with these little picks on the end. So I took them to a man who sharpened skates and I got them shaved off, so I played okay with it," Huff says. "As the months went on, I picked up a pair of boys' skates from the Goodwill store and played hockey. I loved it."

The shift from figure skates to hockey skates or, as most called them, "boy's skates," was a significant development that removed one more barrier to women's participation. As Harold Ribson told *The Windsor Star*, some women who chose to wear "boy's hockey skates" for the first time, or who had filed toe picks off figure skates, found the adjustment difficult. "The girls have been wearing white figure skates and using the points of the skates to push away. Some of the girls have had to learn how to skate all over again."[2]

Despite the level of competition, players were almost always portrayed as ladylike, rather than athletic. In the local newspaper, images promoting upcoming tournaments involved members of the Hornettes preening in the mirror, applying makeup, and wearing dresses. One Wallaceburg player, described as one of the team's "best forwards" was introduced by referencing her victory in a recent beauty pageant: "One of the last places you would expect to see a beauty queen is taking her turn on the ice in a hockey game."[3] During the week of the tournament, a two-page spread appeared in the *Wallaceburg Courier Press*, each woman encapsulated in or accompanied by a heart, with the title "Here are Wallaceburg's Sweethearts" emblazoned atop the page. Other articles referred to women's hockey as "powder puff" or "distaff" hockey. Often, the women themselves were "patsies."

It would take almost a decade for the narrative to shift from curious spectacle to serious athletic endeavor. Strikingly, as the quality of play improved, media coverage declined; instead of mocking women in sport, newspapers were forced to acknowledge that players had earned a measure of legitimacy. Previewing the 1976 tournament, *The Windsor Star* observed that, "If you think there is no place in the bruising game of hockey for women, the eighth annual Wallaceburg Jaycee Lipstick Hockey Tournament . . . might change your mind."[4]

Weeks after the first Lipstick Tournament, the first Dominion Ladies Hockey Tournament was held in Brampton, Ontario. Held annually in April, it would go on to become Canada's longest running and largest women's hockey tournament. Women in the greater Toronto area had been competing in league play for years, but this new event brought a bigger spotlight to the sport. As with Wallaceburg, spectators came with skepticism but left impressed.

The revitalization of women's hockey was part of a broader social movement. Less than a week after the first puck drop in Wallaceburg, on February 16, 1967, Prime Minister Lester Pearson announced the creation of a Royal Commission on the Status of Women in Canada. In response to persistent pressure from more than thirty women's groups, the Commission set out to "ensure for women equal opportunities with men in all aspects of Canadian society." Later that year, on November 7, the United Nations General Assembly released the Declaration on the Elimination of Discrimination Against Women that read, "All appropriate measures shall be taken to educate public opinion and to direct national aspirations towards the eradication of prejudice and the abolition of customary and all other practices which are based on the idea of the inferiority of women."

The report on the Status of Women in Canada took three years to complete. When it was published in 1970, it confirmed what every player at the Lipstick and Dominion Tournaments already knew: "Ball parks, ice rinks with scheduled hockey practice, and summer team sports are almost the exclusive province of boys. We know of no programme for girls, for example, that includes the numbers of participants as those included in Little League Baseball or the variety of hockey leagues open to boys." The Commissioners made 167 recommendations, including to "provide girls with equal opportunities with boys to participate in athletic and sports activities," "establish policies and practices that will motivate and encourage girls to engage in athletic and sports activities" and to conduct research to discover "why fewer girls than boys participate in sports."

The last Lipstick Tournament was played in 1993. By then, it had done the heavy lifting. In conjunction with the Dominion and other tournaments, it had showcased women's hockey and created space for women to organize and advocate for change. "It was the forerunner of the women's hockey association," says Grace Small. "Back then, you didn't really think of the significance of it until years later. When it was done, it was something important, but when you're a kid, you're just out there to play the game of hockey, to have fun with your friends, and have a good time. You don't really stop to think of what you've done and what you've started."

CHAPTER 7

Power Plays

When I was in Grade 12, my Exercise Science teacher assigned us debate topics. The one my partner and I were given was "in the National Collegiate Athletics Association (NCAA), men's sports deserve more funding than women's." My partner—another male athlete who played football, basketball, and volleyball at our school—and I were tasked with arguing in favor, while two women from our class were appointed to argue against. It was the first time in my life I'd been asked to consider such a topic. It was also the first time I learned about Title IX.

One word in the resolution was particularly troubling: deserve. Men didn't deserve more funding, although at the time they received the bulk of it, primarily for sports like football, basketball and, at schools that had a team, hockey. Travel, stadiums, and equipment for football alone tipped the scales. To run these programs, schools needed to pump more money into men's sport, but men didn't "deserve" more money. They weren't inherently more worthy.

It was a difficult resolution to argue in favor of, but that was our assignment. I distinctly remember sitting across from our opponents and delivering our points as diplomatically as possible. My partner, however, lost his composure and, in a moment I'm sure he'd like to take back today, challenged both of the women sitting across from us to an arm wrestle.

I wish I could go back to that Grade 12 classroom, lay down my pen and paper, and calmly state, "There are no reasons. Men do not deserve more than women in any aspect of life, and I will not debate otherwise." I would have loved to fold my hands and open up space for the women in the room to safely explain their perspective, which might have changed some minds. Instead, I did what men have done for years—I tried to define the undefinable in a way that met my purposes: in this circumstance, to get the best mark and "win" the debate. I sat back and watched the debate devolve to a point where men were telling women what they'd been told for years, that unless they could beat us, whether it be on the ice or in an arm wrestle, they did not belong.

•

The winds of change that brought the UN Declaration and the Royal Commission on the Status of Women were also blowing in the United States. On June 23, 1972, US President Richard Nixon signed Title IX of the Education Amendments into law, ensuring that, "No person in the United States shall, on the basis of sex, be excluded from participation in, be denied the benefits of, or be subjected to discrimination under any education program or activity receiving Federal financial assistance." Seven months later, on January 22, 1973, the US Supreme Court's landmark Roe v. Wade decision upheld a woman's right to abortion.

In 1975, Title IX was revised to specifically include athletic programming and opportunities at the university level: "No person shall, on the basis of sex, be excluded from participation in, be denied the benefits of, be treated differently from another person or otherwise be discriminated against in any interscholastic, intercollegiate, club or intramural athletics offered by a recipient, and no recipient shall provide any such athletics separately on such basis."

In order to be Title IX compliant, schools needed to ensure that the enrollment on men's and women's teams was proportional to overall registration. Beyond participation, schools were required to increase opportunity. According to law professor Deborah Brake, "The law focuses on the institutional structures that suppress and discourage women from expressing and developing their athletic interests and abilities. In this respect, the law reflects strains of feminist legal theory not widely embodied in sex discrimination law."[1]

Title IX revolutionized sports for girls and women, significantly increasing access and participation. But the rapid expansion of sports also exacerbated the existing power imbalance. As Brake points out, when women lack access to decision-making, "athletics becomes another arena where men exert control over women . . . Female athletes may be more vulnerable to abuse of the disparate power inherent in the coach–athlete relationship when they are coached by men."

In Canada, women were already organizing and running their own leagues. In the United States, men still controlled the main opportunities in women's hockey—Assabet Valley Girls Hockey prime among them.

From the outside, the beige metal siding and stained sloped roof of the Valley Sports Arena in West Concord, Massachusetts, is slightly less impressive than many equipment sheds across the Midwest. Despite its nondescript appearance, the home of Assabet Valley Girls Hockey has been a mecca for generations of girls with hockey dreams.

The architect of the Assabet program was Carl Gray, who founded it alongside the New England Girls Hockey League in 1972, just as Title IX was introduced. In an interview with Shira Springer of public radio station WBUR, he explained, "I've always said to people, 'If you have a son or daughter, wouldn't you want to have the same treatment for your daughter that you do for your son?' It really is a very fundamental question you need to ask yourself."[2]

Gray developed an elite program just as women's hockey at the NCAA level was beginning to grow in the Northeast. In the modern era, Brown was the first school in America to launch a women's hockey team in 1964, followed by Cornell in 1971. Because a women's hockey team could accommodate twenty or more athletes, NCAA programs anxious to become Title IX compliant often favored it over sports with smaller rosters. Soon schools across the eastern states, including Yale, Dartmouth, Providence and Princeton, were forming teams. All of them relied on the pipeline of players from programs like Assabet, which attracted the best. Hundreds of Assabet alumni went on to play NCAA Division I hockey, and the American national team has included Assabet alumni since its inception.

As *The Boston Globe* explained, "In a blood sport dominated by an abundance of testosterone, Carl Gray chose a different path: He started a girls' hockey program in 1972, just before Title IX reared its liberating head. In 1975, he and his partners bought the rink in West Concord so that no one could deny his girls equal ice time." Describing him as "the acknowledged king of girls' hockey," journalist Bella English went on to profile the man. "Gray's legendary gruffness is matched only by his legendary wins. If you want to play for him—and girls who take hockey seriously do—you learn to take 'Mr. Gray' in stride . . . During one recent game in which he yells that they are playing '(expletive) hockey,' one of the players says, 'That's just Mr. Gray. He says a lot of swears.'"

Gray made no excuses for his demanding approach. "I tell them I take the girls right to the edge of a steep cliff, but I won't take them over. They might lose their lunch the first time, but the second time, they're OK." Players and parents generally accepted Gray's rough manner. "A few parents have spoken up, too. But not many. They know he has great contacts, that coaches scout his games, that he has helped his girls get into elite prep schools and colleges."[3]

"From a standpoint of development, by the time a young girl reaches age 13, it is very important as you go through the process that they feel comfortable about themselves," Gray told the *Boston Herald* in 2012. "They're going through big changes physically and psychologically. They are very sociable and if you work at that inner relationship around the rink, they'll work their butt off for you. You don't have to push them. They'll just do it from within."[4]

In her *Boston Globe* article, Bella English described Gray as a "Svengali-like character," a reference to a fictional character who made a young girl a star by exploiting and manipulating her. It was a more apt description than she knew.

•

Cindy Curley stood knee-deep in Boon Lake. The ice was thin along the shore and she'd broken through. With her skates resting on the muddy bottom, she retrieved the puck that had slid beneath a boathouse and sent it back across thicker ice to where her brothers and neighbors waited to resume the game. She climbed out of the water, removed her skates, and sprinted for her house. She changed her wet clothes and then sprinted back to the lake, putting her feet back into wet skates. All she wanted to do was play hockey.

Only a few miles from Cindy Curley's house, Estey Ticknor was skating on a pond in Concord, Massachusetts. She'd watched her brother play hockey at the local rink and knew that's what she wanted to do as well. "My brother was helpful in making sure the guys let me play. If he wasn't there, they either wouldn't pass to me or wouldn't let me play. I was just constantly fighting."

Ticknor wouldn't play in an indoor arena until she entered ninth grade at Concord Academy. "By the time I got on the ice with the girls, I had a lot of skills," she recalls. Her talent was quickly recognized by Carl Gray, who invited her to play at Assabet Valley. There, she joined Cindy Curley in one of hockey's first dominant programs for women.

"Girls' hockey was in residence in Concord. It was the biggest program there; the Assabet girls' program ruled that rink," says Ticknor. "At Assabet, we got the best ice time, because it was primarily a girls' program there," explains Cindy Curley, who started in the program at age ten.

Assabet players were granted unparalleled access and resources, but at a price. "Carl was a gruff man, he liked to yell, and he was hard on players, often too hard," Curley says.

"Carl . . . he took on this girls' hockey thing as his call to arms. It fueled his narcissism, but he put all his resources into it and it provided so many opportunities for girls, which is why he's so controversial. He loved being the king of it all and feeling like he made these players. He had power over being somehow responsible for 'creating us,'" Ticknor explains. "Carl screamed and yelled and berated me all the time. I was very scared of him; he made me desperate for his approval."

In their senior year together, Curley and Ticknor powered Assebet to the 1981 national championships, held in Lake Placid on the same ice where the USA had experienced the "Miracle on Ice" against the USSR only months before. But triumph on the ice also marked the beginning of a nightmare for Ticknor. That season, Carl Gray began pursuing a romantic and sexual relationship with her.

One evening in 1981, Ticknor, then seventeen, and her 43-year-old coach sat on a blanket in Minute Man National Historical Park, a place they often went. When flashing blue lights interrupted their rendezvous, she hoped for rescue. Instead, Gray, a mountainous six-foot-four man, sauntered toward the police car, had a brief conversation with the officer, then returned to Ticknor and explained they had to leave because no one was permitted in the park after dark. For Ticknor, it was one more reminder that Carl Gray was a man with power.

When she attempted to end the abuse, Gray arrived at her house and sat at her kitchen table, tearfully pleading with her mother. "He started drawing circles on paper about how he saw things going, with his wife as one circle and Estey as another circle," Matilda Ticknor told *The Boston Globe* years later. "He wanted Estey as his mistress. I said, 'What are you talking about? This is impossible.'"[1]

At the end of the 1981 season, Curley and Ticknor went their separate ways. Curley attended Providence College where she met another man working to promote women's hockey, Lou Lamiorello, then the athletic director. "When I got to Providence, I remember it was so different, not being yelled and screamed at," she said. "I didn't know any different from Assabet. If Lou saw something in your game that he didn't like, or that could be improved, he was going to tell you, but he was also going to help you. Lou always wanted women's hockey to be successful at Providence, and he made sure we had opportunities that women at other schools didn't. I remember we'd talk, and he knew I would sometimes get out of the way of the puck, that I needed work on my tipping. So, after practice, he'd send one of his men's players out there with me, and I'd stand in front of the net and they'd just blast the puck at me until I learned not to move and got comfortable tipping the puck."

One of the all-time greatest to play at Providence College, where she was an Eastern College Athletic Conference Player of the Year, Curley was one of the pioneers of the American hockey program. She represented the USA at the inaugural Women's World Championships in 1990, setting a single tournament record that would stand for decades, scoring twenty-three points in only five games. She would go on to represent the USA at the next two world championships as well, winning silver at each. When Curley was inducted into the United States Hockey Hall of Fame in 2013, one year after Lou Lamiorello, he sent her a personal letter of congratulation.

While Curley chose Providence, Ticknor chose Dartmouth. "Even though my entire family had gone to Harvard, I turned on Harvard because I didn't want to be in Cambridge where Carl Gray happened to work. Dartmouth was two hours north of Boston. I chose it because I wanted to be farther away."

At Dartmouth, Ticknor encountered the disparity between men's and women's hockey programs for the first time. Assabet had been all about women's hockey; here women's hockey players were second-class citizens. "Certainly there were men who were dismissive and would scoff at the idea of girls playing hockey, but the things that made me the angriest were the structural things, like the men's team at Dartmouth getting the prime ice time," Ticknor explains. "They had a bigger budget.

"I was completely fixated on hockey. It was the only thing I cared about and the coach there was a really great guy. He was not a big hockey guy but he mentored us and fought for the women's program to get equal treatment. When he resigned, they hired a local guy who had been working at a skate shop for us; they didn't want to bring someone in, or pay someone, and this guy didn't know a thing. Dartmouth was such a sexist, conservative, horrible place. Dartmouth was an awful place to be a young female athlete. It was very homophobic. It was all men up until just before I got there, too. The men's team had this gorgeous, palatial locker room; we had to climb stairs to get to our room and it wasn't even as nice as the visiting men's locker room."

The barriers were structural and systemic, but also very personal. Ticknor felt the weight of the abuse she had endured from Carl Gray. Every team they played included Assabet alumni; she was afraid everyone was talking about her, that they knew what had happened.

"During college I dealt with my internalized shame. I went to therapy, and realized it was Carl's fault," says Ticknor. "I confronted him at one point. I was still going home in the summers, and so, in order to get ice time, I had to go to the rink he owned. I confronted him and said, 'You did this thing to me, you were wrong,' but he maintained how 'special' I was. By this time, I was twenty-one and I was pretty clear in myself, but he was still in charge of my access to women's hockey outside of Dartmouth. If I was going to participate, I had to reconcile with it all and take back my own power."

Ticknor chose to stick with hockey. She was the 1982 Ivy League Rookie of the Year at Dartmouth, and twice a First Team All-Ivy star. She captained the school team in the 1984–85 season and, in 1987, represented the USA at the first unofficial women's World Hockey Tournament.

Thirty-two years later, in 2019, more than two dozen former Assabet players, some as young as eight, came forward to accuse Carl Gray of emotional abuse and unwanted physical contact. Some girls claimed Gray had sexually assaulted them.

Hockey officials were not surprised. It seemed his behavior at Assabet was a poorly kept secret. Following a parent's complaint about the treatment of their eleven-year-old daughter, the chair of Mass Hockey's discipline and SafeSport committee, Christine Mayer, responded in writing: "Unfortunately this type of behavior exhibited by Carl Gray has occurred before and probably will again . . . We believe the whole 'culture' at Assabet needs correction."[2]

When Estey Ticknor read the newspaper article, she felt compelled to tell her story. Gray "retired" shortly after her interview was published, turning the Assabet program over to his daughter, Paula.

Separating the man from the program is a challenge, one that Cindy Curley and others struggle with. "I have no doubt that he did some awful things and made a lot of bad choices, so it's difficult to reconcile. He was so important to building women's hockey, not only at Assabet but for the USA as well, especially for women, but he also caused a lot of harm, including to some of my teammates."

CHAPTER 8

Changing on the Fly

In the darkness, buckled into the passenger seat, I would try to steal a few more minutes of sleep while my dad drove me across the county for early morning hockey practice in nearby Chatham, Ontario.

I knew this ride by heart; my eyes would pop open at the same bumps and turns. Midway between Wallaceburg and Chatham, we'd pass the spot where I had been born at the side of the road. Just past that intersection was a tiny farming village called Electric. In the 1950s, most of Electric's population had one last name, Coveny, a name synonymous with championship fastball teams in the area.

The Covenys, particularly eldest son John, loved baseball and, with ten siblings, could field their own team. During the winter, the family skated on the frozen creeks that divided farmers' fields. At the age of four, Marian, or Mern as the family called her, put on a pair of bob skates and started pushing an old metal chair along Bear Creek. Soon, she advanced to figure skates, her father filing off the toe picks so they would more closely mimic the hockey skates she dreamed of. As the youngest in a family of ten, however, Mern used hand-me-downs until she was a teenager. "Every Christmas I would ask for a hockey stick and puck and hope for new skates," she recalled. "However, I purchased my first pair of new skates on my own when I started playing organized hockey. Up until then, we just shared skates within the family."

Coveny began playing organized hockey when she entered high school. Her sister, Carmen, had been invited to play for a new team, but it was Mern who couldn't wait to suit up with the Wallaceburg Hornettes. "I jumped at the opportunity as soon as my mom said it was okay."

After her first practice, there was no looking back. "I remember absolutely loving playing the game of hockey ever since stepping on the ice for the first time in Wallaceburg. My fondest memories are all to do with the Lipstick

Tournament. I remember when I was young, the big teams from Toronto would come in and I would watch their games and hope that someday I might be able to play at that level. They were an inspiration to me." In 1972, in front of a packed crowd, Coveny starred for her hometown, leading the Hornettes to a B-division title.

From the Hornettes, Coveny moved on to play Ontario Women's Interuniversity Athletic Association hockey for McMaster University, where she was studying to become a physical education teacher. She led the McMaster Marauders to a pair of Ontario championships in 1976 and 1978 and was inducted into the McMaster Athletics Hall of Fame in 2002

In 1977, while still playing for McMaster, Coveny became a founding member of the COWHL's Hamilton Golden Hawks. As team captain, she demanded that women's hockey be treated with respect. When her team was forced to start late because the preceding men's game ran over its allotted time, she insisted the women be given sufficient time to finish their game. When, during the third period, the Zamboni began to clean the ice for the next men's game, she jumped on board and ordered the driver off the ice.

Nothing was going to get between her and the game she loved. "She was a keener from the word go, very intense. I never saw someone get so excited about hockey games. I think hockey excited her more than anything in this world to be honest," says teammate Sharon Sanderson.

•

While Mern Coveny was playing hockey and studying physical education at McMaster, Sylvia Wasylyk was doing the same at the University of Delaware. After taking a course in hockey, Wasylyk was smitten. "It's indescribable how I feel about hockey," Wasylyk told Wilmington's *The Morning News*. "I just can't get enough. For other girls it's fun. For me, it's my life."[7]

As there was no women's program, Wasylyk played in goal for the University of Delaware Hens men's team, winning the Delaware Valley Collegiate Hockey League title in 1976. She also played for the Russell Flames in the New Castle County Recreation Ice Hockey League and other men's teams in the area.

"Men's leagues were kind of desperate for goalies," she recalled in an October 2, 1979, interview with Beth Miller of Delaware's *News Journal*. "I stopped the puck and that's what they needed, so they didn't mind . . . Guys would shoot for my head. They figured if I can't take it, I shouldn't be there, so I took it."

Wasylyk was determined. "When the other teams first find out I'm a girl, it's really funny to them. Then they say, 'We'll show her'. It darn sure inspires me, too. I want to show them I can play with them. I've spent my whole life meeting challenges."[8]

"Some people think I'm a hot dog—one team even calls me that," she said. "I get a lot of remarks, relentless ribbing. For a lot of the guys, it would probably kill them to give me a compliment. I guess if they didn't kid me though, I would think something was wrong."[9]

Reporters were skeptical. "But Sylvia Wasylyk is a girl, for Heaven's sake!" wrote Ray Finocchiaro. "Girls aren't supposed to be goalies. When was the last time Nancy Drew cracked some nefarious scheme in an ice hockey rink? Do the Girl Scouts give out merit badges for blocking flying pucks? Okay, so Sylvia Wasylyk isn't a Nancy Drew fan and the Girl Scouts don't turn her on. Ice hockey does."[10] Chuck Lewis was dismayed. "It seems women's liberation has pervaded what many men regard as the center of masculinity."[11]

Looking for more opportunities to play, Wasylyk founded the Delaware Valley Women's Hockey League, later known as the Mid-Atlantic Women's Hockey League, in 1975. The team, which started with figure skates and street hockey sticks, attracted women from all walks of life, many of them inspired by the Philadelphia Flyers' back-to-back Stanley Cup victories in 1974 and 1975. One of them was BC (Karen) Biesinger, who saw a poster Wasylyk had posted at her high school. "We always played street hockey and followed the Flyers, but there was never a women's team," she said. Biesinger would later go on to lead the league in scoring.[12]

In its inaugural season, the league featured three teams: the Delaware Bobcats (also founded by Wasylyk), Boulevard Hookers (now the Philadelphia Freeze) and the University of Pennsylvania club team. While she often played in goal, Wasylyk also played forward and led the league in scoring, recording twenty-one goals and twenty-six points, as her Bobcats won the first league title.

By the 1977–78 season, the league had expanded to include nine teams.

Louie Strano, who described by Wasylyk as "a playmaker, but also the top goal-getter on her line," served as president while also playing forward for the Bobcats. Her husband, Al, coached the team, which remained at the top of the standings. Their success brought some grudging respect. As Rod Beaton wrote for Wilmington, Delaware's *The Morning News* on November 2, 1978, "Players like Sylvia Wasylyk and Louie Strano and their colleagues on the Delaware Bobcats ice hockey team have proven that the rugged, often violent world of hockey is not exclusively a male domain."

•

Like Sylvia Wasylyk, Michele Emerson was a goalie on a boys' team, the Waukegan Shields. In 1978, she and her team traveled for almost twelve hours from Illinois to Sarnia, Ontario, to play in the International Silver Stick Tournament. When she arrived, the only goaltender for her team, she was told she could not play because, according to Ontario Minor Hockey Association executive John Slobodnik, "The OMHA provides hockey for boys only." Tournament director Hugh Sutherland confirmed that, "to the OMHA, she is an illegal player."[13] Michele Emerson had played for Waukegan for three seasons; she was nine years old.

"I just can't believe this is happening," Michele's father, David, told the media. "Those kids have practiced six days a week. They drove eleven hours to get there. Now their goalie can't play because she's a girl. I'm definitely going to sue if my daughter can't play. She's a member of the Amateur Hockey Association of the US which sanctions Silver Stick competition in this country. AHAS rules permit her to play. And they knew she was coming up there. I'm just sick about this."[14]

"I don't get it," Emerson admitted. "Why don't I get to play because I'm a girl? . . . I got a lot of trophies playing hockey, you know. I don't see why a girl doesn't get a chance."

"We asked if we could move the game to the United States," said Waukegan manager Ron Williams. "We figured with all the little league cases, the precedent had been set. But they told us OMHA rules would apply in Port Huron, too."[15]

Referees were instructed not to drop the puck if Emerson was on the ice. She took warmups, and then retreated to the dressing room to watch her team play the opening game of the tournament without her. Playing with six skaters and no goalie, the Waukegan Shields lost 6–4 to Coniston, Ontario. The team returned to Illinois without getting a fair chance to show their mettle against the top competition in their age group.

"When I first found out I couldn't play, I cried a lot, but then when I saw the game, I just got mad. We all worked hard and we wanted to win," Emerson said. Her manager agreed. "I'm not a crusader or anything, but this whole thing is pretty stupid," said Williams. "She's one of our best players. The only difference between her and the rest of the players is that she combs her hair after the game."[16]

The following month, the Shields were scheduled to face a team from Kitchener, Ontario, at an event in Kenosha, Wisconsin, part of a "friendship" series between American and Canadian teams that still would not include Emerson. "We've told our team just to skate off the ice and wait for the next game," Kitchener coach Pat Doherty said.

This time, Emerson was prepared. "I planned for this for a long time and I'm gonna suit up against them," Emerson told Associated Press. "If they want to walk out, it's their tough beans."[17]

Another team, the Chicago Saints, brought flowers onto the ice for Emerson, and the players all wished her luck to let her know she belonged. Even so, continued discrimination from Canada was taking a toll. "I don't think it's right," she said. "I realize I can't play up there, because of their rules. But why should they be able to keep me from playing down here? . . . If this is gonna happen every year, I don't want to play. it's just not worth it."[18] Loving the game wasn't always enough, despite the fact women had now been playing for nearly a century.

The year, after Emerson gave up her fight in North America, eleven-year-old Laura Cooper was banned from boys' hockey in Melbourne, Australia. Cooper wanted to join her two older brothers but "was told girls weren't allowed to play." After a five-year battle, she finally won the right to play right wing for Melbourne's Footscray Pirates in 1984. "When I first began playing," Cooper said, "the opposition team members used to wink at me but they soon found out I was as tough as the boys."[19]

•

In 1981, yet another girl, eleven-year-old Heather Kramble, stepped on the ice in the suburbs of Winnipeg, knowing it could be her final game playing for the Transcona Pirates. Kramble had always loved playing hockey on the street and at outdoor rinks but the closest she could get to organized play was ringette. There was a five-team women's league in the province but the players were all in their late teens and twenties, so when Kramble decided to make the move to hockey, she joined a boys' team. "'I like hockey better than ringette. It's harder, but I like it better, so it's easier," she explained to The *Winnipeg Sun*'s George Jacub. After playing most of the season with her team, Kramble was suspended by her own association because girls were not permitted on boys' teams in Winnipeg, or in much of Canada. Three other Winnipeg players were in the same position: fifteen-year-old Paula Brasier, twelve-year-old Bernice Chartrand, and thirteen-year-old Lorin McLachlin.

The Transcona Pirates refused to accept the ruling. "They have no right to suspend her. We've done nothing wrong in the way of registration and she's a paid-up member of the club," said coach Jerry Hartwell. The ten boys on Kramble's team said they would not return to the ice as members of the league without her. "She's like any one of us boys. The rules are stupid," said one of her young teammates. "If she wants to play, let her play."[20]

"I remember my teammates, the boys I played with, being super supportive," Kramble says. "There was all sorts of nonsense about where I was going to change, where would I shower? Nobody was showering at that point; I would come basically dressed. It was really a non-issue, and I remember the support of my teammates."

Following that February 17 game, the Greater Winnipeg Minor Hockey Association suspended Kramble's coach and forced her team to forfeit the game. "It's been a hard week. She's been pretty down," said her mother, Elaine. "We're pretty disappointed in the whole situation. We feel that really the persons who are getting hurt the most are the girls."[21]

To Elaine and Bryan Kramble, hockey was hockey, and if their daughter wanted to play, she should. "My parents would never have said that hockey is a boy's sport to me, never," Kramble says. "We were allowed to sign up, I was allowed to play, it never occurred to me that this was a 'boys' sport.' It never has and it never will. It's just been a sport, a great sport."

A week after Kramble's case made headlines, Mac Rousseaux, coach of the Waverley Heights Wings, complained to the press following a disciplinary hearing resulting from his refusal to bench Paula Brasier. "It's a bunch of crap," Rousseaux told the *Winnipeg Sun* on February 23, 1981. "They already had their minds made up," he said. "You were supposed to say something they like to change their minds. I wouldn't say I wouldn't play Paula, so I'm out. I told them it was blackmail."

Officials were adamant. "The girls are not eligible to participate in the program and the coaches are suspended," said Russ Farrell, the Greater Winnipeg Minor Hockey Association's president. "The Canadian Amateur Hockey Association and the Manitoba Amateur Hockey Association are in complete agreement that our position is correct."

In fact, Farrell sent a letter to the Transcona Minor Hockey Association and the Kramble family stating that the Canadian Amateur Hockey Association had revoked Heather's registration and pulled her from her team. The letter was clear that, "should this girl participate in male minor hockey," she would no longer be insured.

Kramble's parents brought the issue to anyone who would listen. "My mom and dad pursued a whole bunch of different areas to allow me to play—Manitoba Human Rights, the Mayor of Winnipeg, Members of Parliament—I didn't recognize how much work they did to move it forward," she realizes now. "But what I remember is just the support from my teammates and family. I just played hockey."

The Manitoba Human Rights Commission and the Canadian Advisory Council on the Status of Women both asked the association to allow girls to play, and the matter was even raised in Canada's House of Commons. The City of Winnipeg also advocated on the girls' behalf, passing a motion on February 18, 1981 "THAT Council support the immediate reinstatement of Coaches and players who have been suspended due to the fact that a girl or girls have been playing minor hockey."

The City of Winnipeg also discussed the possibility of banning the association from using civic rinks should they refuse, but the Winnipeg association and the Canadian Amateur Hockey Association refused to budge. "There was so much pressure not to play me," says Kramble. "Our community club was backing me, but they were told that if I were to play every team playing out of that community club would be suspended. That was a lot of pressure for one little girl."

Although she loved hockey, Kramble went back to ringette. "I was just a kid, so I went back to playing whatever I could play," she says. "I loved sports. I went back to ringette because I had no choice." If it were up to her, she would never have left the game. "I would have continued, absolutely, but I had no choice."

Kramble wouldn't play again until she enrolled at the University of Manitoba in 1987, where she joined their newly formed women's hockey team. Having taken up the game again, she didn't stop. She played while she was pregnant and into her forties and continues to follow the sport as a fan. Her daughters, however, chose ringette, not hockey.

For Kramble, her sacrifice, and those of other girls and women of the era were part of a much longer fight resulting in incremental, yet slow change. "I think things happen for a reason and change is slow," she says, reflecting on that time in her life. "I'm happy, now girls can play. If they try out for a team and they make it, they can play. They also have the option to play with girls and with women who are pretty highly skilled. Playing at the time, there weren't a lot of girls playing hockey. It just takes these incidents over a number of years to enact change. You see that not just in sport, but in a lot of aspects of life. It doesn't seem that long ago, but I guess it was—that you'd be kicked off because you were a girl and for no other reason."

•

Although she was forced out of hockey, Heather Kramble's fight became the catalyst for change. As pressure from government officials, parents, players and coaches continued to build, the Canadian Amateur Hockey Association recognized that the only way to keep women out of men's hockey was to create a league for girls alone. By spring, a resolution was set, and on May 24, 1981, the CAHA endorsed the formation of a women's hockey council to oversee women's hockey in Canada. The following day, at the opening of the Association's annual meeting, the resolution was approved, and a seat on the Association's board of governors was reserved for a representative of the new women's council. "There has been hot and cold interest for a number of years in helping to establish women's hockey," CAHA president Murray Costello explained. "We felt we should take an active role in making it happen."[22] While many informal or independent associations existed locally and provincially, a national governing body had not existed since the Dominion Women's Amateur Hockey Association was dissolved in 1940.

Recognition by the CAHA brought more consistent schedules, rules, and standards as well as financial stability. It also paved the way for a national championship, the 1982 inaugural Women's National Hockey Championships. After decades of opposition, this also marked the first time the CAHA allowed sponsorship.

As women's hockey became more organized, the caliber of competition increased with a commensurate focus on training. In the years following the introduction of the birth control bill, the landmark Roe v. Wade decision, and scientific research that debunked myths about the harmful effects of exercise, gyms began opening their doors to women. For the first time, dry-land training, popularized for men by the example of the 1972 Soviet men's hockey team, became a part of many players' regimens. Mern Coveny was one of many who recognized that off-ice training could help her outwork her opponents and excel. "I was obsessed with working out, weightlifting and running, in order to be at the top of my game," she admitted.

As part of putting a national championship structure in place, the CAHA decided that the Lipstick Tournament would become the official Ontario tournament, crowning a provincial champ and determining Ontario's representative at Nationals. For the first two years, the tournament champs (the Agincourt Canadians in 1982 and the Burlington Ladies in 1983) went on to secure the national title. Mern Coveny's now-powerhouse Hamilton Golden Hawks won consecutive Lipstick Tournaments from 1984 to 1987. The team parlayed its 1984 and 1985 provincial titles into silver and bronze medals at Nationals and, in 1986, won their first national championship.

Mern Coveny scored two goals as the Golden Hawks defeated Saskatchewan's Maidstone Saskies 7–2 to capture the Abby Hoffman Cup.

Coveny's American counterpart, Sylvia Wasylyk, also excelled on the national stage. Spurred on by Title IX, the first girls' US national championships were held in 1978, the same year that Michele Emerson visited Ontario. Wasylyk's Delaware Bobcats, who won three straight regional championships from 1980 to 1982, earned their way to the national championship tournament in 1981. The Bobcats finished as national runners-up, beating the Detroit Miniwings in the semi-finals 4–3 before falling to the Cape Cod Aces 4–0 in the final.

A long-time firefighter, Sylvia Wasylyk continued playing with the Delaware Bobcats for more than twenty-five years, well into her forties, serving as player/coach in 1999–2000, when the team again won a Mid-Atlantic Women's Hockey League title. Wasylyk passed away in 2014 but her legacy continues—the Mid-Atlantic Women's Hockey League remains the longest continually operating league in the United States.

CHAPTER 9

Fran's Got a Plan

Sitting on the bench of Mattamy Athletic Centre, formerly Maple Leaf Gardens, I watched Hall of Fame member Geraldine Heaney stand at a whiteboard surrounded by players waiting for drill instructions. She was there to coach Team Canada at the 2023 Premier Hockey Federation All-Star weekend, assisted by fellow Hall of Fame member Kim St-Pierre. Only days before, a young NCAA graduate named Daryl Watts has signed with the league's Toronto Six, coached by Heaney and managed by another legend, Angela James. Her US$150,000 contract broke all previous records. It was a celebration weekend.

I snapped a photo of the moment on the ice: hockey stars past and present preparing to compete in an all-star event for a professional women's hockey league. Shortly afterward, my phone buzzed in my pocket. Text and social media messages were piling up on my screen, all with the same link: "'Hurricane Hazel' McCallion, longtime mayor of Mississauga, Ont., dead at 101."

It was the inhale and exhale of women's hockey history. Stops and starts. None of the women in front of me would be here without the support Hazel McCallion had once provided to the pioneer of international hockey, Fran Rider.

•

Fran Rider was born in Etobicoke, a suburb of Toronto. Her family loved sports but "women weren't supposed to be athletic back in the 1960s," Rider remembers. "If a girl liked sports, it wasn't always deemed favorable." Fran was not to be deterred. In the summer, she played all pick-up sports, including football, and was an avid waterskier. When the cold arrived, she played backyard hockey with figure skates on her feet. When she wasn't playing, Rider would sit beside the radio listening to Toronto Maple Leafs games, alert for the mention of Ron Stewart, her favorite player. Fran and her brother tried to stay near the radio, because if the Maple Leafs scored while they were absent, they'd be banished for the remainder of the game. The Riders were superstitious in support of their team.

Fran's father, a Toronto firefighter, and mother, a loyal Toronto fan, would take her to Maple Leaf Gardens to see the Leafs live. As she watched the team win multiple Stanley Cups in the 1960s, her love for the game solidified and soon outgrew her Etobicoke yard. She wanted to play for real, but hockey was not for girls. At least that's what she thought.

In 1967, the same season the Leafs won their last Stanley Cup to date, Rider spotted an article in the *Toronto Telegram* about Brampton's upcoming women's hockey tournament. She contacted the reporter who'd written the article, who connected her with Brampton's association and, within days, Rider was playing hockey. She was placed on a team from Cooksville that included players ranging from nine-year-old girls to women in their mid-forties. There were no age brackets—teams would take anyone they could. The following year, Fran started playing with the Brampton Canadettes. She played, she volunteered, she kept time, anything to be involved.

"As a player walking into an arena in the 1960s, you were called names that I won't repeat for even daring to play the game," recalls Rider. "You just had to shut it out and draw strength from your teammates and the other players, because all we wanted to do was play hockey. It's a great game and we loved it; what was wrong with us playing? You were looked at like some kind of freak by others and called all kinds of horrible things just for wanting to play the game. We had to keep saying, 'We're not doing anything wrong here, we're loving hockey.' Some people said, 'How dare you, you're trying to take over the men's game,' but it was not to be compared. We were developing a game there was a need for, a desire for, we were playing it and enjoying it and we weren't hurting anyone."

The Canadettes played Sunday mornings at 7:00 am. It was the only time the arena would give them. Once, they were given an 11:00 pm practice time. The arena manager joined them on the ice, wanting to skate himself, and they practiced and played until two in the morning. Every second on the ice was valuable and created lifelong memories.

Like Alexandrine Gibb before her, Fran Rider had always been a proponent of being empowered and supported to run women's sports and of allowing women's hockey to develop its own, autonomous identity..

By 1982, Rider was president of the Ontario Women's Hockey Association, sat on the Ontario Hockey Association's board of directors, and was a member of the Canadian Amateur Hockey Association's new women's council. The trophy awarded to the runner-up at the new national tournament was the Fran Rider Cup. If hockey was happening for women anywhere in Canada, Fran was there, pushing it forward.

In the Central Ontario Women's Hockey League, Rider was playing alongside the best players on the planet. She was also aware of the unprecedented growth of women's hockey in the United States in the wake of Title IX, and in countries like Sweden, Finland, the Netherlands, West Germany, and Switzerland. While women had been crossing borders to play hockey since the Ottawa Alerts traveled to play a three-game series against the Pittsburgh Polar Maids in 1917, international competition outside North America was novel. In 1984, the Maidstone Saskies, winners of that year's Fran Rider Cup, toured Finland and Sweden, winning all seven games. Fran saw the promise and made a plan: she would use the starting point of her own hockey career, Brampton's annual tournament, as a springboard to showcase international teams in Canada.

In 1985, as the director of the Brampton tournament, Rider enticed teams from West Germany and the Netherlands, as well as American teams from New Jersey and Massachusetts, to play in an international division of the tournament alongside Canadian teams from Quebec and Ontario. The tournament would demonstrate that women's hockey existed outside of Canada. It was also an opportunity for Fran to implement the next phase of her plan. "We had a lot of meetings with Germany when they were here for that tournament," Rider says. "I had wondered, for years, why are these players not in the Olympics? Why don't we have a world championship? It just didn't make sense because the caliber of play was so good. Perhaps I was naïve. I didn't understand the extent of the roadblocks and walls. If I'd known then what I know now, I would have thought it was impossible. But I didn't understand that. I thought, 'It could be, so it should be.' I immediately started working toward a world championship."

Rider set a goal of hosting the first women's world championship in Toronto only two years later. "We approached Hockey Canada to get a world championship and we were turned down," Rider recalls. Canada's governing body for hockey wanted nothing to do with a women's international tournament. Men remained in control of the game, and women had yet to gain a seat at the table. Even Hockey Canada's female council could only recommend; they could not make any decisions about women's hockey in Canada.

Rider decided to go it alone. Sanctioned or unsanctioned, a tournament would happen, and she would show Hockey Canada and the International Ice Hockey Federation (IIHF) that women belonged. "What we could do was hold a world tournament," says Rider. "We could not get a world championship, which would have brought all kinds of sponsorship and money from all the participating countries, but we could do a world tournament. We were determined there would be one."

Fran again invited West Germany, the Netherlands, and the USA. She was communicating with eleven nations, finding contacts in Sweden and eventually Japan. Discussions were ongoing with Norway, Britain, and Australia, but only months before the proposed event, as Rider recalls, "We didn't have teams, we didn't have money, we had nothing but expensive phone calls and telexes we used to communicate."

While international participation was being confirmed, arrangements were being made domestically. Organizers decided that Team Canada would be represented by the national champion Hamilton Golden Hawks, who had just defeated the formidable Edmonton Chimos. Due to the struggle to get teams, the host team, Mississauga, would participate as Team Ontario.

As the longtime captain of the Golden Hawks, Marian Coveny was set to become the first captain of a Canadian women's national team. "What was most impressive about Mern was her leadership. She would drag our team on her back if she needed to in order to win, or if we set a goal," says former teammate Pat White. "At the beginning of the 1986 season, our goal was to get to the Nationals. When we found out about the world tournament, that was our next goal. Mern was just laser focused. She demanded a lot from the team, but nobody worked harder than she did. She would skate through a brick wall if it meant succeeding."

Rider was the tournament's driving force, but she was not alone. She had the backing of women's teams in the area, and notably Mississauga's mayor, Hazel McCallion. "She was championing her vision to create women's world championships and establish female hockey as an Olympic sport," McCallion wrote of Rider. "I enthusiastically joined Fran and the believers and together we accomplished the 'impossible' and made everlasting dreams come true."[1]

Born in Port Daniel, Quebec, McCallion (née Journeaux) began her hockey career in the late 1930s, playing for her hometown team in the Gaspé Hockey League, that also included teams from Chandler, Port Daniel, and New Carlisle. After moving to Montreal, she joined the Kickees of the Montreal and District Ladies' Hockey League at the beginning of 1940. "The Kik," as McCallion called them, took their name from Kik Cola, a Quebec-based company.

"The club has just persuaded Hazel Journeaux, ex-Port Daniel star to sign on the dotted line," wrote Myrtle Cook. "The player, who hails from the Gaspé Coast League, is reported to be a fast skater and a hard shot . . . 'Her ability should soon place her among the best ranking players here,' comments the delighted Kickees manager."[2] McCallion's love for the game lasted decades and was a driving force behind her advocacy for growth, including through the promotion of the 1987 tournament.

"Hazel McCallion actually embarrassed the mayor of Hamilton, Bob Morrow, into supporting us," explains Sharon Sanderson, another member of the Golden Hawks. "We had to raise our own money to go to this tournament, so Hazel embarrassed Morrow into giving us money, because all the girls had to take time off work. It was just a whole different ball game back then than it is today."

Then it almost fell apart. Rider received a telex from West Germany announcing the nation had decided to pull out of the tournament. They were unhappy that organizers had decided to omit bodychecking from the competition. By the next day, as she skated onto the ice with her Brampton Canadettes, she had lost hope.

As Fran lined up to face off against the Hamilton Golden Hawks, Mern Coveny approached, her face eager and intense.

"It's going to happen, isn't it, Fran?" Coveny implored.

Rider was uncertain. Then the message came again, this time from net-minder Cathy Phillips, who told Rider the tournament must go on. "Every shift we were out there, Mern was coming up to me, and when I was near the net, Cathy Phillips would come up to me," recalls Rider. "We were struggling so much; I was making the call the next day to pull the plug. There were so many obstacles we faced and so many people against it. I'll never forget that game and the look in Mern's eyes."

Rider woke up with renewed purpose. She wanted women's hockey to someday be an Olympic sport. She wanted a world championship. She wanted equity and opportunity for women. "I called Mern and Cathy the next day and said, 'It's not over yet, let's try again.'"

For Coveny, the tournament was a dream come true, and she was acutely aware of the gravitas of the situation. As she stepped onto the ice for the first game ever played by a Canadian women's national team, Coveny whispered that she was taking "one giant step for womankind."

"I didn't think anyone heard me," Coveny told reporters after the game. "To think that I am the captain of Team Canada just blows my mind."[3] Not only did Coveny step on the ice as the first national captain, she scored the first goal in national team history, opening the scoring in what would turn out to be a lopsided 10–0 win.

Team Canada and Golden Hawks manager Jackie Hughes maintains that, "Mern was the most competitive person I've ever met in my life. She just wanted to win, every time those blades touched the ice. She was a great playmaker, and she wanted the puck all the time." Perhaps that's why Team Canada went undefeated in that first world tournament. "Mern put her heart and soul into the game of hockey, it was the most important thing in her life besides family, friends, and her teaching. She was the captain of Team Canada, and she led us that way."

Coveny led Team Canada to a gold medal, ousting the USA in the semi-finals before beating the Ontario entry 4–0 for the gold. Looking back, she called the tournament "a story of a lifetime." "Being part of Team Canada was huge for me. Growing up in rural southern Ontario, I only dreamed of being able to play hockey, never imagining I would ever play for a Team Canada. I was thrilled for myself, but also for so many other women that I had played with and against over the years."

"She made a difference," says Fran Rider. "The future of the game revolved around her. She wasn't just playing for an event, she wasn't just playing for a championship, she was playing for the future of the game, she was representing the future of women's hockey. The players finally had an opportunity to show who they were and what they could do on the world stage, and Mern was the leader of that entire movement, because she was the captain of Team Canada and Canada was the center of hockey. That was all on her shoulders, and she stepped up to the plate."

"After the tournament, people all wanted our autographs. We'd never signed autographs, that was something new," recalls teammate Sharon Sanderson. "The team from Sweden, they were great girls, but a lot of them had borrowed equipment from the boys. It was just so different from today when the kids are outfitted with the latest and greatest and best of everything. But they were still over here representing their country. It was one of the greatest experiences of my life."

"I don't think Mern ever got the recognition she deserved," says Jackie Hughes. "For being the captain that she was, the player that she was, and the part of her life that she dedicated to this sport."

Current and future greats—Cathy Phillips and Marian Coveny, Angela James and Geraldine Heaney, Sharon Sanderson and Shirley Cameron, Cindy Curley and Estey Ticknor, Kristina Bergstrand and Line Baun Danielsen—all saw themselves in international play for the first time. It was a glimpse at what was possible. When the 1987 tournament began, sixteen-year-old Vicky Sunohara led her new heroes onto the ice carrying a national flag. During an intermission skate that featured a group of local ten-year-olds, Cheryl Pounder looped the ice. By the time they retired, Pounder and Sunohara had collected a combined seventeen gold medals at the Olympic Games and World Championships

"If it wasn't for Fran Rider, there wouldn't be women's hockey the way there is today," maintains Sanderson. "She was just phenomenal. She got the Worlds going, she supported women's hockey and the Nationals, every little step of the way. It was unbelievable, what she did for women's hockey."

"Nowadays athletes . . . they have so much opportunity, and so much is given to them. But when we played, we played because we loved the game," explains inaugural Team Canada member Pat White. "There was no carrot being dangled out there for us with respect to world championships and the Olympics."

"My generation is standing on the shoulders of the work that she did," said longtime Team Canada star Brianne Jenner. "I don't think we would have the opportunities that we have now if it wasn't for the women who came before us and laid the foundation. Our hope is to do the same thing for the next generation. It's people like Fran and her work that inspire us to do the same."4

After Rider opened the door, more and more women flooded onto the ice. Off the ice, there was a shift toward equity. For the first time, girls and women were seeing themselves in positions that had been reserved for men for nearly a century. "You have to start from somewhere," Cheryl Pounder said in an interview with *The Athletic*. "That somewhere was Fran Rider saying, 'We start here.' That's a pioneer."

A two-time member of Canada's Olympic team, Pounder appreciates her good fortune. "I came along at the right time for everything. I'm a beneficiary of that initial impact. That time when no one was sort of paying attention is when the advocacy was critical—and Fran was at the forefront. Would I have had an opportunity if not for Fran Rider raising her concerns or battling for her vision? Probably not."5

In November 2021, Mern Coveny donned her Team Canada jersey, the one she wore in 1987, to watch a Rivalry Series game between Canada and the USA. She had continued playing after the unofficial world championship and even won a pair of Canadian Ball Hockey Championships. Just the year before, her 55+ hockey team had won their district title, and advanced to the national championships before COVID-19 canceled the event. Shortly afterward, Coveny was diagnosed with Stage 4 pancreatic cancer and given only months to live. More than a year later, Cheryl Pounder, now a broadcaster, took advantage of the rivalry game to acknowledge Mern's battle with cancer and her contribution to women's hockey on air. Mern Coveny passed away on January 6, 2022, a winner to the end.

CHAPTER 10

Hockey Nation

In the underbelly of Brampton, Ontario's CAA Centre, my feet danced, trying to stay warm until players emerged from their postgame talk with their coaches and team. Nearly forty years after the first international competition on North American soil, I interviewed Switzerland's Alina Müller, then Sweden's Emma Söderberg, Czechia's Tereza Vanišová, and France's Chloé Aurard. We analyzed the games and talked about their chances at the tournament. One common thread emerged when I asked about the future: they all had no doubt they'd be playing professional hockey.

At the 2023 Women's World Championships, any European or Asian player could list hockey role models from their own countries and abroad. Perhaps for the first time, they were exclusively women. When I returned to the 2024 World Championships, this time in Utica, New York, it was clear that no generation would ever again struggle to see themselves represented on the ice. Today's players were now role models for girls across the globe. But, with new names striding into the spotlight, it felt as though the thousands of women who played and pushed to get the game here were rapidly being forgotten, with unknowing media and fans calling today's players "pioneers."

•

Long before any of the women at the 2023 or 2024 Worlds were born, women's hockey was crawling along worldwide, including in Europe and Asia, where skating and versions of the game had existed for more than a century.

From 1931 to 1936, international competition between Britain and France was "a platform for the expression of a new modern womanhood. Hockey was both an activity and an aesthetic—an arena for new ideas about female movement, grace, style, verve." After World War II, however, resources disappeared, and a new definition of womanhood emerged. "In both Britain and France, war decimated the women's game. It was disrupted in England by the need to reallocate labor power, resources, and space. In postwar Britain it was shouldered aside by a new cultural definition of the game as even more strenuously masculine, aggressive, and violent, personified by the rough-hewn Canadian troops who dominated wartime competition.

English audiences must have concluded that women could not conceivably return to that game. In France, the end of women's hockey was even more blunt: it was simply outlawed."[1]

Women's ice hockey fared better in Australia where, in 1949, it returned to Sydney after only being played in Melbourne for the previous twenty-three years. Reporting on a game between the Eastern Cats and the Western Witches, *The Australian Women's Weekly* was optimistic. "[The] match created so much interest it seems likely women's ice hockey will become a permanent affair."[2]

It wasn't until the 1970s that women across Europe again started organizing formal teams and leagues and overcoming obstacles similar to those in North America: lack of ice time, blatant sexism, insufficient equipment, poor or no coaching, and zero funding from national governing bodies.

In Denmark, twelve-year-old Line Baun Danielsen first strapped on a pair of skates in 1972. Her father, a sports journalist, often attended hockey games and tagging along sparked her lifelong love of the sport. "I was the kind of girl doing all kinds of sports, and after seeing my first hockey game I just knew this was what I wanted to do," says Baun Danielsen. "I started looking at where to play, but it turns out there were no clubs offering girls' hockey at the time."

Eventually, she spotted an advertisement in a local magazine placed by a group of girls inviting others to play hockey. A phone call later, Line Baun Danielsen was standing on the ice at the Forum in Copenhagen. It was well past her bedtime, the clock creeping toward midnight, but she didn't care—it was the only time girls were given to play.

"We were lucky we got one hour for training, ice time, Friday night at midnight," she recalls. "My dad would take me and eventually there were a lot of girls from the area who joined. After a season, we started trying to build our own team in our local club."

Today, Line Baun Danielsen is one of the most recognizable faces in Denmark, a famed television personality. In 1972, however, she faced men who looked at her and saw a girl, not a hockey player. When she approached her local club to start a girls' program, they pushed back. "The resistance was enormous because it was ruled by men, and we were just young girls," Baun Danielsen explains. Luckily, the chairman of the club was a local teacher who, recognizing some of the girls from his school, agreed that, as long as they managed themselves, he'd provide the group with ice time.

"We started off practicing late Friday night and then again early Saturday morning. After that, eventually other girls became interested in hockey in Jutland, another part of Denmark. Then there was another team in Copenhagen, and gradually it started to build up. We succeeded in creating a tournament for Copenhagen, one in Jutland, and another in the Zealand area."

After finding her first team in a magazine, another publication helped Baun Danielsen and her teammates bridge the Atlantic. In the early 1980s, picking up an edition of *The Hockey News* that her boyfriend at the time had left lying around, Baun Danielsen found an article mentioning Fran Rider. Wanting to see what else existed for women in the world in hockey, Baun Danielsen did the only thing she could do at the time: she wrote Rider a letter. "I was captain of my team and wanted to find out what was going on in hockey in the big world around us and maybe learn from other people," she recalls. "I told her that I had this team, what our credentials were and so on, and asked if she could make it possible for us to come to Canada to learn from other women's hockey players."

Not expecting a reply, Baun Danielsen was shocked when Rider invited her team to Canada and coordinated a tour for the team with games in Toronto, Ottawa, and Huntsville, Ontario. It was another building block toward international play, cemented by Rider. According to Professor Julie Stevens, Rider was participating in an "effort to build the game globally" reflecting "a type of cultural diplomacy," not only benefiting the image of Canada and Canadian hockey, but building the image of women's hockey globally, which remained under attack from men.[3]

Returning to Denmark motivated, Baun Danielsen and her team-mates started a national tournament, watching enrollment grow from fifty players to three hundred in those early years. Although largely ignored, Baun Danielsen's father did his best to highlight his daughter's dream. Showcasing the sport in the media helped expose the game and draw interest from more and more women and girls. "My dad, he wrote a lot in the newspapers, so he made sure we got a little attention in the media, and on television, and I think that was part of the reason why we grew relatively fast in numbers at that time."

•

At roughly the same time, across the Baltic Sea in Sweden, nineteen-year-old Kristina Bergstrand put on hockey skates for the first time. She loved orienteering, table tennis and basketball, and skating at the neighborhood park in the suburbs of Stockholm. In 1982, her basketball teammate, Susanne Mörne, invited her to try playing hockey in the upcoming Gurka Cup tournament in Västerås with a team known as Nacka HK. Much like the Lipstick Tournament, the Gurka Cup was an annual event that sustained the sport. Sweden was still three years away from hosting its own national championship that, even then, was unofficial.

"I put on the equipment and took part in that tournament. Then it was over because this was the funnest thing I've ever done," recalled Bergstrand in a 2018 interview with *Hockey Sverige*. "I didn't know much . . . there were no series or particularly many tournaments at this time. It was once a year that the Gurka Cup in Västerås took place and you played against other teams," Bergstrand explained.[4]

Much like her North American counterparts, Bergstrand was often dissuaded from participating in hockey. Even though Sweden was a country known for progressive policies and gender equity, sport, including hockey, remained a domain controlled by men. "[T]he decision-making bodies in sports mainly consist of men, and this means men have control over both men's and women's sports . . . Even though Sweden is considered a country with a rather developed sense for gender equality, the sports arena is still unequal."[5]

"There have always been prejudices and everyone has talked about that, but I'm not the kind of person who takes such things," said Bergstrand. At one point, Rickard Fagerlund, who served as the chairman of the Swedish Ice Hockey Association from 1983 until 2002, tried to dissuade Bergstrand and her teammates from continuing in hockey. According to Bergstrand, "He said that we should do equestrian sports instead."

Despite these barriers, Baun Danielsen, Bergstrand and hundreds of other women across Sweden and Europe continued to organize and play. At Sweden's first national championship in 1985, Bergstrand led her club team, Nacka, to a pair of wins with six goals and nine points in the two playoff games. "To be able to play matches where something mattered was absolutely fantastic," Bergstrand recalled.[6]

That offseason, Line Baun Danielsen arrived in Stockholm to start a job with a language school. "When I got there, I took the Yellow Pages and I looked under ice hockey and called a local club. They told me they did not have women's hockey, but they had a farmer league, and there is a women's farmer team outside of Stockholm called Nacka. So I called them and it turned out they were the women's champions of Sweden. I thought I'd never get a chance to play. They invited me to a training session and the coach— he was showing me this big bucket of a hundred pucks—told me, 'If you practice your shot at the end of every practice, shooting all of these, I think I can use you.' I was part of the team for two years and we won two Swedish championships."

Already acquainted with Fran Rider from Denmark's trip to Canada years earlier, Baun Danielsen was not surprised when the Canadian builder reached out to international federations about the unofficial world championship in 1987. Baun Danielsen, living in Stockholm and playing for Nacka, received dispensation to play for Sweden. Years later, when she returned to Denmark, she became one of the few players to play on the national teams of two countries.

National federations and clubs were still unwilling to fund women's hockey. To get to North America, players had to pay their own way. Börje Salming, a Swedish star then playing for the Toronto Maple Leafs, helped fund Team Sweden. "I knew they were having trouble getting a sponsor and I was pleased to be able to help them," Salming said at the time.[7]

•

More than 8,000 kilometers away, Tamae Satsu wondered how she, alongside her Japanese teammates, would pay for a once-in-a-lifetime journey to Canada to play in an international women's hockey tournament.

Satsu had grown up watching the two semi-professional men's teams in Tomakomai on Hokkaido Island, home to two factory teams. One employed men at the local paper mill; men on the other team worked for a lumber importer and exporter. During the 1978–79 season, one of the teams, Iwakura Tomakomai, featured Darryl Sutter, who would go on to captain the Chicago Blackhawks before becoming a coach and general manager in the NHL. Satsu remembers that "it was always a huge battle. When they had a game, the entire town would empty. We had three shifts, and people would come between shifts. There was no beer, people would bring saki to watch the games. It was a crazy hockey town. When I was eight years old, I saw a goalie and thought, 'Oh my goodness, I want to play hockey. But my mom was a beautician, a single mother, and she couldn't afford it. I could not ask, but I put it in my head that I wanted to play hockey."

In the early 1980s, the town formed a women's hockey team that included ex-Olympic speed skaters and factory workers. Fifteen-year-old Satsu could not afford to play, but learned the team was offering a free spot to any woman who wanted to play goalie. Satsu accepted, riding her bicycle to and from hockey practice five times each week, including in the snow.

"It wasn't a normal thing for women, playing sport in Japan at that time," recalls Satsu. But "as women playing hockey in Japan, everyone was so helpful. My high school guy friends would throw a stone at my window. It was 9:30 pm. They came to my condo and they took me to the outdoor hockey rink; my guy friends would shoot at me to train me."

Soon, the five-foot-ten Satsu would travel across the world to play in Toronto, a member of Japan's first women's national team. "We didn't get Team Japan uniforms or jackets; we got leftovers from Mizuno. They put money into men's hockey, not women's," she explains.

Without national funding, team rosters were dependent on which eligible women could afford to pay for the trip themselves, or through fundraising. Despite the fact Satsu was already working at an architectural firm, she still needed to borrow money to be part of Japan's team. "We had to pay $5,000 to go. I borrowed half from my mother and half from my team manager. But it was such an amazing experience."[8]

•

The 1987 tournament was an eye-opening event for women across the globe.

Canada and USA were dominant, decades ahead of development in Europe and Asia, where women's hockey was still in its infancy. Behind Canada, USA, and Team Ontario, Sweden was the clear fourth-place team. In a 4–0 round-robin loss to Canada, Baun Danielsen earned game MVP, an award presented on the ice after each game by Fran Rider's father. Canada would again beat Sweden in the semi-finals, an 8–2 decision, with Baun Danielsen and Bergstrand scoring Sweden's goals. Japan suffered a worse fate, falling 11–0, 14–0, and 16–0 to Canada, Ontario, and USA respectively. But Japan defeated the Netherlands 5–2 and played tight games against Switzerland and Sweden.

As Kaori Takahashi, one of Satsu's teammates, told the *Toronto Star* at the time, "To play against Canada is an honor. It will take one or two generations to beat Canada. Technically, we are not ready, but in our hearts we are."[9] Tamae Satsu faced a barrage of shots, spurring her rapid development.

"When we played the United States, those girls, they were enormous," recalls Baun Danielsen. "We were normal, but the women we met over there, size-wise and talent-wise, were much better than we were. I remember that difference; I got the puck and tried to dribble down the ice toward the goal and this huge, huge defender came toward me, and I got knocked out."

While the games often ended in lopsided results, the opportunity to see what could be and to appreciate the skill of the North American women inspired international participants. Each nation took back lessons from both the on-ice style and off-ice preparation they observed.

Team Sweden learned one of those lessons one hot afternoon when the players decided to enjoy the sunny weather while the more experienced North American squads prepared for their next contest. According to Baun Danielsen, "When our coach found out we'd been sunbathing before our game, he got so annoyed and told us how unprofessional it was. I learned a lot from that, how you have to focus. That was part of it, part of our learning. It was so fantastic to take part in this. We were not professionals. We were just young, happy girls, thankful. We were in Canada, we'd been to the Hockey Hall of Fame, to Maple Leaf Gardens to see the Maple Leafs play, so it was an amazing ten days."

Kristina Bergstrand, considered by many to be the top player in the world outside North America, remembers the skill discrepancy. "What I am reminded of sometimes is that in the years around 1986 and 1987, I was the best in Sweden," Bergstrand said. "Many thought I would go over and dominate this unofficial World Championship. It turned out that Canada and the US had many who were at least as good as me."[10]

Team Sweden was one of many who returned home with renewed motivation to grow. "I think that Fran Rider should have applause for that first tournament, without her it would not have happened," said Baun Danielsen. "Without Fran Rider, without her, international women's hockey is not where it is. And we are many who are grateful for that."

As Julie Stevens wrote in *Hockey: Challenging Canada's Game*, "It is difficult to capture the true extent of Rider's contribution under the gamut of builder. It could be said that women's hockey in Canada and around the globe is the 'house that Fran built' as she had a hand in every aspect thereof."[11]

Line Baun Danielsen used her new knowledge and experience to help her home country. "After that tournament, I returned to Denmark, and the national hockey federation in Denmark contacted me and asked if I would help establish a women's national team," she says. "I said, 'Of course I would,' so I got a position on the board—not a voting one—but I was part of it. Eventually, I got a group of people around me who were interested in building up women's hockey and, by the end of that year, we had established our first women's national team."

Baun Danielsen's success hinged on convincing board members to discard antiquated attitudes. "Back when I started, there were the old-fashioned guys sitting in power in the clubs," says Baun Danielsen. "The basic argument was that it was dangerous for women to play hockey. They told us it can cause breast cancer, that was one of the messages we got. Then people said this was too tough of a sport for a girl to play. It's not appropriate."

Nonetheless, Denmark had a national team in time to compete at the first International Ice Hockey Federation (IIHF) sanctioned European women's championship. Held in 1989, the tournament would decide the qualifying nations for the first official women's world championship scheduled for 1990. That year, Denmark finished sixth in the eight-team pool. The next year, however, Denmark won a bronze medal, upsetting Norway 2–1, and qualifying for the 1992 Women's World Championships. "It was so special.

It was everything. I mean, we were nothing, but we were everything in our own minds and we had the greatest time of our lives."

The following season, 1993, Baun Danielsen and her teammates remained underdogs, taking trains, buses, and boats to tournaments while other nations flew. She recalls arriving at events tired and sore, no one having slept on the journey. Denmark was relegated out of Europe's top division following a sixth-place finish at the European championships. It was a devastating outcome. "We lost all momentum. All the money and media attention were gone," says Baun Danielsen. She retired after that season.

It took the Danish national women's team until 2019 to earn promotion back to the top division of European women's hockey. Due to the COVID-19 pandemic, Denmark wouldn't play in the top division until 2022, when the nation hosted the ten-team tournament in Herning and Frederikshavn.

Denmark finished the tournament with a single win and three losses and were again relegated to the Division 1A grouping.

I remember that tournament vividly. It was the first women's event I'd been assigned to cover as a reporter with *The Hockey News*. I wrote previews and daily recaps, analyzed the games and highlighted the tournament's top players. I watched as Canada won gold in a 2–1 nail-biter against USA, and Czechia won a historic bronze medal, the first in the nation's history.

At the gold-medal game, Line Baun Danielsen sat among the 1,738 fans in Herning. A seasoned broadcaster herself, Danielsen flinched each time "growing the game" and "newfound visibility" for women's hockey were discussed in the media. She listened to a generation of Danish players talk about lacking role models. After all, only one member of Denmark's national team, defender Simone Jacquet Thrysøe, was alive when Baun Danielsen helped Denmark form their first women's national team. She was born on the third day of the 1987 unofficial world tournament, a day when Baun Danielsen was helping Sweden defeat Switzerland 3–0, the nation's first international win. Jacquet Thrysøe was only four when Denmark won bronze at the European Championships in 1991.

Neither the players nor the fans knew where the game had come from. The players were too young to remember, and the pioneers of the 1980s were largely forgotten. They didn't know the women, whether it was Kristina Bergstrand, Line Baun Danielsen, or Tamae Satsu, who had fought to create space for future generations. Even Baun Danielsen, a celebrity in her nation, was forgotten—she had not received an invitation to participate as an honored guest. Instead, she bought her own tickets. "I was at the final," she says. "I thought it was sad though, hearing the Danish women say they had no role models. We were those role models."

CHAPTER 11

Playing Like Girls

Every morning, I woke to my mother's voice telling me it was time to get up; I would descend to be served a glass of juice and a bowl of cereal. My mom would check that we had the lunch she had prepared, and she'd call us when she could see the headlights of the bus coming down the road. Then she would dress and drive twenty-five minutes to a neighboring town to start her job.

My mother worked as an optician, but she also did invisible work, unpaid and unthanked labor. She remembered our schoolwork, scheduled our dental appointments and knew when we were about to run out of milk. If we scraped our leg, she bandaged it. She kept the world magical, making sure the Tooth Fairy and Easter Bunny left their treats, and that Christmas stockings were full. She helped us choose Halloween costumes and, when we were invited to a birthday party, she made sure we arrived with a gift in hand. My hockey equipment was dried, my skates were sharpened, and my registration fees were paid. I never missed a practice because she'd meticulously mark my schedule on the calendar, arranging rides to and from the arena.

It wasn't until years later that I came to appreciate my privilege, the vast number of things I never had to think about, the things that men in hockey never had to think about. Will there be enough ice time to train? Is there a changing room in the arena? Will I be allowed to take time off work to play? How will I cover the cost of the tournament?

The best men's players in the world never had to worry about getting paid to play. They never had to worry about a lack of coaches, a lack of sponsors, a lack of training facilities. They never thought about losing their jobs—or needing jobs. As women's hockey began to emerge from its long hiatus, its top players juggled all of that and more.

•

Shirley Cameron felt the weight of her bag on her shoulder. It wasn't her hockey bag; it was a letter bag. She was the only woman working as a letter carrier in Edmonton, a role she loved for the opportunity it provided to be active. With even strides, she moved from house to house, sometimes silently tucking letters into mailboxes, other times stopping to chat, making small talk with the people on her route. There was a crunch of snow beneath her feet as the Edmonton winter pierced her thick jacket.

Less than eight hours earlier, Cameron had been on the ice with the Edmonton Chimos. She'd known she'd be tired this morning and would have to walk several kilometers to complete her route. She was one of the top women's hockey players in the world, but there was no way for her to earn a living. There was no equivalent of the NHL's Edmonton Oilers for women.

Growing up on a farm in Northern Alberta, Shirley Cameron had never seen a woman play hockey. She'd played on ponds with family and neighbors, but playing on a team was not an option.

At age eighteen, Cameron followed her sister from rural Alberta to Edmonton, initially taking a job in computers. Her love for the outdoors and for being active soon drew her to an occupation her uncle had long held. She was the first woman to hold the role in Edmonton, which came with issues. The postal service thought Cameron was too small to handle the labor. "I felt a bit of pressure being the first one, and if I couldn't handle it that they would never hire another woman," she says. "I started working out on the farm, picking rocks and roots and throwing bales, milking cows. Playing hockey outside on the farm growing up, our feet would be frozen and we didn't care, we just stayed out and played, so I was prepared. I could handle it."

Cameron proved the doubters wrong. "It was a mixed reaction from men," she recalls. "Some were very accepting and some were very critical. The first place I worked, there wasn't even a bathroom for women. They'd turned the main floor of an old hotel into a station for letter carriers, and I had to go up the stairs and into the old hotel to use the bathroom."

Listening to the radio one day in 1973, Cameron heard an announcement that would change her life: a group of women and girls were meeting to play hockey at an indoor arena. "It was crazy showing up there, because there were thirteen- and fourteen-year-old girls and grandmothers. There were people there in figure skates, people there in hockey skates. The only thing we all had in common was the excitement about women playing hockey."

Following that first skate, there were enough interested women to create two groups. At first, Cameron considered the game as just recreation, a social outing. After their Tuesday evening skate, her group would go to a local bar for a beer. When the women raised their glasses, "One of the girls said 'chimo,' which was an Inuit greeting. And that's where our name came from," explains Cameron. "When we started—I don't know if it was just luck—but we were quite dominant. Eventually more teams were formed; the Northern Alberta Female Hockey League came after that."

Unlike elite male players, women like Shirley Cameron were required to foot the bill for their participation. "Sponsorship was non-existent, because people weren't going to put money into women's hockey. We realized the only way to play was to take on fundraising: we did casinos, we did bingos, we sold chocolate, we delivered phone books, we played the old-timer teams. We just hoped we'd get enough to subsidize our practices. In terms of ice time, we all paid that out of our pocket. All of my years in hockey were paid out of my own pocket."

Shirley and her teammates would do anything to play just one more game, one more period, one more shift. "We had to work for it and find the money, because no one was going to give us anything. We got tired of asking people for money, but it was the only way. The first help we got—one of the girls worked for an insurance company that bought us jerseys. Up until then, we were buying our own jerseys too."

The Chimos rarely lost a game, but competition was scarce. The nearest city with a rival team was Calgary, a three-hour drive away. In order to keep playing, the team started barnstorming across Northern Alberta to play old-timer men's teams. "When we first started, women's hockey was full body contact, so the men's teams wanted to play us for entertainment value, and we would play to full arenas," Cameron says. "The men could not take full slap shots and they couldn't hit, but they wanted us to hit. The people in the crowd, the women especially, loved the fact we were trying to hit these men. They would give us part of the gate for our expenses; it was kind of a fundraising thing for us, and a way to develop the sport in the province for other young girls who might come out and see us play."

When the Chimos wanted to travel, they were forced to squeeze hockey in among other commitments. Often that involved jamming players and equipment into teammate Kathy Berg's van. With Shirley Cameron in the front seat and up to ten players piled onto bags and against each other behind, the group would travel through Alberta snowstorms on weekend nights to play. When they returned, no matter how late, Cameron and her teammates would wake up early the next morning, some to care for their families, others to return to work. It was the second shift women in sport have always known.

When, in 1982, Cameron's Edmonton Chimos had the opportunity to participate in the first national championship tournament, her request for time off was denied. She refused to let her team down. "I got a medical certificate that said I had a knee problem. I did whatever I could to play, but that's how hard it was." Unsure of whether she'd have a job to come back to, Cameron packed her hockey bag, picked up her stick, and headed east.

Her ruse was discovered when the *Toronto Star* wrote about her risking her career to play the game she loved. "I was naïve. The first national championship I went to was the first time I was exposed to the media," Cameron recalls. "I had a reporter interested in getting some background on the Chimos. I said, 'I'll give you whatever information you need but please don't use my name in the article.' I explained the only way I could get here was doing this, so he made a headline out of it, 'Shirley risks job to help Alberta gain final.'"

When she returned to Edmonton, Cameron was suspended for five days. "It's only because I had a union I didn't get fired."

The Chimos remained dominant, winning all but one provincial championship from 1982 to 1997 and representing Alberta at sixteen national championships. The team won the national title in 1984, 1985, 1992 and 1997.

When Cameron made Canada's first national team for the 1990 Women's World Championships, she didn't tell her coworkers or supervisors. Instead, she booked vacation and quietly traveled to Ontario to compete. "When I went to the Worlds in 1990, I asked if I could take time off, and they said I had to take my holidays, even though there was a men's curler who got time off to compete at his world championships," she says. "People thought I was on vacation and were shocked when they saw me play on TV. Ironically, when I came back and they realized this was real . . . they gave me back my two weeks of holiday time. But it was only after that."

After the inaugural 1990 Women's World Championships, Cameron watched the game grow but, at thirty-seven, progress came too late for her career. The International Ice Hockey Federation still did not place women on equal ground, hosting a women's championship every other year instead of annually. Even though she helped the Chimos win a national championship in 1992, she failed to make Team Canada that year.

Instead, she became involved as a coach and administrator. From a coach in Hockey Alberta's high-performance women's program to serving as head coach of Team Alberta for the Canada Winter Games and coaching minor hockey for the Edmonton Blazers, Cameron gave back to the game. "There are so many opportunities that I never even imagined would happen. I was able to be part of it as a coach, but not as a player," she said. "When I started there were Westerns and then Nationals, but there was no opportunity to get into the Olympics."

Had Shirley Cameron been born in a different era, she would have been recognized by the Hockey Hall of Fame. One of the best in the world for decades, she worked shift after shift to play. Interviewed during her first and last world championship appearance, she summed up her experience this way. "I hope that hockey won't be looked upon [any longer] as a man's sport, but just as a sport that men and women can play."[1]

Over the course of her career, Shirley Cameron helped change the perception of women on the ice and in society. Speaking with journalist Dan Barnes, Chimos teammate Deanna Miyauchi described it this way: "The women's movement was part of that and it felt like I was part of it by sort of striking out in hockey, in yet another realm where girls had been excluded for no good reason. I would say those of us who came up in that time were aware we were all fighting together to be more full participants in society and we knew that playing hockey was part of that, and it carried on. That was what gave us strength to fight back against the naysayers and the people who put obstacles in our way. We knew not only in hockey, but society as a whole was starting to get behind what we were doing. But the main thing was always the love of playing."[2]

CHAPTER 12

Faceoff

After my daughter was born, when I saw my wife exhausted, I would temporarily take over and feel like a good dad. I read to my daughter, I made dinner, I changed diapers, I did bedtime or bath. When I told myself that my father and his father, or my wife's father, had never done this, it was selfish still. I wasn't changing the underlying structure. More wasn't enough.

The same dynamic, upheld and passed down, pervades public spaces like arenas. Women in hockey, the unpaid trailblazers working to establish teams and leagues, were consistently told they did not belong. After all, only men made money playing hockey, so there was no value in this pursuit for women.

The 1987 international tournament opened a door. When the 1990 Women's World Championship was televised, decades of invisible labor—planning, organizing, fundraising, balancing, scheduling—became visible. It was an announcement that the past was gone and would be followed by a new path, a new understanding of women in sport. The small steps men had taken, the breadcrumbs they had handed out so far, would no longer be enough.

•

When twelve-year-old Justine Blainey emerged from the dressing room, the short walk to the ice felt like miles. As she turned the corner, with the door to the ice in sight, a splash of coffee landed beside her; popcorn rained down on her helmet. Adults were throwing things at her. She stepped more quickly, the sound of her skate piercing the ice dulling the chant from the crowd: "Kill the girl, get the girl."

Born in Toronto, Blainey was introduced to sport in the gendered way familiar to many girls in the 1970s. She scrubbed floors, washed dishes, and learned to cook while her brother took out the garbage. She was enrolled in figure skating, dance, and gymnastics, while her brother tried football, lacrosse, and hockey. Family and friends came to watch her brother, but no one watched her. She can still picture her brother scoring a winning goal, smiling through his mask as his teammates mobbed him, the crowd on its feet.

She wanted to be part of it. "I was jealous," she recalls. "I would ask to play hockey. I'd say, 'Mom, Mom, can I play hockey?' and she'd say, 'No way. Girls don't play hockey, that's not your role.'"

After years of pleading, Blainey's mother finally relented, finding her a girls' hockey team the year she turned ten. "It didn't take long for me to realize, that first year, that my brother got way more things playing boys' hockey than I did in girls' hockey," she says. "Way more games, way more practices, practices that were inside instead of 6:00 or 7:00 in the morning outside. They had sponsors, they'd get gloves and jerseys, and leather coats. The girls—you'd get a jersey and socks . . . and then you'd have to return them. And then, very importantly, he was able to go up and play rep hockey." The "final kicker" was seeing her brother allowed to bodycheck, something that was no longer available to girls.

So Justine Blainey decided she was going to play boys' hockey alongside her brother and, in 1984, tried out for the Toronto Olympics, a team in the Metro Toronto Hockey League (MTHL). She made the team but was denied her place in the league due to an MTHL regulation prohibiting female players. She was allowed to attend practices and participate in hockey schools, but she could not play in a game alongside boys. To do so, she would need special permission that would only be considered if no girls' hockey program was available locally. For the 1984–85 season, twenty-two girls received permission in Ontario, none in the Toronto area.

The eleven-year-old decided to take her power back. "I wrote a letter to the newspaper saying, 'Hey, I'm a girl, I want to play, I'm good enough, but they won't let me.'" That letter caught the eye of a local reporter, and eventually a lawyer, Anna Fraser, who decided to take on Justine Blainey's fight, filing a complaint under section 19.2 of the Ontario Human Rights Code that prohibited discrimination on the basis of gender.

Precedent appeared to be on her side. In 1977, Françoise Turbide, a fourteen-year-old goaltender, had appealed to the Quebec Human Rights

Commission after she was denied a spot on the boys' team she'd played with since 1974 because of her gender. The commission found that she had "the competence and abilities required for the team and was considered the best player for the goal-minding position had she not been of the feminine sex."[1] The case continued when the CAHA and Quebec Ice Hockey Federation appealed. Quebec's Supreme Court ultimately "ratified the commission's judgment and ordered that girls be allowed to play on boys' teams if separate and equal facilities for girls didn't exist." Even though Turbide, who had been prohibited from playing for a year, did not return to the game, the ruling set an important precedent for future generations. From that moment forward, no woman in Quebec could be denied.

The Ontario Human Rights Commission, however, decided it had no jurisdiction in the Blainey case because the "Ontario Human Rights Code, which permits discrimination by sex in athletics, is not illegal."[2] Blainey and her lawyer appealed the ruling to the Ontario High Court of Justice, arguing the ban violated the 1982 Canadian Charter of Rights and Freedoms that provides that rights in Canada "are guaranteed equally to male and female persons."

Says Blainey, "The initial court cases . . . I didn't understand anything, it was all a new language to me. A few male teammates came and supported me and sat with me. Outside the courtrooms and at school, it was on the media all the time, all over Canada and the US. It was very overwhelming; I had no experience and no idea how to answer questions. I became hated by my friends at school and hated by my teachers. I was somehow destroying women's hockey, destroying men's hockey, I somehow thought I was too good for the girls, I was egotistical, I was gay, I was sleeping with the coach, that's the only way I'd made the team, I'd never have kids—these were the things that were said on TV, so I lost all my good friends. No one would talk to me, no one would walk beside me or sit beside me, they'd play pranks on me, teachers tried to fail me, they'd slam doors in my face. Being in the courtroom was actually easier."

Blainey's mother sat beside her. Justine could feel her shake each time a witness took a shot at her daughter's ability. "I thought, 'I don't know what's going on so I'll just smile.' I didn't sit with the lawyers, I was at the back," she recalls. "The impression I got was that these adults are talking about

CHAPTER 12 • FACEOFF

something I don't understand and discussing the fate of my life—because hockey was my life at the time—and I had no say. I was trusting this lawyer I'd really just met to fight for what I wanted so badly—to play hockey."

While the case proceeded, Blainey did what she could to play. "I pretended to be a boy . . . Justine to Justin, but it was super uncomfortable," Blainey says. "'Justin' Blainey was able to participate in unsanctioned exhibition games or compete in the United States with her former teammates but remained banned from league competition. "It was the same age I started to like boys, and I noticed boys, and I didn't want to be a boy. Pretending to be a boy proved to be very difficult for me."

One night at a hotel in Buffalo while traveling for a tournament, Blainey was approached by a man from another team demanding oral sex. It resulted in a fight between parents and coaches, with the hotel owner pulling a gun. At the rink the next day, only Blainey's brother and one of the team's goalies would sit in the dressing room with her.

It was when she returned to the ice, now in girls-only hockey, that adults threw coffee and popcorn on her, and chants of "kill the girl" rose from the stands. She was an outsider, a disrupter. Teammates would not sit beside her, and she wasn't invited to team parties and functions. In public, she was pushed down the stairs at a subway stop and chased from public transit.

In 1985, the court ruled that the MTHL regulation did not violate any law "because the charter does not apply to private organizations such as hockey leagues." Blainey's lawyer, Anna Fraser, said it was "a sad day for everyone."

The coach who had originally selected Blainey based on her ability, was incredulous. "I can't believe that in the 1980s, with a team the girl has proven she can play for, this would happen." Standing outside the courtroom, Blainey, twelve at the time, was surrounded by microphones and reporters asking for comment. "I feel very upset, not only for myself . . . but for all other little girls who won't be able to play in higher levels of hockey." [3]

"My mom, at every step, would ask me if I wanted to quit, and she'd say, 'Why don't you sleep on it and decide the next day.' Every time, in the morning, I decided I could take a little more and that this would be something for my daughter someday, or for other girls," Blainey says. "I always thought it was the right thing to do, and it couldn't get any worse. But it always did."

"All across the media, the headline was, 'Blainey's a loser' and that was hard to handle," she remembers. "If I look back at those times, I'd say I was depressed even though I didn't know what that word meant at the time. I didn't fit in anywhere. I didn't fit in at boys' hockey, at girls' hockey, at school, or even in my family. It was the most challenging time of my whole life. People ask if I could do it again, I say absolutely not. The ignorance and innocence of my age at the time was all that got me through it."

The decision reverberated throughout the hockey world. Emboldened, the Ottawa District Hockey Association used the ruling to ban four girls, aged ten and eleven, from playing boys' hockey, a decision they were later forced to reverse due to an absence of girls'-only programs in the area. Fran Rider, in her role as president of Ontario Women's Hockey Association, supported the decision, arguing, "It's not a step forward to put girls on boys' teams,"[4] even as men's hockey stars Darryl Sittler and Marcel Dionne spoke out in support of Blainey.[5]

Through it all, Blainey persisted, continuing to play hockey while bringing the case to the Ontario Court of Appeal. "In the appeals court, I was put on the stand for the first time. They'd criticize my skating, my stickhandling, and they were trying to trip me up with questions. They were making fun of how I played and said that I wasn't good enough. It was so hurtful. It was degrading," Blainey says, the pain in her voice palpable almost forty years later. "Someone challenged me, saying I'm a liar or threat or had something to gain when all I wanted to do was play hockey. It was very challenging, but none of it was as difficult as losing friends, and how people treated me who I thought liked me."

In 1985, the Court of Appeal ruled that Ontario's provision allowing sports organizations to discriminate based on sex was a violation of the Canadian Charter, opening the door for Blainey to pursue her complaint with the Ontario Human Rights Commission.

The ruling sent a clear message to women and girls. Ontario's Attorney General, Ian Scott, observed that, "It seems to me that it is only natural justice that if a female has the ability to play a particular sport as well as the male applicant for a team, she cannot be denied a place on the team strictly because of her gender . . . It will end the powerful message the law now sends out to women, and particularly to young girls, that they are simply not allowed to play with males. At a very young age this can discourage those youngsters from career paths in male-dominated occupations."[6] The Metro Toronto Hockey League attempted to appeal the decision to the Supreme Court of Canada but the country's highest court decided not to hear the case.

When Blainey won her appeal, she didn't realize that her fight was far from over. "When I won the appeal, I remember being ecstatic, so I got dressed and went to the game," says Blainey. "I was at St. Mike's Arena, and I was ready to play. I was getting dressed, and Lois Kalchman came up to me and said, 'Nope you can't play', and I was like, 'I just won.' And she said, 'Nope, you still can't play.'"

Like Myrtle Cook and Alexandrine Gibb, Lois Kalchman advocated for women's sports for more than thirty years. Writing for the *Toronto Star* and other publications, she covered sports stories, including the 1987 world tournament, that would have otherwise gone untold. She also served on the Committee for the Prevention of Spinal Cord Injury Due to Hockey, and the Parent Education Committee for the Ontario Hockey Council. When she approached Blainey, it was to warn her that her fight was not yet finished.

"She explained that it's against the law to go through a red light," Blainey recalls. "She said, 'Of course, people still do it.' She said, 'Now it's against the law for them to stop you, it's discrimination, but now you have to charge them, you have to fight to stop them from discriminating.' So, I wasn't able to play. I was trying to be tough and not cry, but I had to stay in the stands and cheer my team on for the rest of the season. Eventually they stopped me from even practicing. Even after winning in the court, I still wasn't allowed to play."

When Justine's case came before the Ontario Human Rights Commission, she faced opposition from all sides—organizations across Ontario wanted to keep girls in girls' hockey. Dr. Charles Bull, head of Team Canada's medical team and surgeon for the Toronto Maple Leafs, maintained that "most women are too weak to survive in a physical sport such as hockey . . . Even the Gretzky of females would only be in the middle category of males. [T]he aggressive nature has been proven to be stronger in males than females. They [women] don't have this fighting hormone."[7]

Fran Rider, speaking on behalf of the Ontario Women's Hockey

Association, agreed, testifying that overall, "Girls are too weak to compete on boys' teams." The OWHA knew that almost all of the top women were practicing with men, and Rider worried that "if the top-level females were to leave the teams . . . we've taken a valuable role model out of that league." Such action would seriously undermine the OWHA. "If we took the top three or the top five from each of those teams, that would eliminate all of the hockey. You've lost your entire hockey system. If one or two girls were to leave each team, we would lose teams and leagues. We feel team sports are suffering because of this push for individual rights."[8]

"Fran Rider and Angela James were the two main parties against me," Blainey recalls. "James was really a great hockey player; I respected her on the ice. She also practiced with the boys and dealt with a lot of discrimination as a Black woman. All I knew was, when we went on TV or on the radio, it was always 'Blainey versus James.' She was fighting for her own spot to be on the national team, and was friends with the OWHA group, and I wasn't. If the top female hockey player in the world was saying, 'Stop Blainey,' what do you think my other women's hockey teammates were saying?"

Blainey and James would go on to play senior hockey together in the Central Ontario Women's Hockey League. "She later apologized when she was my teammate," Blainey says, "and we found a way to be friends and teammates."

In December of 1987, Judge Ian Springate ruled that Blainey's constitutional rights had been violated for the three years of her battle, and unequivocally stated that "discrimination on the basis of sex in athletics is now unlawful in Ontario." Caroline Blainey, Justine's mother, saw it as a victory not only for her daughter, but for women. "If a kid can skate and shoot, then let her play," she told Canadian Press. The ruling was "absolutely wonderful not just for Justine but for other girls who are good enough and want to play on boys' teams. What kind of private parts the players have under their uniforms doesn't matter."[9]

Justine Blainey was finally allowed to play. But, because the decision had been delayed until December, midway through the season, her coach had been forced to give Blainey's spot away to another player. Blainey recalls sitting at the kitchen table with her brother and mother, listening to the coach apologize over the phone. There was no room for her. Still sitting at the table, Blainey's brother, who had stood beside her throughout the entire ordeal, called the coach back. "He said, 'If there were a spot on the team, could my sister have it?' The coach said yes. So my brother said, 'Fine. I quit. My sister can have my spot.' And he did. He quit, and I took his spot."

Blainey spent the next three seasons finally playing alongside boys before switching to girls' hockey with the Scarborough Sting. In 1992, she accepted an academic scholarship to attend the University of Toronto, where she would play for the school's women's hockey program.

When she arrived, it felt like she was ten all over again, watching her brother get everything. "I was playing for the university, and still the girls' team had nothing. The men had equipment, training, dressing rooms, and we had nothing."

In 1993, the university was contemplating cutting women's hockey altogether, even though their Lady Blues had been the reigning provincial champions since 1988. Blainey again found herself in the news as she rallied for equal funding and treatment for women's athletes. She organized a one-week fundraising blitz, personally calling one hundred alumni and organizing a "Save the Team" night that raised over $8,000. In 1995, the University of Toronto moved to equalize funding, recognizing the historic inequity between men's and women's hockey, along with other sports at the school. As the university's vice president, David Neelands, said, "On every level, men get more, from team costs to officials to equipment, travel money, lodging and per diems for food. In some cases, it looks like we assumed men ate and women didn't."[10]

Blainey's crusade opened doors for the next generation but, behind closed doors, it left its scars. "I still struggle from the challenges from back then: in trusting, in building new friendships, in wanting to be liked," she admits. "Being nervous on buses and subways, maybe easily hurt by comments. Some people have a thick skin to handle jokes, but I don't because I've been hurt and so many bad things were said in the past."

Long after Blainey's case defined girls' sports in Canada, the outcome remains controversial. "This action by the OWHA had an adverse effect on the progress of women's hockey in Ontario because by 1990, the OWHA was still paying its expenses dedicated to the Blainey case, which amounted to approximately $100,000 . . . The OWHA executives feared a successful outcome of this case could lead to the end of their league or at the very least drain it of the top female players. In the end, the Blainey case led to the dismantling of a discriminatory clause in the Ontario Human Rights Code that specifically exempted athletic organizations and activities from its sex equality policies."[11]

"Our members are still paying the cost of the case," Fran Rider stated in 1992. "They felt women's hockey would have been further ahead if we had won. Now if girls want to go for any male team, they register, sign up, and play."[12]

Justine Blainey is unrepentant—this is exactly the outcome she fought so hard to achieve. "It definitely was worth it; it's something I'm proud of. I'm surprised I made it through, and there were some desperate times, but it was definitely worth it."

•

Thirty years later, Abby Stonehouse was the star on the ice in my home-town, playing boys' AAA hockey for the Chatham-Kent Cyclones, the same organization that Olympic MVP and three-time gold medalist Meghan Agosta had skated with in her youth. Stonehouse was also playing in the local girls' hockey program, beginning the transition that would make her eligible to compete for Team Ontario and Team Canada at the U-18 level.

In 2017, the Cyclones made national news when they converted a girls' change room at East Kent Memorial Arena into a dedicated locker room for the boys' team. Girls playing in the arena were first assigned a tiny room, roughly six feet by eight feet, without benches, a sink, toilet, or shower. When the door opened, the interior was visible from the lobby. The next solution was assigning the girls an accessible washroom, a space that also opened to the public and could accommodate about three people at any one time.

"By leasing the girl's dressing room to a Chatham Cyclones AAA Hockey Team, the municipality has created the situation where the female players are treated inequitably," said Shawn Allen, president of the South Kent Minor Hockey Association, the arena's primary tenant. "Their efforts to create a substitute dressing room have exacerbated the situation by creating additional inequities."[13]

Pressure from the hockey world continued to mount in 2018. "Really people? This is the crap I was dealing with in 1985. It's 2018!![14] Just make it right. Period!" Hockey Hall of Famer Hayley Wickenheiser wrote on social media. Shortly after, the Municipality of Chatham-Kent renovated a new locker room for girls' hockey players at the arena, and the council committed to reviewing all arenas in the Municipality to ensure safe and appropriate spaces were available for all players.

Following the COVID-19 pandemic, Stonehouse moved on to play women's hockey with the OWHL's London Devilettes. During the 2022–23 season, now a U-18 world champion, she stood on a blueline in Östersund, Sweden wearing a Team Canada jersey and a gold medal, singing the Canadian anthem as a flag was raised to the rafters. Stonehouse was living her dream after spending years developing in boys' hockey, an opportunity and choice that may not have been afforded, and a gold medal that may not have been earned, had it not been for Justine Blainey.

CHAPTER 13

Powerful In Pink

I sat down in an old plastic chair, uncomfortable with my surroundings. I'd grown up in church, but it had been years since I'd been in one. I believe in God, or some greater power in this world, but not the God I was taught about. Not the man in the sky who would sentence a man to eternal fire for loving another man, or deny a woman's autonomy over her body, or condemn a hungry individual for envying the wealth of those who would not give. Certainly not the god who taught everyone I knew that it was a woman's responsibility to sacrifice her life for her husband, father, and brothers. I was tired of presidents bowing their head in prayer and dropping bombs on innocent civilians, and I resented the lifelong struggle the church sent me on to relearn kindness, to embrace people for who they are. I still struggle.

Sitting alongside my family, I listened to the minister jovially reinforcing tropes and stereotypes about our gendered roles. I looked around at the children listening intently, at the older men and women nodding in agreement, interjecting an occasional "Amen." I tried to zone it out, but my wife was squeezing my hand violently. It was the squeeze of a person struggling to breathe or trying to pull themself out of the path of a barreling bus. It brought me back to my surroundings, where the pastor was now explaining explicitly that pink was not a boys' color; that men do not wear pink. His story elicited laughter and agreement from the congregation. My wife and I sat, hands clasped, until the benediction released us from our seats. When we stood, our fingers pulsed as blood returned. I wanted to tell him pink was never mentioned in the Bible, not once. I wanted to grab his shoulders and explain the harm he was doing, the role he was playing in hurting women and men, and how that hurt, instead of love, would fester in their lives. I wanted to tell him his belief that pink was soft, delicate, and gentle, which his antiquated views ascribed to women, was wrong.

This remains one of my most vivid memories of church; I'm certain it's because of my own silence, rather than his message. Today, I think we would have been brave enough to stand up and object, or at least to leave.

•

As international women's hockey moved from unofficial in 1987 to an officially sanctioned IIHF World Championship in 1990, the balance of power also started to shift. Hockey scholar Julie Stevens observed that, "Although the event was an invitational tournament as opposed to a sanctioned IIHF championship, it challenged the status quo, where men held hockey's world stage, and moved the male-dominated hockey federations who controlled the international forum a few steps further along the gender-equity path."[1]

People within the women's hockey world were determined to push for an official tournament. The sport was also approaching a serendipitous moment—women's hockey was now of interest to the International Olympic Committee, members of which were "being lobbied by numerous groups who were unhappy with the inequity in the ratio of women to men competitors in the Olympic Games."[2] The easiest way to rectify this imbalance would be to add a large team sport like hockey that involved more than twenty participants per team and needed at least eight teams to form a tournament.

Before it could earn an Olympic berth however, women's hockey would need to prove it was played at an elite level globally. Organizers from the IOC and IIHF recognized that the CAHA was the only national body capable of showcasing the sport and hosting such a complex tournament. It would be up to Canada to put on a world-class event, that proved there was an on-ice product, fan interest, and media support sufficient to justify a place on the world stage.

While the IIHF promised the CAHA $150,000 to host the 1990 event, the funding came with a caveat: organizers were required to find a television network willing to broadcast at least four games.

Both of Canada's national networks, CBC and CTV, declined due to pre-existing commitments. Eventually, organizers found a network, TSN, willing to broadcast the games—for a price.

Unlike standard media deals where the network purchases broadcast rights, Women's World Championship organizers would have to pay TSN $17,000 per game to air the tournament.

Leading up to the event, organizers were struggling to attract media, sponsors, and fans. Ottawa showed little interest, perhaps believing that the ringette championship the city had the previous month had satisfied the public's curiosity. Media fatigue for international women's competition resulted in lackluster ticket sales. Few sports believed themselves to be a man's domain more than hockey.

Women's hockey had never had such a large stage; there had never been more at stake. In an attempt to attract attention, tournament director Patrick Reid opted for a gimmick: they would exchange Canada's traditional red and white uniforms for pink and white.

The choice was controversial, sparking a discourse that played out in the media leading up to the event and for years following. "Hockey traditionalists were outraged," Roy MacGregor wrote in a 2013 article in *The Globe and Mail*. "The issue was even raised in Parliament. But the media ate it up, both pro and con."[3] Instead of recognizing the inherent sexism, the media spun the symbolism into a message of empowerment. "The unofficial motto of the Canadian women's hockey team is 'powerful in pink' and no one is arguing with the boast yet."[4]

When speaking with players from this team, I always asked about the pink jerseys. The question was met with a consensus chuckle, followed by "Don't get me started," or "What a joke that was," but eventually landing on the idea that, as much as players disagreed with the change, it had drawn much-needed attention. At the time, players publicly supported the jerseys, but almost exclusively with the caveat that they would have worn anything for the opportunity to play the game they loved on an international stage. Having waited a century for this moment, the athletes on Team Canada were in no position to push back and risk losing everything they had gained.

"I think putting the team in pink was a great thing, a smart thing, because a lot of people clued into the pink team and they tuned in and saw women could play hockey and we were pretty good," says Canadian goaltender Cathy Phillips. "Women's hockey grew so much the following year."

Shirley Cameron recalls, "I went from wearing the traditional Team Canada jersey in 1987 to going to the pink and white pants and white gloves outfit. At that point in time, I don't think there was a player in there who cared what color it was. The fact we were having an official World Championship was the most important thing to everyone. Those pink and white jerseys, because they got talked about so much, turned out to be a pretty good marketing ploy. There were very mixed reactions to it being pink and white."

And so, Cameron, alongside future Hall of Famers Angela James and Geraldine Heaney, young standout Vicky Sunohara, and stars of the era like Dawn McGuire and Cathy Phillips, stepped into the spotlight for the first time and ushered women's hockey into a new era, wearing pink.

•

Cathy Phillips' voice is labored. The brain tumor has taken her speech, her balance, her job and her love—hockey. Her voice breaks as she speaks of her father, who passed away before seeing her play in the first Women's World Championship. We are speaking by phone, her story keeping me company on my three-hour drive to Toronto. She travels back inside her memories to the best period of her life, when she was the top goaltender in the world.

Cathy grew up playing road hockey with her brothers on a neighborhood tennis court. She scored at will but grew frustrated that those she faced couldn't stop the ball. She shifted to defense, where she could still shoot but could also stop the opposition from scoring. It wasn't enough. Eventually, with her baseball glove on one hand and stick in the other, she climbed into the net. Soon, she was frustrating her opponents, stifling their attempts to score.

Phillips knew women played hockey, but also knew teams were scarce. She'd always see ringette advertised, a game she described as "hockey, kind of" but with different zones and a requirement to "play with a broken hockey stick." It wasn't for her. She couldn't find a team, but her brother's team had only one goalie, so Phillips started practicing with them, acting as a second goalie during training.

As Phillips turned thirteen, a neighbor approached her while she was playing road hockey near her home and said, "'Cath, I found you a hockey team,'" Phillips recalls. "I took off like a shot. I thought, 'Holy cow.' He told me the guy he works with was going to be coaching his daughter on a team in Burlington. He had told him to watch out for me, that I was going to sign up and play. I finally had a hockey team of my own."

Phillips stayed with Burlington for years, establishing herself as the best goaltender in Canada. After a coaching change, Phillips switched to the Hamilton Golden Hawks, a team that included some of the best players she'd faced. Her father joined her, taking over as coach. On both teams, Phillips was dominant. She was named the Central Ontario Women's Hockey League Goaltender of the Year fourteen times and league MVP twice.

In 1986, Phillips had a conversation with Fran Rider. "My father had passed away and I remember meeting Fran on a baseball field. 'Cath, I'm trying to get a world championship going, and I'm trying to get it done this year,' she said. 'I'll know by Christmas.' And by Christmas, she said, 'We're doing it.' After losing my father, it was something nice, something to look forward to. I was surprised that other countries had hockey."

During the 1986–87 season, Cathy Phillips was nearly unbeatable. When she learned that her Hamilton Golden Hawks would represent Canada, she started looking for sponsorship. "I thought it would be nice if we had team jackets so that at least we looked like a team off the ice, not just on the ice. I remember walking into one place and meeting the gentleman and saying, 'I'm looking for a sponsor to help my team play in a world championship.' He pulled out his checkbook and asked, 'how old are the kids?' And I said, 'Oh no, it's us, it's women,' and he slowly slipped his checkbook back into the drawer. Women's hockey was a no-no."

No one would take Cathy Phillips' love for the game from her. Following the 1987 tournament, however, she started experiencing vision issues. On the baseball diamond, she could no longer see a ball approaching. On the ice, the puck tended to disappear; then she began seeing double. "I can remember once watching the puck go across the net. I followed it and, when the player took a shot, all of a sudden there were two pucks coming at me, and I thought, 'Oh my gosh, which one is it?'" Next came the head-aches. Knowing something was wrong, Cathy began undergoing tests. The doctor believed she had multiple sclerosis and scheduled her for a spinal tap. Phillips, however, knew it was something else, and insisted on an MRI.

Leading up to the 1989 tryouts for the first official world championship, Phillips, an electrician, went to work like any other week. But this time, she couldn't shake her migraine. It became piercing, debilitating. In her words, "The world turned upside down on me." At the urging of her coworkers, Phillips lay down in a dark room. Team Canada tryouts were the coming weekend and everyone knew how important this moment was for her. Whatever was ailing her was threatening her dream.

At Canada's national team selection camp, she endured. At one point, Phillips had to leave the ice because of her headaches and double vision. Staff knew how good she was, but told her that, to make the team, she needed to play. So Phillips returned for the team's final exhibition match, played a spectacular game, as she always had, and made the roster. She was named to Team Canada, and when the puck dropped on the inaugural game, she proudly stood in her crease. "To be able to represent Canada and be on the world forum where everyone across the world could watch, it was a big thing, it was something that was serious." She had fought for this moment and was ready to take on all comers wearing Canada's pink and white.

The games were fierce. Initially, bodychecking was permitted but, as the tournament went on, organizers began asking officials to assess penalties, despite the IIHF's own rules. Once again, men dictated what women were capable of. It caused mass confusion but, as always, the athletes adapted. Stopping shot after shot, Phillips starred as the tournament's top goaltender. In the gold medal game, she put on a performance to remember and was instrumental in helping Canada secure the victory.

But what was a beginning for many was the end for her. That same month, Phillips found out what had been causing her migraines and blurred vision. "I went to the MRI; there were these three doctors sitting there. I went into the cave, this tunnel of a machine and when I came out, I wanted to talk to the doctors, but they'd all gone. I thought they'd seen something and they didn't want to tell me."

It turned out she was right. When Cathy returned to her doctor, he said, "You have a brain tumor." It was the end of her playing career, and the beginning of a new fight. Recounting this memory, she's overcome by emotion. Her voice fails, and she stops talking.

As I drive, I hear only silence. I pass the exit for Burlington, Cathy's hometown, on my way into Toronto, creeping through the congestion. Slow progress forward with many stops and starts. "I'm sorry," I say to her. And I am. "Did you find a way to heal, to come to terms with losing hockey?"

"No," she replied.

•

Cathy Phillips was among a generation of fighters, forgotten women who only wanted to play a game they loved. When men decided to dress women in pink, Team Canada took the opportunity to showcase their skill, claiming their own power. Off the ice, fans showed their support by wearing pink as well. By the time the gold medal game was played, the color dominated the streets of Ottawa and the arena itself. Even the Zamboni was adorned with pink flamingos.

The excitement extended to homes across the country, where the women were visible to a national audience for the first time. Jayna Hefford, then thirteen, remembers the impact on her life. "A big turning point for me was the 1990 Women's World Championships," she says. "I remember watching it on television. It was in Ottawa and it was on TSN. I remember my mind being blown that women played hockey, that there was a Team Canada. I remember them coming out in the pink jerseys, and the other thing I remember is the arena was completely sold out, it was packed. I had no idea that even existed prior to that. That was really the impetus for me; at that point, that was what I wanted to do. A few years prior I probably realized I wasn't going to play in the NHL or win a Stanley Cup, but that was the moment I really understood that this was something I could achieve. The World Championships was something I could dream of."

The success of the tournament, and the caliber of play, ensured the issue of jerseys did not return. "What began with silly hype over uniform colors and lopsided preliminary games ended by winning fans with surprisingly fine hockey," the *Ottawa Citizen* reported. Or as Patrick Reid, who had first suggested the use of pink jerseys, said, "We won't have to talk about pink uniforms anymore to get people out to see women's hockey."[5]

Above: The first known photograph of women playing hockey. Isobel Stanley, daughter of Governor General Lord Stanley, is seen wearing white. Ottawa, Ontario, 1891.

Left: In 1915–16, Albertine Lapensée became a hockey phenom, so dominant that she was repeatedly forced to prove her gender. She regularly attracted crowds in the thousands and led her Cornwall Victorias team to an undefeated season. When organizers refused to compensate her, the "Miracle Maid" retired following the 1917 season at the age of eighteen.

Above: The Vancouver Amazons enjoy a lighthearted practice at the Banff Winter Carnival, 1922, the year they won the Alpine Cup.

Below: When the Fernie Swastikas claimed the Alpine Cup the following year, the town closed the schools so everyone could celebrate their victory.

Library and Archives Canada / Glynn A. Leyshon collection / a150991

City of Toronto Archives Fonds 1257, Series 1057, Item 3059

Myrtle Cook (above leftt, winning gold for Canada in the 4x100-meter relay at the 1928 Olympics) and Alexandrine Gibb (above right, in 1934) both became sports journalists and tireless advocates for women's sport at the conclusion of their athletic careers.

Below: The Preston Rivulettes were nearly unbeatable. Between 1931 and 1940, the team played 350 games, losing only twice.

City of Cambridge – Courtesy of the City of Cambridge Ontario Archives

Above: Hilda Ranscombe, star of the Preston Rivulettes, was considered "the best female hockey player in the world" in the 1930s.

Right: Abigail Hoffman suiting up, March 8, 1956. One of the best defenders in the Little Toronto Hockey League, "Ab" Hoffman was named to the all-star team. Despite support from her coaches and teammates, the discovery of her gender led to girls being formally banned from boys' teams.

Above left: Grace Small, founding member of the Wallaceburg Hornettes, with the endorsed little hockey stick, created for the inaugural Lipstick Tournament, February 12, 1967.

Above right: Marian Coveny of the Wallaceburg Hornettes received a gift of roses in recognition of being chosen Miss Valentine for the 1969 Lipstick Tournament.

Right: Bev Beaver played hockey for almost four decades, and in 1980 won the national Tom Longboat Award as Canada's top Indigenous athlete.

Left: In 1981, when Heather Kramble's parents lobbied local, provincial, and national hockey associations for her right to play on a boys' team, officials canceled her registration and threatened to ban all of the club's teams if they continued to support her. Heather reluctantly switched to ringette.

Right: Not content with the second-class treament girls' teams received, eleven-year-old Justine Blainey appealed to the Ontario Human Rights Commission. In 1987, after three years, five court cases, and several death threats, she finally won the right to play on a boys' team.

Above: After the first international women's tournament in 1987, Team Canada's captain, Marian "Mern" Coveny (l) and goalie Cathy Phillips (r) hoist the championship trophy with Mississauga mayor, Hazel McCallion.

Below left: Fran Rider celebrates Canada's win at the first international women's tournament, 1987. *Below right:* Shirley Cameron is honored by her team after winning the 1992 national championship, her last game.

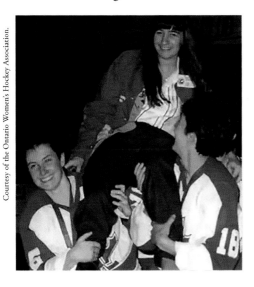

Above: Team USA captain Cammi Granato, pictured here with superstar Mark Messier, became one of the first faces of women's hockey when she began promoting hockey equipment designed especially for women.

CHAPTER 14

Red Line

When I was seventeen, my Junior hockey team was down a goal in a game in Essex, Ontario. I was playing defense in front of our net, trying to move out one of the biggest forwards on the opposing team, when he dropped his gloves, pulled off my helmet and gave me a beating. I held on but didn't fight back or drop my gloves; I was eventually knocked to the ice. Our team received a power play, during which we tied the game. Minutes later, we scored the winning goal. I was on the ice for both.

We came into the dressing room elated and sat down to hear our coach speak. He praised the win, but then said, "We won even though one of our biggest players was too much of a fucking pussy to fight." He turned to find me and stared straight into my welling eyes, "If you ever do that again, it will be the last time you see the ice." That moment stuck. It changed me.

Years later, I told this story to young players. When I asked how many had called someone or been called a "pussy," every player in the room—girls and boys—raised their hand. We unpacked the term together. "Why did they call you that, or why did you call someone that name?" I asked the group.

A long silence ensued. I changed course. "Okay, what does the word mean when someone uses it?"

After another moment of hesitation, an uncertain hand emerged. "Weak," they said.

"Okay, anyone else?"

"Soft," someone else chimed in. "Not tough," another joined the chorus. "Wimp," yet another offered.

Moving delicately with these teenagers, I brought up the other use of the term. "Is it also used as slang for a woman's genitalia?"

This was met with a few sheepish nods and awkward giggles. I could tell that none of the twenty-five teenagers in the room knew where this was going, so I proceeded. "So, when you use that word, when you call someone a pussy, you're relating the term to female genitalia. You're calling someone who is weak and soft, someone who isn't tough, or is a wimp, you're relating that to being a woman?"

"No, that's not what it means," called out a boy who went on to play in the OHL, noticeably defensive. But there were others nodding with more certainty now. They saw the correlation.

"I'm not weak. I could kick the ass of half the boys in this room," declared one of the girls, the captain of the high school hockey team I coached. Her grandfather had played more than 600 games in the NHL, and she could have played college hockey, but instead chose to accept an NCAA Division I track and field scholarship.

"You absolutely could," I said to her, smiling. Many of the boys were also smiling in agreement.

From there our conversation flowed. It was that simple. No one in that room had thought about the power of the word, the hidden meaning that told every woman that they were weaker, inferior. I asked them to consider their words, and to think about where that word came from, and what message it sent to women and girls. After that, I rarely heard it. From time to time, it still slipped out on the ice or in the gym but was almost always followed with an apology, an immediate recognition of the message and its meaning. It was a tiny step in unlearning and relearning what they'd all been taught, what I'd been taught, since the first day any of us stepped on the ice.

•

Hockey has always been a physical game, but it was not one that originally discriminated based on gender. "It is critical to recognize that organized women's hockey, particularly from the early 1920s to 40s, included rough play and fighting . . . Heavy body checks, hooking, slashing, fighting were all part of the women's game, which emulated the contemporary male hockey model. In the early 1900s, women and men played by the same rules, and women were more than capable of handling the physicality of body checking."[1]

Throughout the 1930s, headlines referred to on-ice fights: "Sticks and Fists Fly Freely as Girl Hockeyists Battle," "Girls Wanted Another Fight but Referees Stopped Them" and "Girls Draw Majors for Fistic Display."

Bodychecking in women's hockey only became an issue during the planning for the 1987 tournament. As Fran Rider recalls, "We were communicating with around eleven countries. Nations like England and Australia were very weak, but teams like USA and Canada were very strong. So we made a decision to play with no bodychecking to allow developing nations a fair chance. As soon as we communicated that, we got a telex from West Germany saying they weren't coming because, without intentional bodychecking, it wasn't real hockey."

For many players, the removal of bodychecking was unwelcome. "I loved the checking that we had back then," said American defender Kim Eisenreid. "I wasn't afraid to take a hit or give a hit."

Bodychecking was banned partway through the inaugural 1990 Women's World Championship tournament. Rule makers worried that a game that had featured checking, and sometimes fighting, for the better part of a century would repel spectators watching for the first time. More specifically, the men who governed the sport felt it their obligation to "protect" the women they saw as delicate, soft, and weak. The line between the rulebook and on-ice behavior became blurred and it was left to the officials on the ice to determine the boundary. One of them was Deb Maybury.

Maybury's life changed in 1973 when she saw a newspaper advertisement for a new girls' hockey league in Kingston, Ontario. She remembers jumping up and down with excitement. She then spent the next decade playing.

When Maybury got to the University of Waterloo, there was no women's hockey team. To stay in the game, she started officiating the school's intramural men's league. The next year, she transferred to York University and returned to playing hockey, initially for Brampton. In her third year, the 1986–87 season, she played for Mississauga. She was on the ice almost every day, some days playing for York University's women's team, others with Mississauga, and was still officiating as well.

After losing to the Hamilton Golden Hawks in the Ontario final, Maybury and Mississauga were forced to wait and watch as the national championships between the Hamilton Golden Hawks and the Edmonton Chimos played out. The winner would become Team Canada. If Hamilton won, Mississauga would become the host team, playing as Team Ontario. If Edmonton won, Hamilton would become the host. Hamilton won the

1987 national title 3-2 over Edmonton, and after a strong round robin at the World Tournament Maybury and Team Ontario found themselves in the semi-final facing Team USA.

"I think everyone expected us to lose. Everyone was kind of cheering for the other side because they wanted that US and Canadian final. The stands were filled," recalls Maybury. "Team USA were a better team than us, but we just shut them down." Ontario squeaked out a 5-4 win over the Americans before eventually falling again to Hamilton, now Team Canada, in the final.

"It was so exciting, just to play against other countries. To see the crowds and watch Team Canada and Team USA play, it was back and forth, the fastest games I'd ever seen," Maybury explains. "It was a catalyst, a stepping stone. We'd worked so hard in women's hockey; we wanted the right to play at a higher level and have the game recognized."

Following that tournament, Maybury shifted her focus to becoming an official, refereeing her first national championship the following year. Soon, there was a conversation about an official World Championship, and the possibility of Olympic involvement was on the horizon. She had a decision to make. "I went from playing, to playing and refereeing, to playing, refereeing and coaching. At that time, I needed to choose and decide how I was going to achieve what I wanted to achieve. I knew I would be the best I could be as an official."

Her experience and ability earned her an invitation to join the officiating team at the inaugural World Championships. It was a moment where everything changed; when, finally, women were not only playing in an IIHF-sanctioned event, but they were officiating as well.

"We got helmets, and we got skates that we were supposed to wear, and we were getting paid," she recalls. "It was like 'oh my gosh.' Any time I went to the Nationals, I wasn't paid. A lot of the time, you had to pay for your own flights. I went to seven and I paid for my flights every time. It didn't matter because it was so important to go.

"But in 1990, we got paid, and we got equipment. I got $400 for the week, a huge amount of money. We had an officials' skate to get to know each other. Most of us were Canadian and most of the others spoke English. There was a combination of male and female officials, but I was the only female referee. There were certainly others at the time who were capable of refereeing, and some people really fought to get females into those roles, but the powers that be wanted only men. Being a referee is a different game: there are no accolades, you get yelled at, you get questioned. You really need to have a strong core and they didn't feel women should do it. I remember the referee-in-chief talking to us as officials, telling us what to call and what not to call, telling us how we were going to referee after the exhibition game."

Maybury approached her first game, a pre-tournament exhibition contest between Canada and Sweden, as she had any other game in her career. "That tournament was to be a bodychecking tournament," she maintains. "I'd been playing bodychecking hockey since 1973, There was always bodychecking, except for university. That was non-checking, but there was still body contact."

Sweden, unable to match Canada's speed, tried to slow Canada down with a physical game. Maybury knew it was a mistake to push Canada, particularly with a player like Angela James on the ice. "If you wake up people like Angela James, you're waking up a beast who can play with a high level of skill and intensity you've probably never seen before."

While the first period wasn't particularly rough, especially compared to high-level women's hockey in Canada, it was enough to prompt a reaction from officials watching from the stands. "When we went into the room during the intermission, I remember the referee-in-chief coming in," says Maybury. "He stood in front of me and he reamed me, I mean reamed me. He was raising his voice, saying, 'this is not a midget boys' hockey game,' like I needed to be told that. 'You will call this, this, this, and this, and this will not happen.'

"I said, 'Okay, but I need clarification. I know what midget boys' hockey is. I also know what women's bodychecking hockey is. But I need clarification because, if I'm calling checking, everyone needs to know it's non-checking. I don't just mean the players. You need to let that out into the media and tell everyone it's non-checking.' He said, 'We do not want people getting hurt in this tournament, because it's not going to be good for women's hockey.'"

The IIHF worried that bodychecking was too risky given the range of height, weight and age among the players. However, IIHF president Günther

Sabetzki "did not want to risk the IIHF being criticized for staging a less than legitimate first women's world championship by not allowing the longstanding artifact of bodychecking. He also did not want to risk IIHF endorsement of a separate women's hockey routine performed based on an official body-contact artifact, without first having some evaluation of its acceptability to members of the media and the public. His strategy was to publicly state bodychecking was the artifact of the 1990 WWHC tournament, then privately instruct the actors, coaches, and arbiters the tournament was to be played in accordance with the intent of a less violent body-contact regulation."[2]

When she stepped on the ice for the second period, Maybury immediately skated to the closest bench, telling Canada's coaches and players who were gathered there that she'd be calling any open-ice hit. She delivered the same message to the Swedish bench. She made it clear to both teams that, after the game, the coaches could go figure it out and ask the IIHF for clarification. But for the remainder of her time on the ice, she'd be calling bodychecking a penalty, regardless of the rule book. "I went over to the bench and said, 'You've got to take it down a notch or I have to call everything, and I will call everything.' I wanted to be successful in this tournament just as much as they did."

Officials like Deb Maybury were forced to improvise, calling penalties for interference, roughing or holding whenever a bodycheck occurred. "If you listened to the commentators, they still were not aware that the referees were told to call a non-checking, no open-ice hits game." Broadcast host Michael Landsberg and color commentator Howie Meeker repeatedly complained that legitimate bodychecks were being unfairly penalized.

Tournament Director Patrick Reid quotes one such exchange. "Well I think we should yell down [to the referee] and say, 'there is bodychecking allowed here!" said Landsberg on air during the tournament. 'The referee is clearly out of his depth,' responded Meeker."[3]

As the tournament progressed, confusion reigned. "I always loved to hit other opponents," said Canadian blueliner Dawn McGuire. "I played a lot of full contact and it was difficult switching from stepping into an opponent to riding them off into the boards." Or, as Angela James stated, "You know hitting was a big part of our performance and how we played it. They kinda hand-cuffed you with that [body contact] rule and it made you wonder what was going on. Every now and then, you know, I hit someone because it was hockey."[4]

Prior to referee assignments being announced for the medal round, Maybury told officials she did not want to be considered for the gold medal game. As a Canadian who had played with and against the members of Team Canada, she wanted to avoid any perceived conflict. "I said, 'I can't be in that final game because I've played with these players that are on the Canadian team. There can't be any controversy in the game. We can't have that in the first world championship."

She went on to officiate the bronze medal game, then took advantage of a unique opportunity to sit back and watch history being made. "After the bronze medal game, I went and got something to eat. I was sitting there and I watched as thousands of people wearing pink, and with pink balloons, and pink ribbons, and pink flags filed in. It was emotional. It was a dream," she says. "I was watching thousands of people filing into an arena to watch our sport. It was going to be the biggest women's game ever."

The tournament highlighted the need to standardize rules. In Europe, many leagues were not checking, while others were. In the US, the national team was used to bodychecking in their regular games against Canada, but it was not permitted in the NCAA. In Canada, checking was the widespread norm. Following the 1990 Women's World Championship, a single line was added to the IIHF rulebook banning bodychecking from the women's game, which would thereafter be assessed a minor penalty.

It was a decision unique to hockey. Other, equally physical sports, including rugby and mixed martial arts, use one set of rules for all competitors. It was also clearly gendered. "Tournament officials thought that their interference was justified when it came to women's hockey; yet neurologists have a hard time convincing the NHL that paternalistic interference is warranted when it comes to men's hockey."[5]

The elimination of bodychecking immediately made women in hockey feel as though they were playing a secondary, lesser version of the sport. "The players view the limitation of body checking as an obstacle from being regarded as the real sport. They feel that they are real ice hockey players . . . they are made for ice hockey just as men, and they are not frail and weak women. They do not feel any need to adjust any rules or the physical training regimen simply because they are women. The same muscles are used and body checking should be allowed."[6]

"In 1990 when they had the checking, they didn't know how to handle it," Eisenreid maintains. "The referees were asking if they should let it go. They still thought of us as delicate as women, but there were no written rules about how to handle the hitting, so eventually they decided it was far better to eliminate it. For 1992, they took it out completely."

By 1994, the question of bodychecking in women's hockey was forgotten. It was a foregone conclusion that hitting would not be part of the women's game.

Some maintained that the absence of checking encouraged a more fluid, skill-based style of play. "I like the idea of no hitting," said American national team assistant coach, John Marchetti. "It brings out the grace of the game." For most, however, the reason remained protective. "I don't think the women's game is ready for it," said Les Lawton, head coach of the Canadian national team for the 1994 Women's World Championships. "There's a lot of disparity in skill level and the better players would just dominate that much more."[7]

•

In 2022, twenty years after the IIHF changed the rules, Sweden launched a pilot project to reintroduce bodychecking at all levels of women's hockey. The goal was to become more competitive internationally, and to inspire women to use their bodies in a powerful way. They started with their top professional league and second division league, then moved down through junior and youth ranks.

"We have tried to pursue the checking issue before at IIHF but have not been heard," said the Svenska Damhockeyligan's (SDHL) sport manager Gizela Ahlgren Bloom. "It feels inspiring that we now make a decision for our own league and not only pave the way for Swedish women's hockey but for the entire women's hockey world."[8]

When the puck dropped on the new PWHL in 2024, arena microphones picked up the sound of bodies hitting boards. "There's a lot of physicality," said PWHL Senior Vice President of Hockey Operations and Hockey Hall of Fame inductee Jayna Hefford. "That was our priority, to let the game be physically . . . the way . . . women want to play the game."

PWHL forward, Becca Gilmore, said, "We're strong players and to be able to play that physical game, obviously cleanly, it's awesome to give us energy on the bench. I think the crowd loved it and to let us play, that is just another step (forward) in women's hockey's growth."[9]

CHAPTER 15

Don't Tell Me What I Can't Do

Growing up, I remember questioning whether or not I should get braces. I never did because, as my family joked, I was likely to lose them playing hockey anyway. I didn't lose my teeth in the end, but it became normal to see teammates putting their fake teeth in and out before and after games. When my competitive hockey career ended, I joined a men's league where players wore visors, cages, or nothing at all over their faces. Soon I heard players on my team hurling insults at opponents who chose to wear neck guards—a common refrain in Junior hockey—and mocking those who wore a cage. You weren't tough or a real man if you wore a cage. The word "pussy" was flung around in all directions among men with families and careers for whom hockey was now simply recreation.

After I left that league, I walked away from playing for a decade, a time I filled with coaching and scouting. When I turned thirty-five, I joined an old-timers' league—that age was the official definition of an old-timer. With the pace slowed down, I succumbed to peer pressure and took off my half-visor. On the second week of our season, my wife and new daughter decided to come watch; I waved at them through the glass. Less than five minutes into that game, I circled the net in the offensive zone and set up to the right of the crease, calling for a pass. Instead, a player on my team took the puck into the high slot and unleashed a shot that, had he been twenty years younger, may have been more accurate. The puck hit me square in the mouth, pushing several of my bottom teeth through my lip. Blood ran down my chin, dying my beard red and filling my mouth.

A few weeks later, I returned to my old-timers' team, this time wearing a full cage. In truth, I don't think I'd ever play another game without one. I can't explain why I, an adult with multiple degrees who knew the dangers, hadn't worn one all along. Why wasn't this the norm at all levels of the sport?

Why was it only youth and women who were required to wear these vital pieces of protection?

I know the answer. When people saw my face, they reacted with a congratulatory smile when I told them it was an injury induced by a puck, a response I expected from a world that glorifies the toothless grins of grizzled NHL players. Would the world react the same way to a woman spitting out teeth as she fought for a PWHL title? I think I know that answer as well. I also know there are many who want full face masks to be optional for women. I'm on the side that thinks full masks should be mandatory for everyone. But I'm mostly on the side that thinks women should decide for themselves.

•

Growing up in New England in the 1970s, Kelly Dyer was a product of the Bobby Orr explosion. On the streets outside her house, neighborhood kids emulated their hero. Dyer pieced together a set of goalie pads from garbage she found in dumpsters, using her sewing kit and shoe glue. Soon, Massachusetts began building more arenas, and it was on one of these rinks that Dyer first stepped on the ice.

"I started as a figure skater because at the time that was the only way girls could get on the ice," Dyer recalls. "But my brother, David, who's two years older, was a hockey player so I would get off the figure skating rink and run over to the hockey rink to watch. I always wanted to play hockey and begged for two years until my father found Assabet in Concord, the next town over. My first day of skating with Assabet was in my brother's equipment with figure skates."

It didn't take long for Dyer to skyrocket up the ranks at Assabet, aided by the Acton-Boxboro high school program that included future NHLers Bob Sweeney and Jeff Norton. Her goaltending partner at the school was future Hockey Hall of Famer Tom Barrasso. She went on to play four years of NCAA hockey at Northeastern, graduating just in time to try out for the national team ahead of the inaugural 1990 Women's World Championships. As tryouts took place at Northeastern, Dyer didn't even need to move the equipment from her stall. She just changed the color of her jersey when she was named to Team USA.

Suiting up for Team USA in the gold-medal game changed her life forever. "It was one of the greatest events of my life, probably second only to the birth of my child," Dyer says. "It was amazing to see and feel the energy in the arena for a women's hockey game. The amount of excitement and intensity and honoring us as athletes. Canada was a tremendous host. All of these things that we had never experienced before: team masseuses, team apparel, even the orchestration of the team meals. It was truly amazing to be treated how we perceived an NHL athlete was treated, to the highest level of recognition our sport had."

After that tournament, there was nowhere for Dyer to play. She stayed on to help at Northeastern in order to stay on the ice and also suited up for a men's league. "It was a huge problem," says Dyer. "I was working on Newbury Street in Boston and getting on the ice with Northeastern as much as I could and then catching a high-level men's league game. At times, though, there was a high level of alcohol involved in the game, and the skill level was inconsistent, which really doesn't do a goaltender much good. It wasn't really game play. There was a lack of backchecking and no strategy, so there was a huge gap." In 1994, Kelly Dyer joined the Sunshine Hockey League in Florida and spent three seasons backstopping the West Palm Beach Blaze, one of a handful of women to play men's professional hockey at the time.

Coming home from the first World Championships in Ottawa, Dyer saw a huge gap in the women's game, one that often left women's bodies unprotected. Even the top players in the world were forced to use equipment designed for men. There was no alternative.

"It was a little disappointing," recalls her teammate, Lisa Brown-Miller. "I'm not sure how great the backing was from USA Hockey. I don't think it was awesome because we had gear that didn't fit. We had warmup clothes that were much, much too large. Mine, especially—I'm only five-one. My gear was so big they had to hem up my jersey, and the covers for my pants had to be shortened, so that part was really a bummer. We had no matching hockey bags so we looked like a team of rag tags."

Eventually, a sponsor came through and provided team bags. "I remember just being grateful for anything that we got," said Brown-Miller. "But how ill-fitting most things were, I don't know, it seems like we were an afterthought."

Dyer also recognized that women were an afterthought in the hockey equipment industry. As a goaltender, she had always loved equipment and wanted to know what stick and glove, what brand of helmet and skates, each player on the ice was wearing. Now she saw an opportunity. "I would see players—Cammi Granato is a perfect example—I think she played at 5'7" and let's say 130 lbs. So she'd have to wear a men's medium pant for the pad to come down to her shin guards. But then she'd have to take the waist and cinch it in tight because she was slender. So now her kidney pads are in front of her belly," she explains. "Bending forward to tie their skates, players had to re-open their pants to let the hard plastic kidney pads flare out and then do them back up. So players were carrying this extra bulk where they needed dynamic movement and had no protection on their kidneys. I thought, this is ridiculous."

Dyer had one mission in mind: to find a company willing to manufacture sticks and protective equipment specifically built for women. "Coming from USA Hockey, we just had hockey pants that the men wore. They were heavy and weren't good for performance or for protection. So that became my motto, performance and protection. Protection because our equipment kept the padding in place where players needed it, and performance because it fit and it didn't shift all over.

"I had a good amount of attention coming back from the 1990 Women's World Championships. I just came home and I was so pumped and so full of energy and visions in a thousand directions of where women's sports could go," she explains. "I just picked up the phone and called every single person I could think of and I called every single hockey manufacturer. I had a long conversation with Bauer and they were seemingly supportive but then they just couldn't commit the time or the manufacturing to it."

One company, however, said yes. And it changed the game forever.

Hillerich and Bradsby, the company that had taken over Wally Enterprises just in time to sponsor the first Lipstick Tournament, was already well-known for the famous Louisville Slugger line of hockey sticks and baseball bats and also manufactured men's gloves and hockey pants. For goaltenders, they produced chest and arm protectors and goalie pants. When Kelly Dyer contacted them following the 1990 Women's World Championships, they were already taking the leap into producing protective equipment for men.

"I ended up with Louisville Hockey because they were Canadian so there was less time delay in trying new equipment as we were tweaking it," she explains. "They were small enough to be flexible, and they were committed to me, so I switched to wearing their product in 1992. I really became part of the family as soon as I started work." She would spend the next seventeen years working with the company.

In the back of Team USA's bus, Kelly Dyer sketched out ideas, using her teammates as models: Lisa Brown-Miller for size small, Cammi Granato for size medium, and Kelly O'Leary for large. "Everybody was constantly pulling their pants up and you couldn't keep them up," Dyer explains. "The same with shoulder pads. We had kids wearing these massive shoulder pads, so I really saw a need. With gloves, women don't have the depth in the fingers, so you have all this material taking away from maximizing your strength. Just thinning out the gussets on the fingers and then narrowing them meant that when you went to make a grip you were using the full strength of your hand. Instead of having your hand spread out, you were actually maximizing the transference of your energy through the stick. Before, a lot of girls would cut their palms out, but then they'd have all this extra material dangling off the back of their hands."

It was a significant shift for women who had been filing the picks off figure skates and wearing their brothers' equipment for decades. "The sticks—first we did wood, but then we went with composites. Louisville bought Fontaine so we had the wood blades with the melt-in composite shaft. We made women's sticks with a smaller radius, we made gloves, we made shoulder pads with breast protection, and we made pants that were shorter on the torso and longer in the legs."

For Brown-Miller, having equipment designed for her body was a game changer. For the first time, she had shoulder pads that fit—and pants and gloves and shin pads—and then sticks built for her. "Kelly just approached me and said, 'Hey, this is what we're going to do and I'd like you to be our small model.'" It took a vision from Dyer to fill a need that had existed since women first stepped on the ice.

"Makers of sports equipment have finally realized there's another sex," wrote the *Chicago Tribune* in 1996, as Louisville prepared to announce their groundbreaking line of women's hockey equipment. "The industry is quickly learning that there are millions of women out there who want to play sports, and they have purchasing power," said Mike May of the Sporting Goods Manufacturing Association. "They need stuff to fit their bodies."[1] The plan was to fill a growing void in the market and tour the equipment prior to the debut of women's hockey at the 1998 Olympics—and to be prepared for an explosion afterward.

In another first for women's hockey, Dyer began signing athletes to endorsement deals to join her as ambassadors for the Wallaceburg company. "I didn't want to make it all about me, so then we signed Erin Whitten, and we did a Whitten goalie stick. Then I thought, well, we need a Canadian, so I signed Geraldine Heaney."

Says Brown-Miller, "It was fun to be a part of something groundbreaking, because nobody had ever done that before, or even really had the thought. At that time, it was like, 'Okay, women play hockey, but what is the market?' Louisville and Kelly realized there was a market. So it was really exciting to be a part of that, and I felt special because I was picked to be one of the representatives. We were part of something new."

"From the moment I first tried on the new equipment I could tell that it was different from anything I had ever used before. It's designed for female proportions. It holds the pads in the right places, providing protection that unisex equipment cannot offer," Cammi Granato said in another Louisville advertisement. Granato also appeared on an iconic Louisville poster alongside Mark Messier, each wearing the other's jersey and looking back at the camera, decked out from head to toe in Louisville hockey equipment.

Granato and Heaney, both future members of the Hall of Fame, became the faces of the women's equipment industry, promoting "proportionally designed hockey equipment for female athletes." Emblazoned on their photos in large yellow letters was the campaign's slogan: "Don't tell me what I can't do."

CHAPTER 16

Power Forward

In 1998, for the first time ever, I sat down in front of my television to watch women play hockey. I was playing AAA hockey that year, captaining the Chatham-Kent Cyclones, and would soon make my Junior hockey debut at age fourteen with my hometown Wallaceburg Lakers. At the time, I'm sure I made sexist comments—I was already years into being told not to "play like a girl." But by the time the Olympic tournament ended, I had come to respect the game and the players. In addition to the men's stars present, I now knew Geraldine Heaney, Hayley Wickenheiser, Jayna Hefford, Vicky Sunohara, and Cassie Campbell. I also knew their American arch-rivals, among them Cammi Granato, Lisa Brown-Miller and Angela Ruggiero.

•

Pierre de Coubertin, co-founder of the International Olympic Committee, believed that "the Olympic Games must be reserved for men. [W]e must continue to try to achieve the following definition: the solemn and periodic exaltation of male athleticism, with internationalism as a base, loyalty as a means, art for its setting, and female applause as its reward."[1] Beginning in 1900, women's participation was limited to genteel sports such as golf and archery.

France's Alice Milliat disagreed. In 1918, Milliat, who had previously played in the first women's football match as a member of Fémina Sport, was the president of France's Fédération des sociétés féminines sportives, the world's first national sports organizations for women. She lobbied for the inclusion of women in the 1920 Olympic games but was denied. So, in 1921, she founded the Fédération Sportive Fèminine Internationale (FSFI), the first international body for women's sport. The following year in August, Milliat stood before 20,000 fans in Paris, France, to announce the opening of a women's competition, the Jeux olympiques féminins.

The event drew little attention from men's sporting bodies, who were preparing for the 1924 Paris Games. But the unauthorized use of the term "Olympics," a deliberate irritant, got a reaction. "[S]he set her sights on the Olympics. And she would use that word for her event, scheduled every four years between the cycles of Coubertin's mostly male Olympic Games. Members of the Olympic Committee remained gatekeepers of the games, subjugating women in sport for decades longer."[2]

In 1926, during an address to FSFI members, Milliat continued to argue that the Olympic Games could only be complete with women. As reported by John Branch in *The New York Times*, Milliat maintained that "participation in the Olympic Games can only be understood if it is total, women's sport having proven itself and should not serve as an experiment for the Olympic Committee. Such limited participation cannot serve the propaganda of women's sports."

Eventually, her ploy worked. "Milliat agreed to stop using 'Olympics' if the Olympics let women compete in athletics. A deal was struck, and in 1928, the Summer Olympics in Amsterdam had women's track and field for the first time," Branch wrote. "Milliat wanted ten events, but women were granted five. Milliat was selected as a judge, the only female face in a sea of men."[3]

Partial inclusion was not enough for Milliat, who continued to operate a parallel event for women, now dubbed the Women's World Games, in 1926, 1930, and 1934, with an ever-increasing number of events and participants.

Milliat knew the work could not stop, and implored all those who could, like disciples of the gospel, to share the news of women's sports. "I urge you all to continue to do good work and spread the good word on every occasion and to fight the good fight with us for a cause which we always defend with the same spirit and the same faith . . ."[4]

The Olympics were now in direct competition with the Women's World Games, a situation that pleased neither organization. In 1934, Milliat presented the IOC with an ultimatum: either integrate women into the upcoming 1936 games to be held in Berlin, or permanently cede control of women's athletics to her organization. The ensuing IOC resolution passed by one vote: ten to nine.

Originally included in the 1920 summer games, men's hockey had been part of the winter Olympics since 1924, when women were only allowed to participate in figure skating. When women's alpine skiing was added to the 1936 Olympic docket, the subject of women's hockey was raised, then quickly dismissed. "They laughed off the suggestion now that women's hockey will eventually be recognized on this Olympic card but wait and see!"[5]

In an era when champion clubs were generally chosen to represent their countries, the Preston Rivulettes were the logical candidates to represent Canada should women's hockey be included. To drum up international interest in the sport, Myrtle Cook and the Dominion Women's Amateur Hockey Association sought to send the Preston team on a European tour. "A trip to England prior to the opening of the 1935–36 season with Rivulettes representing the Canadian side, would do a lot towards persuading the moguls in the European territory that the time is not distant when they can vote for women's hockey in the Olympic program and not suffer at the gates," Cook wrote in 1935.[6]

It was a discussion other papers quickly latched onto as well. "The question of sending a women's team to Europe this fall for a series of exhibition games will be discussed at a later meeting. A suggestion was heard that delegates express an opinion on the desirability of entering a team in the 1940 Olympic Games. A resolution tabled provides for an official request from the association to the International Olympic Committee to include women's hockey as a demonstration event for the 1940 games."[7]

During the 1930s, there were many nations already fielding women's hockey teams, and the popularity of the sport was on the rise. "With England, France, Russia and Germany developing women's hockey it will not be long before Canada and USA will be stepping into an international tournament to decide who's who in women's world hockey. If they ever get it on the Olympic games as a demonstration event, that will be the start."[8]

Sadly, with teams defaulting due to a lack of financing in regional and national competitions, the costly tour never happened. Cook, however, remained the predominant voice pushing for women's hockey's inclusion in the Olympic Games until her death in 1985.

Cook lived long enough to witness the renewed campaign for Olympic participation that accompanied the resurgence of the game in the 1970s. Sylvia Wasylyk left her Delaware Bobcats for two seasons between 1976 and 1978 to play for the Massport Jets in Boston, believing women's hockey would be on the docket at the 1980 Olympics in Lake Placid, New York.

"We were training for women's hockey for the Olympics in 1980," she said. "We were sure they [the International Olympic Committee] would vote it in, but they didn't. I can't understand it, they have women's bobsledding, skiing and so on. Slowly but surely, things are improving. I might waste my whole life trying for the Olympics. I'll probably retire the year they go with it."[9]

Women's hopes for 1980 were dashed. By 1990, in the wake of the successful Women's World Championship, remarkably little had changed. Walter Bush, Chairman of the Board at USA Hockey, said, "I wrote a letter to the IOC and suggested they put women's hockey into the Olympics. I got a letter back, about four lines, that said, 'Thank you for your inquiry, but you must understand that we already have women's hockey in the Olympics in the Summer Games. It's called field hockey.' We took movies of the tournament and sent them to the IOC, and they said, 'You sped these movies up.' I sent them footage of Canada vs USA, and it wasn't anything like it is today, but it was pretty impressive. They could see that these women could skate."[10]

When, in 1992, the IOC finally voted to include women's ice hockey at the Olympic Games, organizers hoped women could compete in Lillehammer, Norway in 1994. However, programs had been finalized and there were not enough facilities available. Japan agreed to host the inaugural event in 1998 with one stipulation: that it could include their team.

"This is the beginning of the most exciting stage in the history of women's hockey in this country," said Shannon Miller, head coach of Team Canada at the time. "The players all have made sacrifices to be here—some of them taking leaves of absence from jobs, others interrupting their university studies."[11] One of those players was American Lisa Brown-Miller.

The first time Lisa Brown-Miller took a shot was in the living room of her friend Chris' house in West Bloomfield, Michigan. The six-year-olds took turns putting on his goalie equipment and shooting tennis balls at each other. One day she came home and told her parents she wanted to play hockey.

All anyone in her family knew of hockey was the helmetless, maskless men playing for the Detroit Red Wings, getting in fights or hit by pucks. Her parents were nervous, and when Brown-Miller arrived at Lakeland

Arena in 1972, she was the only girl on the ice. "It was definitely not the norm," Brown-Miller recalls. "I knew of no other girls who played hockey."

Brown-Miller was unique. Hockey became part of her identity, the way people knew her and thought of her at school. Even her teachers showed interest, showing up to watch her play. When she turned thirteen, she made the switch to a girls' hockey program her dad found in nearby Royal Oak. "It was as if we were kind of, just a step or two away, as if doors were opening," she says. "Doors would open, and then we took another step or two and we're through that door. And then you're walking along your path, skating along the path, and then there's another door in front of you, and you're just one or two steps there, and you're going to skate through that door. So fortunately for me, when I came into the game, we found this girls' hockey program. Then I heard somewhere along the line that there was collegiate hockey for women, which became my full focus."

When Brown-Miller graduated from high school in 1984, she moved to Providence College to play hockey. As she was finishing her NCAA career in 1988, word came that an official world championship would be held two years later. It felt like another door was opening. She skated through it onto Team USA and onto international ice, winning medal after medal, though never gold.

After finishing her playing career with Providence, Brown-Miller became the head coach at Princeton where in her first season, 1991–92, she was named the East Coast Athletic Conference Coach of the Year. She continued to play for Team USA, balancing biennial world championships with coaching.

When the door to the Olympics opened, the then thirty-year-old Brown-Miller felt time slipping away. In 1996, she walked away from the only viable career path for women in hockey to chase her dream. "I thought, I'm not going to be able to coach and train for the Olympics if this is my last hurrah. I left Princeton to train full-time in hopes of making the Olympic team. I put all my eggs in one basket, so to speak."

It paid off for Brown-Miller. Alongside teammate Cammi Granato, she became one of only two American players to make it all the way from the inaugural 1990 Women's World Championships to the 1998 Olympic Games. The duo was integral to USA's upset of Canada to claim the first

Olympic gold medal. It was the pinnacle of Brown-Miller's career. She'd gone from being a girl in Michigan thinking she was the only one playing hockey to being an Olympic champion.

"There's another door that's opening and it's within reach for me," she recalls thinking at the time. "There were some of my teammates in college, or even some of my opponents who were . . . right there too . . . but maybe just a year or two older. Like Cindy Curley, who just missed that opportunity. She's one of the pioneers of the women's game." Brown-Miller was one of the lucky ones.

She'd prepared for the Olympics like every other world championship before them, in anonymity. "I'd be working out at the gym and somebody asked me, 'You're obviously in great shape, are you training for something?' I said, 'Yeah, I'm training for the World Championships.' Nobody had ever heard of it."

Following 1998, that all changed. Not only had the game moved onto the world's largest stage, but for the first time, USA had beaten Canada for gold. Inevitably, Canada's stunning loss in the gold-medal game led to second-guessing. Many believe that the absence of superstar Angela James was a significant factor. "'I believe to this day she should have made that team,' says [Cassie] Campbell-Pascall. 'She was always a difference maker . . . I played defense, but I think she should have made the team over me. I thought that was a really big mistake.'"[12]

James, a Black woman, grew up impoverished in the Flemingdon neighborhood in the North York region of Toronto, joining a boys' hockey team at age eight. Facing pushback, her mother Donna, a single parent raising her children in subsidized housing, threatened legal action to have her daughter included. Angela led the league in scoring and moved up to compete against eleven- and twelve-year-old boys. The following season, 1973–74, the Metro Toronto Hockey League banned girls, leaving James to look for a new team.

James found a girls' program in nearby Don Mills and, at thirteen, began playing women's hockey for the Newtonbrook Saints. When she was sixteen, James joined the Toronto Islanders of the new Central Ontario Women's Hockey League, where she quickly became a star. Joining a new team for the 1982–83 season, she helped the Burlington Ladies win a Canadian national championship. That same season, James also played for Seneca College, where she led the league in scoring and was named the Ontario Colleges Athletic Association MVP, all while holding down multiple part-time jobs to help pay for her hockey and support her family. She won the COWHL's MVP honor six times and, beginning in 1987, led the league in scoring for seven consecutive seasons.

At the 1987 international tournament, James was a member of the Mississauga Warriors, who played as Team Ontario. By 1990, when the IIHF had decided to sanction a women's World Championship, James was playing for the Toronto Aeros. She was widely considered the best player on the planet, all the while working as the recreation coordinator at Seneca College.

James was named a tournament All-Star at the first two Women's World Championships, in 1990 and 1992. She was a key member of Canada's gold-medal winning team in 1990, 1992, 1994 and 1997. It was enough to have her dreaming of Olympic glory in Nagano. "Going to the Olympics means everything you have put into the game is starting to mean something," she said in a 1996 interview with *The Hockey News*. "At first, it started with just the national championship and that was our Olympics. Then all of a sudden, there were international championships and that was our Olympics. Now with the actual Olympics, it is such a wonderful feeling knowing we will have representation."[13]

But Shannon Miller, the same coach who had touted Angela James' skill for several seasons, decided to cut the biggest legend to ever play the game from the 1998 Olympic roster. James was devastated. "I feel cheated. I feel like someone ripped my heart out. I think a dog would get better treatment," she told *The Hockey News*. "They did everything in their power to keep me down. Maybe they thought I was an old hag and shouldn't be around."

In the same article, Miller justified her decision. "Angela has been a powerhouse player for many years. She's one of the greatest ever. I'm not surprised she would be upset, disappointed and hurt. [But] we were very clear with everybody, from the very first day, that we were not using Olympic spots to reward people for past performances."[14]

Miller's decision may have cost Canada a gold medal. It definitely cost the hockey world an opportunity to finally see James' greatness. "People would have known her name," Campbell-Pascall told *Sportsnet*. "Her story would have been told. That great story of AJ growing up in basically the projects.

There's no one I know in hockey who's faced as much in their life as Ang and [accomplished] what they did. The adversity she faced throughout her life and her ability to excel—it's incredible."[15]

Speaking with James years later, the Olympics remain a topic best left unmentioned, even though her legacy is not tied to that tournament. She remains the only person of color to captain a Canadian hockey team and, in 2010, was one of the first two women ever inducted into the Hockey Hall of Fame.

Aside from her undeniable on-ice dominance, James' pivotal role in powering women's hockey forward for minorities has often been over-looked. Perhaps it was her absence from the 1998 Olympic roster, perhaps it's the erasure of Black women in history, perhaps it's both. "The accom-plishments of Black queer women are more often disregarded because they fail to conform to the heteronormativity and Whiteness of the dominant culture . . . Hence, James represents the intersectional oppressions in sport that burden Black women and compound their erasure from Canada and from hockey."[16]

Angela James "paved the way for so many young Canadian women to go on to play hockey on the Olympic stage, even though James herself never could." One of those women is Sarah Nurse, who first learned about James at age fifteen in 2010. By that point James was retired, but she'd left a trail for other Black women like Nurse to thrive at the international level. "Just hear-ing about her story and kind of seeing her as a figure that I got to look up to, to say, 'She did all this when it was just beginning—when women's hockey really had nothing.' She was really one of the pioneers for our game."[17]

James' impact was felt on both sides of the border as Black women increasingly entered hockey. One of those women, Laila Edwards, an Ohio product, broke Team USA's color barrier in 2023, appearing with USA's senior national team for the first time in a Rivalry Series game against Canada. In April 2024, as if the torch had been passed from James to Edwards, the twenty-year-old Laila Edwards was named the 2024 World Championship MVP, winning silver with Team USA.

•

When Vicky Sunohara, wearing a Team Canada jersey, stepped on the ice for the opening game of the inaugural Olympic tournament, she became a star. She was flooded with media requests, with stories focusing heavily on Japanese Canadian identity. Her grandparents, Junichi and Mei, had grown up less than thirty kilometers south of Nagano. "My hockey card was blown up into a life-size poster and there were banners saying, 'Vicky Sunohara, we are your relatives.' It was amazing. My teammates were like 'oh my gosh, this is unbelievable.' I really had no idea; it was pretty special."

Following the Games, a local reporter who was serving as Sunohara's translator took her to Ueda, the town where her grandparents were born. There, a group of more than eighty relatives and family friends threw her a banquet. "They had pictures of my mom and dad on their wedding day. My grandmother's relatives were there. A couple of the women looked so much like my grandmother. It was unbelievable. It was all a surprise, it wasn't like, 'I'm going to Japan to get to meet some relatives.' I had no idea they'd be there. It was all such a shock."

The Sunohara family originally immigrated to Vancouver, where Junichi worked designing miniature Japanese gardens. In 1942, the Canadian government, following the lead of the United States, invoked the War Measures Act and dispossessed over 22,000 Japanese Canadians, forcefully dispersing them to internment camps across the country. The Sunoharas, including their six children, ended up in Cedar Springs, Ontario, where they survived by working on local farms.

Dave Sunohara and his brother, Phil, became successful multi-sport athletes in nearby Blenheim, eventually playing organized hockey and becoming local stars. Following high school, Dave moved to Toronto to study and play hockey for the Ryerson University Rams, winning back-to-back Central Ontario Hockey League championships. Alongside Phil, he also starred for an all-Japanese Canadian hockey club nicknamed the Nisei Flyers.

After settling in Scarborough, Ontario, Dave and his wife, Catharine, started a family, including Vicky, who was born in 1970. Dave soon passed on his love for hockey. "Everything was with hockey," Vicky Sunohara recalls. "My dad built a rink in our backyard; we played hockey in the basement. My first words were 'shoot score, shoot score.' I was just two, and he'd always ask, 'Are you going to be a hockey player?' I always wanted to be a hockey player. Whether it was the basement or the rink outside, I remember always wanting to play hockey with him. He'd make the rink at our public school too, and he'd flood it at night, and I remember begging to go with him. I'd be there all the time playing with the boys.

"My mom always told me that when I was just two-and-a-half, he brought me to the rink, and when he brought me home, he told my mom, 'You're not going to believe this, Vicky can skate.' My mom said, 'Awesome, she can be a figure skater,' because she never liked hockey. My dad said, 'Not a chance, she's going to play hockey.' When he put me on skates, that was pretty exciting for him, and I just loved it. I don't remember loving anything more than hockey. Whether it be at our school or in our backyard, it was all about hockey."

When she turned five, Dave enrolled Vicky on a boys' team, where she led the league in scoring with thirty-six goals. Like other girls of the time, however, she was soon banned from playing alongside boys. Sunohara faced the additional challenge of being a woman of color in a sport designed for white men. "When I was younger there were a few times when I would get called racist names. I was being called 'chink.'"

After Sunohara's father passed away when she was seven, she faced a new type of racism. When she arrived at the rink with her mother, a white woman of Ukrainian background, people would say, "You must be adopted."

"Some of the names, it upset me, and there were times I didn't want to be called names. I thought, sometimes, maybe I didn't want to play anymore. I wondered why can't I be like everyone else, why am I being called names? No kid wants to get called names. My mom really helped me out with that. She always said to me if people were calling me names, it was because they just wanted me to stop scoring. She'd say just go play harder, go score more."

Despite the layers of resistance Sunohara faced, she thrived. Her skill caught the attention of Northeastern University, where she played NCAA hockey. *The Hockey News* placed her on their cover, declaring her to be the best player in women's college hockey. The next year, she earned a spot on Canada's first World Championship roster, where she played alongside Angela James. Following the Worlds however, Sunohara slipped from the national team, and went through a difficult period in her life. "I hated everything. I didn't want to go to school. I didn't want to play hockey. I guess I was just depressed."[18]

Despite her personal struggles, Sunohara never left the game she loved.

"I'd go to hockey if I had a bad day, or things going on in my life, and it would be my place of freedom, a place to get away and forget about anything bad. I'd go and step on the ice and it would be my outlet, my happy place." Following her time at Northeastern, where she was named an All-American, she returned home and continued playing and studying at the University of Toronto, winning back-to-back Ontario titles in her first two seasons. She was named Ontario University Athletics Rookie of the Year in 1991. She also continued playing in the COWHL with the Scarborough Firefighters, followed by the Toronto Red Wings. In 1995–96, Sunohara was named the MVP of the COWHL and caught the eye of Shannon Miller, who added her to Canada's roster.

Vicky Sunohara would become one of the most decorated hockey players in Canadian history. TSN named her to their All-Time Women's Team Canada in 2020, the same year she Sunohara received the Sakura Award, an honor bestowed by the Japanese Canadian Cultural Centre upon an individual who has helped to promote Japanese culture and enhance awareness of Japanese heritage in Canada and abroad.

•

Nagano was a catalyst for the global growth of the game. For the first time, the Canadian national team centralized and played a full season together. For the women involved, this was their first experience of being treated like true professionals. Players were paid a stipend, and their job became training to win gold. While the athletes participating in the men's tournament earned millions, Vicky Sunohara and her teammates received $435 per month as nationally carded athletes.

"I remember it being so amazing, first and foremost just to be able to be a hockey player full-time, that first chance to centralize and move to Calgary, and be paid to be as a hockey player and get to do that every day and train with the best players and travel around the world, all of that was such an amazing experience," said Jayna Hefford, a national team rookie at the time. "I think we learned a lot about how to be professional athletes. Whether it was someone like me who was twenty, or someone like France St. Louis who was thirty-nine, it was new to everybody. It was a real learning curve in terms of how to become a full-time athlete and really learn how to train in a serious way."

Lisa Brown-Miller was amazed at the change from 1990, when the US team was given almost nothing, to 1998. At first, she and her teammates were just happy to be there, to feast on the scraps. "Because we were always the 'firsts,' we were always grateful for what we got," she says. "We didn't push the boundaries at that point, because we were just so grateful to play.to wear a USA jersey, to have a USA sweatshirt, to get a second pair of skates. We were just conditioned that way; that was just our world at the time."

Conditions began to improve after the first World Championships. "In that span of eight years, there was a huge surge," she says. "The talent level of the players, and the commitment from USA Hockey gradually improved. It was never really to where we wanted it, and at the time, we felt a bit like second-class citizens being given the leftovers from previous men's or boys' USA teams." Nagano marked a turning point. "I feel like it shifted. It got a bit better, the commitment to having a sports psychologist on hand or a massage therapist. Media relations was really amped up. With this support that we'd never had before, you could see that women's hockey was gaining more legitimate attention."

Like their Canadian counterparts, American women got a taste of what it meant to be treated as professionals. "It was just like nothing we'd ever experienced before," Brown-Miller recalls. "At the Olympics, we were all given a shopping cart and they said, 'Okay, go on and pick your gear.' Things from shoes to jeans to shirts and hats to jackets. It's all the apparel that you receive for being part of the United States and the Olympic team. That was just absolutely crazy to us. And it all fit! For the first time."

There was no going back. "After 1998, that jump was exponentially greater than the one from '90 to '98," Brown-Miller maintains. "Now people all over the world knew that women played hockey. And it wasn't as if they were just starting to play the game. These women had been playing for a very, very long time. And they were good. It was a pivotal moment for colleges to start to pick up collegiate programs. It was a pivotal moment for the growth of girls' and women's hockey. It was big. We didn't know that was going to happen at the time, but you can see it now."

The number of women and girls participating in women's hockey in the United States tripled over the next two decades, rising from 28,000 in 1998 to more than 88,000 in 2023. Jayna Hefford has noticed a similar trend in

Canada. "I know every four years there is typically a big spike in women's and girls' enrollment following the Olympics," she says. "It's out there and it's visible and people are talking about it."

The Olympics opened a door that led to the launch for the National Women's Hockey League, and later the Canadian Women's Hockey League, Western Women's Hockey League, a second iteration of the National Women's Hockey League, Premier Hockey Federation, and eventually the Professional Women's Hockey League.

CHAPTER 17

Man Advantage

My first experience of women playing hockey with men was in a large aluminum shed, fifty feet wide and over one hundred feet long, that my dad built to house our farm machinery. Inside, a concrete slab covered roughly a third of the floor. Here I would play out my hockey dreams, using nets my dad made by tying mesh to old pipes he welded together.

In one net, my dad would strap on road hockey goalie pads, a trapper and blocker, and hold an old wooden stick. My net, on the other side of the cement, would remain empty, fair game for him or his lone defender, my mother. She'd snap on a pair of roller blades, and we would duel for hours, winter and summer. I would deke around her, sliding a tennis ball between her feet before finding opening after opening on my dad, who I'm convinced attempted to avoid more shots than he stopped, especially as I aged and the velocity increased.

In today's game, I could imagine my mother as a checking line energy forward, feisty and tenacious but without the puck skills to score. Or perhaps she would have made a good shutdown defender. Watching her chase me around and seeing the satisfaction she gained from finally sliding our tennis ball into my net, I think she would have loved the game. She was always up for the challenge and clearly enjoyed getting the better of me.

I don't plan on playing hockey again. It's the culture that keeps me away. I don't think there's a more beautiful sound in sport than your blades cutting through fresh ice in an empty arena, no greater feeling than scoring, or the wind on your face as you skate down the ice. If someday I do step back into a game, it will be to feel a pass hit my tape and celebrate a goal with teammates—on a co-ed team that welcomes women.

•

In 1969, eighteen-year-old Karen Koch stepped on the ice in Marquette,

Michigan, to try out for the USHL's Marquette Iron Rangers. Twenty minutes into that first tryout, the Iron Rangers' captain, future NHL player Barry Cook, approached the team's head coach. "Coach, did you know that little squirt of a goalie is a girl?" Cook asked.

The coach, Leonard "Oakie" Brumm, asked his captain to take over the practice while he approached the goaltender who had made "some nice saves." He recalled in a 2011 blog post. "She had given no indication that she was a woman. All players were required to wear helmets, so with the helmets and goalie pads it was impossible to tell she was a female. I motioned her off to the side where we could talk without being run into or hit by a puck. She was extremely apprehensive and wouldn't look at me."

Koch expected Brumm to kick her off the ice; she had been turned away from tryouts from every men's team she'd approached in the Detroit area. She was certain this would be a repeat but, to her surprise, Brumm let her stay.

"She said she had heard nothing but good things about the Iron Rangers and felt she could make the team. She desperately didn't want to be cut without a fair tryout," Brumm said. "I thought to myself, A girl goalie . . .what if she gets hurt? Where is she going to change clothes? Just how good is she? For one of the few times in my life I didn't know what to do. She had done nothing to justify cutting her. So I told her we should see how well she did and that she'd be given a fair tryout.

"Koch's presence on the squad brought complaints from the veteran players, but even they admitted she was surprisingly good and probably equal to our regular backup goalie," said Brumm.[1]

When word got out, national newspapers and television focused on the first-year student at Northern Michigan University. "I'd just like to play without anyone knowing," Koch explained in an interview shortly after. "Really, on the ice, I don't look like a girl. Really, I don't. I have short hair."[2]

When it was time to finalize his roster, instead of selecting the planned eighteen skaters and two goalies, Brumm took seventeen skaters and three goalies, including Koch. She signed a contract with the Iron Rangers that would pay her $40 per game, making her the only woman to be paid to play men's hockey in North America at the time. Koch appeared in multiple games for the Iron Rangers, drawing large crowds.

Her ability to play alongside men had earned her a spot in the USHL, but it was her desire to play like the men that ended her tenure. In the era when men were only beginning to wear goalie masks, Koch preferred not to. Brumm wouldn't have it.

"Unfortunately, she seemed to have a 'death wish' for a facial scar caused by a hockey puck in a USHL game," Brumm wrote years later. "She simply and consistently defied my orders to wear a mask while playing. After flagrantly removing her mask during all of the games after Christmas, I was forced to let her go with about ten games remaining in the schedule."

When she moved to Toronto the following year, the St. Thomas Elgins, a Junior A team in Ontario, wanted Koch to suit up. Coach Keith Kewley sought an amendment to rules barring her, saying there was "no reason in the world" to keep women from playing.[3] But his pleas, along with Koch's, fell short. The same rule that prevented girls from playing on boys' teams now stopped women from playing on men's teams.

"She just can't play, it's a CAHA team rule," said Metro Toronto Hockey League secretary-manager Bill Glover. "Besides where would she dress? There are only two dressing rooms."[4]

"Since I moved to Toronto I've been trying to find a team to play on," Koch told the *Toronto Star*. "I've actually been lying. I've been telling teams that I'm phoning for my brother. I knew if I called up and said I'm a girl and wanted to play on their team, they'd just say no."[5] She fit nowhere.

The Canadian Amateur Hockey Association discussed Koch at the 1972 annual general meeting but refused to budge. After an unsuccessful season in Toronto, Koch bounced between cities before landing in Florida where she turned to teaching the game of hockey while working as an activity director for youth with disabilities. Her playing career would go no further.

•

Two decades later, Manon Rheaume would follow in Koch's footsteps, fighting her way onto a men's team, this time in the Quebec Major Junior Hockey League. She knew what she was up against. "If a girl is as good as a boy, a coach will choose the boy," Rheaume told *The Hockey News* in 1991. "Not every coach thinks like this, but many coaches are prejudiced. It's more difficult for a girl to make her place on a team than it is for a boy."[6]

The following year, Rheaume tried out for the NHL's new Tampa Bay

Lightning franchise. We were heading south to Fort Myers, Florida for a family vacation that year, and made a quick stop to watch the Lightning in their inaugural season. The team played at the bizarre Expo Hall. Quite literally a livestock facility converted to an NHL arena, the ice was too small, there wasn't enough seating, and the team had to install their own ice-making equipment, craning it over palm trees that fairgrounds officials would not allow the team to remove. Both the Lightning and Rheaume acknowledge that her appearance in a preseason game was partly intended to generate publicity for the fledgling team. Nonetheless, she broke new ground and shone a spotlight on elite women's hockey players.

"If this helps women's hockey or brings it attention, that is great and I hope it does," Rheaume said at the time. "But I'm here because I don't want to look back ten years from now and ask what might have happened. I want no regrets."[7]

The same year Rheaume appeared with the Lightning, she backstopped Canada to a gold medal at the IIHF Women's World Championships and was named a tournament all-star. This achievement received a fraction of the media attention devoted to her NHL debut and her two appearances with the International Hockey League's Atlanta Knights. Her ability was only legitimized by direct comparison to men. As Abby Hoffman reflected, "On the one hand, she's said something positive about the capabilities of female athletes, and she will serve as a role model for other women who aspire to achieve at that level . . . But her appearance also tends to support the argument that female athletics is only credible when women can compete at the same level, and that athletic ability is to a large extent measured by standards set by males."[8]

For women from hockey families, success has often been tied to brothers or fathers. During TSN broadcasts of Canadian national team games in the 1990s, interviews with blueliner Judy Diduck, a four-time gold medalist, focused on her brother, Gerald, who was playing for the NHL's New York Islanders. "Rather than focusing on Judy, most of the interview consisted of questions about her brother's role in her success. This typified the approach the media had long taken to the sport, inevitably seeking a link to the male game, rarely confident the female game could stand on its own. It was an angle female players found wearisome."[9] Even when players are not related, female players are often legitimized by referring to male equivalents—Angela James, for example, is often called the "Wayne Gretzky of women's hockey."

As the editorial staff at *The Ice Garden*, one of women's hockey's first dedicated online news outlets, observed, "When commentators link a player to a famous male relative, they shift focus away from the player herself. It distracts from her being seen as an individual athlete who worked hard to get where she is. No longer is she four-time Women's World Championship gold medalist Alex Carpenter; now she's Bobby's daughter who happens to have played for the US National Team."[10] The same could be said of Amanda Kessel and her brother Phil, Jesse Compher and her brother JT and dozens of other talented women.

As women began playing on men's teams, this longstanding practice adapted, reaffirming that men set the standard. Celebrating only those women who compete with and against men while largely ignoring the success of women's sport in general solidifies the view that women's sports are inferior.

"The issues raised by Rheaume's experience illustrate well the contemporary struggle to establish the legitimacy of women's sport," wrote scholar Nancy Theberge. "While the bulk of press coverage of Rheaume has presented her as a role model and 'ice breaker,' some commentators have pointed out the dilemma posed by the celebration of women athletes who 'succeed' in men's sport. The inferiorization of women's athletic achievements is at the centre of this struggle."[11]

The year following Rheaume's tryout with the Tampa Bay Lightning, goaltender Erin Whitten made history as the first woman to win a professional men's hockey game, earning a 6-5 win for the ECHL's Toledo Storm over the Dayton Bombers. In 1994, Rheaume and Whitten would face each other for gold at the 1994 Women's World Championships, with Rheaume's Canadian team beating Whitten's American team 6-3.

Each success was treated as a publicity stunt by the media, if not by the teams. When Charline Labonté, another talented netminder, was drafted into the Quebec Major Junior Hockey League in 1999, Acadie-Bathurst Titan general manager and owner Leo-Guy Morrissette said, "I'm convinced she can become a starting goalie for any [major junior] team next season." Labonté posted a 4-9-2 record with Acadie-Bathurst Titan. Team captain

François Beauchemin, a defender who would go on to win a Stanley Cup with the Anaheim Ducks, said, "Charline has taken her place in the lineup and she's considered a regular goalie for us. She's a teammate."[12]

Edmonton's Shannon Szabados was another netminder who grew up finding space in boys' hockey, making her way to the Alberta Junior Hockey League's Sherwood Park Crusaders, a Junior A team, in 2002. "There is no decision to be made," AJHL president Kim Marsh said. "We know we can't stop a person from playing if they have the ability."

"I'm so relieved, all I want is a chance to play like anyone else," Szabados said. It was a stark contrast to Karen Koch's experience decades before. Her teammates recognized the significance of a barrier falling. "I think it's a big step for all females in sport," said Crusaders defender Dan Wanchuk. "I hope she makes the team, so other girls will look up to her and realize that they can do it."[13]

In 2002, Szabados became the first woman ever invited to attend a Western Hockey League camp, when she accepted an invitation from the Tri-City Americans at the age of sixteen. "Without the ponytail, I wouldn't have known she was a girl. She looked good and fit right in. I was impressed," said Pat Iannone, a member of the Americans who would go on to represent Italy at six world championships.

Szabados played a game for the Tri-City Americans, becoming the first woman to ever appear in a WHL game, the highest level of amateur competition. But her gender remained a factor in how far she could go. "When I saw her play she was outstanding," said general manager Bob Tory. "If she'd have been a boy, she'd have been on a protected list or would have been taken in the Bantam draft. She's worthy of the opportunity."[14]

Szabados would go on to play men's collegiate hockey, and eventually professionally with the Southern Professional Hockey League's Columbus Cottonmouths. In women's hockey, she was twice named the Olympic Games' best goaltender, and also won National Women's Hockey League's Goaltender of the Year honors in her lone season in the league.

•

Growing up in rural Saskatchewan, Hayley Wickenheiser often played among boys and, following the 1998 Olympics, attended NHL training camp with the Philadelphia Flyers for two years. Fran Rider, who had been so steadfast in her opposition to Blainey, was disappointed. "We've worked very hard to battle the perception that a girl is better because she's playing with boys because often it's not true," Rider said. "We're striving for stand-alone credibility. Women's hockey is not a second-rate place to play."[15]

The camp inspired Wickenheiser, who went on to win gold with Canada at the Women's World Championships in 1999 and 2000, and lead Canada to their first Olympic gold medal in 2002, being named Best Forward and Olympic MVP. Following that Olympic cycle, and with the experience of two Philadelphia Flyers' training camps, Wickenheiser set her sights on not just training with men but competing against them at the professional level.

According to Manon Rheaume, Wickenheiser was simply too good to continue playing with women. "She's too good to play in the women's league right now," Rheaume told the Canadian Press. "It's fine when she plays on the national team and they play the US. If you don't have an Olympic year, and you go back to play in the NWHL, right now she's playing defense because nobody can skate with her on offense. If she wants to bring her game to the next level, she needs to move up, and the only place she can move up right now is with men's hockey."[16]

Wickenheiser set her sights on playing in Europe. The Italian Hockey Federation banned her from skating with the Merano Eagles but Swedish Ice Hockey Federation president Rickard Fagerlund, who once encouraged Kristina Bergstrand to give up hockey, opened his country's doors. "I think we will see more and more women qualify for men's teams," he said. "The women are as fit as the men, and there is no problem. If the same situation showed up in Sweden, there is nothing to stop her. We'd welcome her."[17] Instead, Wickenheiser signed with Finland's Kirkkonummi Lightning.

When, in February 2003, Wickenheiser scored her first professional goal, she provided proof enough for men that she belonged. When International Ice Hockey Federation president René Fasel, who reportedly did not want women competing alongside men, suggested Wickenheiser quit the team, *The Hockey News* was robust in her defense. An editorial entitled "Fasel's Paternalism Disservice to Women" pointed out that "René Fasel was follow-ing a well-worn path when he suggested recently that Canadian star Hayley Wickenheiser might want to give up her venture into men's pro hockey . . . for her own safety, of course. Ah, that makes us feel better. We thought this was about keeping women in their place. We stand corrected . . . After all, who better to look out for the best interests of adventurous, barrier-breaking women than . . . male administrators! Mr. Fasel should have realized by now that in most other fields this paternalistic path has long since been covered with weeds."[18]

Despite Fasel's insistence, women continued to challenge for opportunities in men's professional hockey. During the 2005 season, Angela Ruggiero's brother, Bill, goaltender for the Central Hockey League's Tulsa Oilers, recommended her when the team was short a defender. The team obtained a special waiver for her to play for a single period and, once again, public discourse flitted between marketing and ability.

Tulsa's head coach, Butch Kaebel, understood "why her participation is viewed as a promotional gimmick . . . This is absolutely exciting for hockey. It's exciting for our league. I don't think this is just another game for us. There's an expectancy out there for Angela, our players and even our fans. It's not like she can't play hockey. She's an exceptional player. She can turn heads. She can play. Her resume is impressive."[19]

Ruggiero, a twenty-five-year-old blueliner known for her physical play, told the media, "I don't want to be a sideshow. I wouldn't do it if I didn't think I could compete on the ice." Her brother Bill said, "People ask me if she can score against me. Well, she can score against anybody. I'm not embarrassed about it. I'm proud of her."[20]

Facing off against Rio Grande, Ruggiero received and delivered checks. And following an in-game decision that allowed her to compete beyond a single period, she did even more. On her final shift of the game, Ruggiero jumped into the play and assisted on a goal by Doug Pirnak, making her the first woman to record a point in North American professional men's hockey.

"It was all I could ask for," Ruggiero said following the game. All discussion of publicity stunts vanished. "She made an impression that top-flight women's players can leave their mark in the rough sport dominated by their male counterparts for years," the *Tulsa World* proclaimed.

"She's a really good player," said Butch Kaebel. "She is a really good passer and a good skater, but she showed she can get a little feisty out there. And her getting that assist at the end was great. I was really hoping she could at least get a point."[21]

At this point in her career, Ruggiero was already a three-time All-American, the first defender to ever win the NCAA's Patty Kazmaier Award as the nation's top player, and had won Best Defender honors at the Olympics and World Championships. But Mike Brophy, writing in *The Hockey News*, proclaimed that Ruggiero had "done herself proud" because she "had proved to the world—and more importantly, to herself—that she could skate with the big boys."[22] One of the best in the world, he still assumed that she needed the validation of men playing several notches below the NHL to be considered worthy. Of course, all of these concerns would be irrelevent had women had their own fully professional league within which they could compete.

•

On September 18, 2023, I sat watching as Billie Jean King stepped on stage in downtown Toronto at the inaugural draft for the new Professional Women's Hockey League (PWHL). King won thirty-nine grand slam tennis tournaments but, like many elite women's athletes, her legacy is often tied to men. Almost exactly half a century before, she had propelled women's sport forward when she defeated men's tennis player Bobby Riggs, a Wimbledon and US Open champion, in an exhibition tennis match billed as "The Battle of the Sexes." Watched by a worldwide television audience of ninety million, her defeat of Riggs in 1973 overshadowed her tennis prowess and pioneering advocacy for women in sport.

Appearing on *The Tonight Show Starring Johnny Carson* on September 8, twelve days before the match, Riggs said, "I really think the best way to handle the women is to keep them pregnant . . . this way they don't worry about getting out in the men's world and competing for jobs, and trying to get equal money and all that baloney, stay in their place, and they help their men, and they're behind the throne . . . the male is king, the male is supreme, and the women should know that."

When King entered the Astrodome stadium to face Riggs, she was carried on a litter by four men. Howard Cosell, the commentator for the match, ignored her athleticism and achievements, saying, "Here comes Billie Jean King. A very attractive young lady if she ever let her hair grow to her shoulders and took off her glasses, you would have someone vying for a Hollywood screen test."

Billie Jean King beat Bobby Riggs in three straight sets. "I thought it would set us back fifty years if I didn't win that match," King said afterward. "It would ruin the women's [tennis] tour and affect all women's self-esteem."[23]

Stepping to the microphone fifty years later, Billie Jean King spoke to the moment, and the movement. "A trailblazer is one that blazes a trail to lead and include others; the first person to do something or go somewhere, who shows that it is also possible for other people," she said. "Trailblazing is bold, it's brave and it can be very scary and lonely, but it's worth it, it's really worth it. It's worth it for each one of us who have fought so hard for this day, and it's worth it for the generations of girls and women who will come behind us. This is an incredible moment, but it's not about a single moment, it's about a movement. Finally giving women professional hockey players the structure, the support, and the platform they deserve, that hockey deserves. I proudly stand here celebrating these trailblazers, and the best part? We are just getting started."

CHAPTER 18

Bench Strength

Sitting on my couch at home, my daughter sits beside me. She's five and filled with dreams of a world that can be. Her mom has raised her to be strong, to lift her chin in defiance of anyone who tries to define what she can and cannot be. I hope I've helped that as well. She picks a color, not a team, to cheer for.

"Are you going for the red or the white, daddy?"

"I like both teams, but I think I'm cheering for red in this game. How about you?"

"Red. I'm cheering for red, too. What city are they from?"

As the game progresses, she'll stand and stare at the television, cheering for her chosen team and announcing the score. Sometimes she'll grab a hairbrush and, pretending it's a microphone, say, "Live from the arena, for *The Hockey News*" in her best broadcaster voice. I see her point at the screen, saying, "I like her" when a close-up comes on. And at least once each game she'll ask, "Daddy, are these girls?" as if to make sure it's true. When I answer, watching her face mesmerized by the action, I see players dashing across the sclera and iris of her eyes before the black puck vanishes into her pupil, traversing nerve pathways to her hippocampus, where a memory is formed, a memory that tells her girls and women play hockey, they play professional hockey, and she can too.

More than seventy years ago, another father inspired his daughter to pursue her hockey dreams. When James E. Norris passed away in 1952, his daughter Marguerite took over as president of the Detroit Red Wings, the first woman to serve as an executive in the NHL. She advocated for arenas to be more woman-friendly, and despite being excluded from the NHL's Board of Governors, reportedly worked out a system of hand signals with general manager Jack Adams to have her say. The first woman to have her name engraved on the Stanley Cup, she led the Detroit Red Wings to back-to-back

Stanley Cup championships in 1954 and 1955. Her family pushed her out the following season, a decision hockey legend Gordie Howe believed doomed the future of the franchise.

"She was good for the club, but unfortunately she didn't stick around for as long as anyone would have liked," Howe said. "I don't think it's a coincidence that Marguerite's time in charge coincided with some of the greatest years in franchise history . . . It's hard to say how many Stanley Cups we might have won if she had stuck around longer."[1]

The Detroit Red Wings would not win another title until 1997. It took even longer for women to once again attain positions of authority. Now, elite players on both sides of the border are in decision-making roles that allow them to continue contributing long after leaving the ice.

•

Hockey was the Granato family's favorite game. Each winter, firemen sprayed the field across from their home to create a rink where three-year-old Cammi learned to skate, prompted by her hockey-playing brothers, Tony, Don, and Rob. They played on the rink, in the driveway, and when the weather wouldn't allow, they played in their living room. When Cammi was old enough, her parents put her into figure skating; in the 1970s, there was no girls' hockey in the Midwest.

"It didn't even cross their mind to put me in hockey. It's just not what girls did," recalls Granato. "There were just no girls who played hockey, and it wasn't considered a sport that girls played. They thought, oh you want to skate, so they put me in figure skating lessons," she explains.

"I just wasn't interested. I was quite miserable. I'd leave the rink and go watch hockey, and I think at that point my parents realized, 'She really loves the game' and saw me playing with my brothers, so they just let me give it a try. I don't think they thought it was going to be a lifelong thing. I commend my parents for supporting me and saying 'just let her do it, even though it's not the norm let's just let her do it,' I think that they went against the grain."[2]

Like many of her contemporaries, Granato began playing organized hockey on a local boys' team, occasionally disguising her gender. Traveling to a tournament in Kitchener, Ontario, Granato's team had to list her name as Carl. "I wore a baseball cap pulled down," she recalls.

Still, Granato found a role model on the ice. "My first female role model was Bonnie Blair, who was dominating speed skating. I just thought, 'She's like my idol.' There's a woman in this position of winning Olympic medals left and right." She also watched Team USA during the 1980 Miracle on Ice. In her basement with her brothers, the Granatos would play out Team USA facing the Russians over and over.

As she entered her teenage years, Granato saw her brothers reaching echelons not possible for her. Her oldest brother, Tony, had starred at the University of Wisconsin and was a draft pick of the NHL's New York Rangers. Her brother Don was headed to Wisconsin as well, and eventually her brother Rob followed the same path. "I really had a hard time understanding when I became a teenager that I couldn't go as far in hockey as my brothers because I was a girl," Granato said in a 2007 interview. "I didn't want to accept it. It was hard because I loved the game just as much as they did. I was good at the game, and I was successful at every level I played at. I just couldn't understand it."[3]

When she turned sixteen, Granato found a brochure featuring the Providence women's hockey team. On the front was a name Granato would never forget: Cindy Curley. "I had no idea women played hockey out East," says Granato. "I got a brochure with Cindy Curley's name at the top and at that moment she became my first women's idol. I said, 'I want to be that, I want to be her, I want to go play college hockey, I want to be at the top of the statistics with her.' It was really cool for the first time to understand that women play hockey."

No one recruited Granato, but when she showed the staff at Providence what she was capable of, she was quickly scooped up and would go on to become the school's all-time leading scorer with 139 goals and 256 points in only 99 games. In 1990, as she turned nineteen, she ranked third in scoring at the World Championships. On the bench beside her was the tournament's leading scorer: Cindy Curley.

Following that tournament, Granato's career took off. She was named Best Forward at the 1992 Women's World Championships and helped the USA win the first gold medal in hockey at the 1998 Winter Olympics in Nagano. In total, she earned two Olympic and nine World Championship medals, including gold at both events.

Although she captained Team USA nine times, her playing career ended when she was unceremoniously cut in 2005 after leading her team to a world championship gold medal the season before. Then thirty-four, Granato believed she could still contribute. "It hurts when you know something is wrong and there is nothing you can really do about it," she told the *Chicago Tribune*. "When I have given what I have given to the program, it is hard to just sit with this." Still, it was a historic career. "I don't want it to end this way, but if this is how it does, holding that World Championship Cup over my head in my last game has a lot more meaning to me now than it did even then."[4] In 2010, Granato was part of the inaugural class of women inducted into the Hockey Hall of Fame.

Like Kelly Dyer, Granato found other ways to remain involved in hockey. She joined the NHL's Seattle Kraken as a scout in 2019, a role she held for three seasons before being hired as an assistant general manager with the NHL's Vancouver Canucks in February of 2022.

Cammi Granato was the second woman hired by the Canucks in a leadership role. The first, hired only weeks earlier, was Emilie Castonguay. Another former NCAA player who grew up playing with boys, Castonguay became passionate about players' rights and obtained a law degree from Université de Montréal to better advocate on their behalf. In 2016, she became the first female NHLPA-certified player agent and developed a client list that included high-profile players in both the men's and women's game.

Following Castonguay and Granato, several women would assume management and development roles with NHL teams. Jessica Campbell was hired as the first full-time assistant coach with an NHL team, making her debut with the Seattle Kraken in 2024. Women are no longer outside the men's game—they are guiding the sport.

•

Other former players focused on developing the women's game internationally, ensuring the long-term viability of the sport by closing the talent gap. Following the Vancouver Olympics, that disparity had raised the possibility of removing women's hockey from the Games. "In 2010, then-International Olympic Committee president Jacques Rogge caused consternation by suggesting women's hockey had to improve its competitive parity or face the possibility of being removed from the Games," wrote Adam Proteau for *The Hockey News*.[5]

Women like Fran Rider and Line Baun Danielsen, who were working to support the growth of international play, recognized that a robust global community was essential to the stability of the sport as a whole. Julie Stevens maintains that the rapid development of women's hockey had occurred against a backdrop of underfunding, an absence of funding at the grassroots level, and systemic inequities at all levels. With media attention limited to once a year at the Women's World Championships and once every four years at the Olympics, these inequities were magnified. "Hence, the criticism about the lack of parity among national women's teams is based upon a partial understanding." Justified or not, preserving recent gains would require a concerted effort. "There is no doubt that nation-to-nation competition is important, but there is also a recognition that it will take a collective effort among women's hockey leaders from all countries to create change within male-dominated hockey,"[6]

Kathy Berg, who spent so many years driving the van for Shirley Cameron and the rest of the Edmonton Chimos, became the director of the Olympic Oval Female High Performance Hockey Program at the University of Calgary in 1997. In 1999, she took on additional responsibilities as the head coach of the Australian women's program. When, in 2007, Australia formed its first women's league, Berg was presented with a Special Commendation Award.

But perhaps no one has been more directly involved in developing international hockey than Carla MacLeod. MacLeod was born in Spruce Grove, Alberta, in 1982, the same year as Canada's first national championship. She would eventually win two national titles with Team Alberta and go on to win two Olympic gold medals for Canada before retiring after the 2010 Games. That year, she took on a coaching role at a Canadian university before moving to Japan's senior national team. Japan had failed to qualify for the 2010 Olympics, and hoped the presence of MacLeod would help close the gap that existed between Canada, USA, and the rest of the world.

"I was arrogant as a player and I never gave these countries the credit they deserved as far as the effort these players are putting in," MacLeod said in a 2013 interview with *The Globe and Mail*. "Their dreams are the same as ours. They're working just as hard. They just don't have the same level of game that we do here."[7]

She approached her coaching role with the same passion she exhibited as a player. "I really believe in what's going on within Japanese women's hockey. Those twenty girls in that room are as dedicated to hockey as the women on Canada's roster, and that's what gets me so excited about the future of women's hockey. We have such negative media attention on the discrepancy between the nations, but many countries are really trying to improve. It's going to take time, but with the right people involved, that gap can be closed."[8]

Roughly a decade after joining Japan, MacLeod took on a new role as head coach of Czechia's national women's team, another struggling program that wanted to compete. MacLeod immediately helped Czechia earn back-to-back World Championship bronze medals.

It was growth that had been coming for a long time, the type MacLeod had seen before. "The game is growing in stages in Czechia, but the women that have come before this team and the women that are on this team just keep plowing through and breaking down barriers to enable the next generation to be able to play, which is a big part of growing our game," says MacLeod. "We lived [that growth] here in Canada in the 1990s and for decades earlier, but it boomed in the '90s, and they're just on the verge of a boom in Czechia.

"This sport is so great, the international piece is so special. I'm probably the luckiest one on the planet–I got to be a player for Canada, and now, I get to coach Czechia . . . I don't know how I got so lucky, but I'll just take it and run."

In 2023, MacLeod was named the first head coach of Ottawa's PWHL franchise. When her Ottawa team stepped on the ice for the first time on January 2, 2024, it was in front of a world record 8,318 fans at TD Place Arena, the same venue that had hosted the first Women's World Championship tournament in 1990. Fittingly, her roster was the most international, featuring players from Czechia, Japan, Canada, USA, Germany, and Hungary. "Thank goodness there is a language of hockey," says MacLeod. "The game continues to grow around the world and there's incredible players everywhere on this planet."

•

While many former players broke new ground in the NHL or internationally, others have chosen to support the university programs that have traditionally provided opportunities for so many.

Following the 1998 Olympics, Vicky Sunohara won five World Championship gold medals plus a silver, two Olympic gold medals and two league titles. Following the 2007 Women's World Championships, the then 37-year-old Sunohara lost her roster spot on Team Canada; she spent one more season in the Canadian Women's Hockey League (CWHL) with the Brampton Thunder before retiring in 2009. She remained a high-profile face in women's sport, lighting the Olympic torch in Toronto as it made its way across Canada before being named head coach of the University of Toronto Varsity Blues in 2011.

Her coaching career has been as stellar as her playing career. Sunohara was named U Sports Coach of the Year for women's hockey in 2019–20 and 2021–22. In 2019–20, she was recognized as the Female Coach of the Year across all sports by Ontario University Athletics.

She's come a long way from the backyard rink her father built. Once, while walking through the old Maple Leaf Gardens to address her Toronto Varsity Blues team, Sunohara paused to look at a display case. The historic arena had been renovated to become the home of the Ryerson Rams, her father's former team. There, through the glass, between trophies and plaques, was a photo of her father staring back at her alongside his Ryerson teammates.

"I looked at this big display, and there was his photo. It was just so emotional. I had to keep it together because I was coaching a big game, but inside, I just wished I could have had a conversation with him. I wish he could have seen it, that he could have seen me playing and now coaching."

Unlike the University of Toronto, where a women's hockey program has existed for more than a century, the University of British Columbia had never had a women's team. That is, until Laura Bennion arrived.

Growing up in Vancouver in the 1970s, there were no options for girls interested in hockey. When Laura Bennion, then seven, and her mother went to register for her first season of minor hockey, they were turned away. "My mom went to line up at the local minor hockey registration day, stood in the long line and got to the front of the line and they looked at her and said, 'Girls don't play hockey.' They turned us away and said, 'There's no girls' participation in this league.'"

Standing in line behind the Bennions, however, was another parent, who also happened to coach in the organization. Laura Bennion and this coach's son had attended the same hockey camp that summer, and he knew she could play.

"He pulled my mom aside and he said, 'Bring her to the rink. We will put Larry on her helmet and she'll play on my team.' Bennion, like so many others, used her equipment as concealer. She dressed at home, and when she arrived at the arena, would put on her helmet and skate guards, and walk directly from the car to the ice. Still, "Word gradually got out that I wasn't actually Larry, that I was Laura."

Little Larry became Laura again when her family found a girls' league in British Columbia, and her life in hockey began. She played for the Killarney Shamrocks, Brittania Blues, and then in nearby Burnaby, but she saw a limited future in hockey. In her final years of high school, Bennion gave up the sport, instead using her five-foot-eleven frame to play basketball.

"In high school, I couldn't see much of a future for hockey as a woman, so basketball became a focus for me," she recalls. "I played junior varsity basketball at the University of British Columbia for two years. After some shoulder injuries, I thought maybe I could do something in hockey, but there was nothing locally, and nothing in Canada."

That year, Bennion watched the first 1990 World Championships on television and saw an interview with Team USA's coach, Don MacLeod, who was also the head coach of Northeastern University's women's hockey team. She looked up the school, wrote MacLeod a letter and sent him a video of her playing hockey. The following fall, she enrolled as a student, and a hockey player, in the NCAA. On a partial scholarship, Bennion worked each summer as a tree planter. Despite the fact she was planting trees and not cutting them down, Bennion became "Bunyan." She said, "Word got out I was a lumberjack. They had this image of me chopping down trees, wearing a plaid shirt and suspenders."[9]

Following her three years at Northeastern, where she played alongside members of both the Canadian and American national teams, Bennion returned home to pursue a medical degree at the University of British Columbia. In 1994, she approached the school's athletic director and asked for funding for a women's hockey team. "I told our athletic director I'd coach the team and volunteer, so the school gave us $10,000, which was enough for ice time and jerseys," Bennion recalls. "And they gave us a little closet, like a custodial closet, to hang our gear in. We got our players by hanging posters around campus."

It was totally different than playing at Northeastern, a well-established varsity program with school funding, scholarships, and resources. "Our coaches were still poorly paid and had to have a separate job outside hockey, but we had things like guaranteed ice time six days a week, our own locker room, access to the gym facilities, a strength and conditioning coach, and an athletic therapist. We didn't have any of that at UBC."

Bennion coached the Thunderbirds women's hockey team for their first two seasons. Starting in Vancouver's lowest city league tier, the team won their way up division by division. When the team reached the city's highest level, Bennion decided to leave the bench, and become a player again. Taking over as coach in 1998, Steve Mathias told the student newspaper that, "Arguably there would not be women's hockey at UBC if Laura hadn't started the program."[10]

1998 was Bennion's final season as a player. That year, UBC traveled to Calgary for the first Canada West Championships. The winner would compete in the first Canadian university national championship tournament in Montreal. "From Day One, Bennion has always wanted to do more for the sport she loves. She and others lobbied the CIAU (Canadian Intervarsity Athletic Union) to recognize women's hockey as a varsity sport and, in an uncharacteristically wise move, the CIAU listened . . ."[11]

"It was the start of something for sure," she says, looking back. "I don't think we knew how far it would go or how long it would last or what was going to happen in the whole women's hockey world, but that year it became an Olympic sport." Laura Bennion was inducted into the UBC Sports Hall of Fame in 2014, having played her own part in the structural growth of hockey in Canada.

No longer playing or coaching, Laura Bennion continued working to open doors for women in the sport. By 2011, she was an associate professor of family medicine at the University of British Columbia, researching exercise and training during pregnancy. It was a stark reversal from the long-held belief that participation in sport could damage a woman's reproductive organs. "Once upon a time, pregnant women were treated like delicate China dolls," Valerie Berenyi wrote in *The Edmonton Journal*. "They were expected to sit back, take it easy and easy and not exercise too much because they might hurt themselves or the developing baby. No more."[12]

Bennion went on to work as a team doctor for the CWHL's Calgary Inferno and with Hockey Canada's national team, combining a specialty in obstetrics and gynecology with sports medicine. "I never used to see many parallels between sports medicine and pregnancy but there are actually tons. Sports medicine people are trying to use their bodies in a way that challenges them and sometimes it doesn't always go right and pregnancy, obviously, is one of the biggest challenges, physically, that a woman will go through in her life. I feel like those two things there are some natural comparisons," she said.[13] She has worked with many athletes, including Olympian and World Champion Megan Mikkelson, helping them return to peak performance following pregnancy. Today, women including Kendall Coyne Schofield, Natalie Spooner, and Madison Packer are professional hockey players with young children at home, breaking yet another invisible barrier.

CHAPTER 19

Breakaways

My alarm rang at 5:00 am. In the dark, my hand traced the edge of the bed, exploring the beveled edge of the lamp, bracing myself to arrive at the switch. Today I would make the three-hour drive to Brampton, Ontario, to begin covering the 2023 IIHF Women's World Championships.

By the time I arrived, my vehicle smelled like coffee. Outside, I saw Team Japan warming up, completing coordinated stretches and brief sprints. Inside, the arena was silent. I grabbed my media badge, a coffee and a donut and found a seat directly above the visitors' net, a spot I'd inhabit for the next week. The glaze of my apple fritter stuck to the keyboard as I typed out my first story of the day. As the building began to fill, I walked the concourse, where items from the 1987 international tournament, the inaugural 1990 Women's World Championship, and the 1998 Olympics were displayed.

Soon, the familiar faces of the greats of the women's hockey world came into view, many of whom I'd now come to know. I exchange a hug with Vicky Sunohara, sip my coffee alongside Fran Rider, and converse with Cassie Campbell, Jayna Hefford, and Sami Jo Small. Wearing her leather-sleeved jacket from the 1987 tournament, I spot Sharon Sanderson in the stands. I plop myself in the seat beside her and put my arm around her while we talk about the stories she'd lived and shared with me. We mention Mern Coveny—if only she could see where the game is now. When I return to my seat, a smattering of media members have joined the press area. Cameras are strewn across chairs, laptops are open, plates of snacks at the ready. Finland and France are on the ice for the first of three games that day.

As with the start of any tournament or season, the event is filled with hope. In the press area, Hall of Fame member Jayna Hefford is discussing the Professional Women's Hockey Players' Association's effort to launch a new league. Others are excited about the Premier Hockey Federation's new salary cap, a record-breaking $1.5 million per team. It feels like the game is on the verge of the sustainability that Hefford and Sunohara, Campbell and Small, Rider and Sanderson have waited so long for.

Prior to the medal-round games, I was named manager of *The Hockey News'* new all-women's outlet, an online platform I'd advocated for as a necessary tool to grow the game. By the time the gold medals were awarded, with the American flag situated between that of Canada and Czechia, optimism continued to swell. As "The Star-Spangled Banner" played, it seemed like women's hockey was destined for more.

Many of the men and women in this arena had worked for decades toward a professional league paying living wages, with all of the support, benefits and fandom that men had benefited from for decades. But if the goal was clear, the path was not. Under the surface, the women's hockey community had splintered into opposing factions that threatened to tear it apart.

•

Following the rebirth of women's hockey in the late 1960s, several leagues had come and gone. Throughout the 1970s and 1980s, the Central Ontario Women's Hockey League, home to legends like Angela James, Jayna Hefford, Vicky Sunohara, Cassie Campbell, Cathy Phillips, and Geraldine Heaney, was the best on the planet. In 1999, it became the National Women's Hockey League (NWHL) and began competing for the Clarkson Cup, named after Canada's Governor General, Adrienne Clarkson.

"When I played in the first NWHL, we didn't know what professional was," says Jayna Hefford. "We had really good teams and typically the best players, so we kind of assumed it was a professional league. We used that word, but it never really was. There were no salaries, there was no infrastructure or resources; I don't even think coaches were being paid at the time. So I don't think we really even knew—although we wanted to be professional— I don't think we knew what that meant."

In 2004, Kathy Berg, Hayley Wickenheiser, and Chimos owner Dee Bateman founded the Western Women's Hockey League (WWHL), featuring the Edmonton Chimos, Calgary Oval X-Treme, and Minnesota Whitecaps. When the original NWHL ceased operations following the 2006–07 season, a group of players that included Sami Jo Small and Jennifer Botterill launched the Canadian Women's Hockey League (CWHL). The WWHL and CWHL coexisted, with the champion of each league meeting to determine a national champion until 2011, when the leagues formally merged under the CWHL umbrella.

Four years later, in time for the 2015–16 season, a new iteration of the National Women's Hockey League was formed in the US. This time operating in direct competition to the CWHL, it created a fissure in the hockey world. The cooperation that had previously existed was gone.

By the 2017–18 season, the CWHL had accepted expansion teams from China and began paying players a stipend—a minimum of $2000 and maximum of $10,000—with team salaries capped at $100,000 total. At the end of that season, Jayna Hefford took over as league commissioner. Ten months later, the CWHL board of directors announced they would be ceasing operations on May 1, 2019. The decision was made without consulting team general managers, among whom was one of the co-founders of the league, Sami Jo Small. She confessed to being "shocked and deeply saddened by the decision," in a *Sportsnet* feature on the closure.

Players and staff were equally unaware, according to CWHL Players Association co-chair Liz Knox. The league had just concluded its championship weekend, and now had no idea what would come next. "Players are left with a lot of questions," said Knox. "My primary concern of course is the players and where does that leave us? And what are some of our next steps? I mean, we're blindsided by it and we don't really have a plan, so I was trying to seek out some information. There was a lot of dialogue, there was a lot of frustration on the players' end, there's a lot of confusion."

Explaining the decision, Hefford said, "As the CWHL evolved into the next step from the original NWHL, it still wasn't professional. We used that word a lot because it had the best players, but it really wasn't. When I came in as interim commissioner, I learned very quickly that this wasn't a business model that could be a professional model. We were literally a charity. That was what needed to happen at the time but it wasn't the model that was going to elevate the league to where we needed to go."[1]

Many members of the now-defunct CWHL refused to join the rival NWHL, leaving them with few options. Some members were unhappy with conditions they had experienced in the early days of the NWHL, others had soured on the league's founder, Dani Rylan. Still others dreamed of something new, something innovative. In an effort to force the hand of powers within the hockey world, dissident players formed the Professional Women's Hockey Players' Association (PWHPA) that would play a single-season tour, the "Dream Gap," until a new league that met their standards could be launched. When a single season proved insufficient, the PWHPA continued to run the Dream Gap Tour, providing competition across North America while they looked for investors to launch another league. Prior to the 2021–22 season, the NWHL rebranded to the Premier Hockey Federation (PHF) and continued attracting more and more talent as they increased salary caps and added Canadian teams in Toronto and Montreal.

Fans saw an obvious solution: the two sides should combine their efforts. Despite the best efforts of many, however, the rift could not be mended. Johanna "JoJo" Boynton and her husband, John, were among those who tried.

JoJo Boynton, née Neilson, had a familiar story. In 1970s Pennsylvania, there were no leagues or teams for girls, but if she showed up in full equipment, she could occasionally sneak onto the ice with a boys' team. The year JoJo reached high school, 1980, the school launched its first girls' hockey team. Four years later, JoJo was recruited to play at Harvard, where, as a captain, she helped the school win back-to-back Ivy League titles in 1987 and 1988. After her playing days were over, she held on to the dream of creating a better future for women in the sport she loved.

By 2014, John and JoJo Boynton were welcoming members of Team USA's women's national program into their home, helping them find billets in nearby Bedford, Massachusetts, as the players came together to train for the upcoming Olympics in Sochi. More often than not, JoJo was feeding extra mouths and helping athletes including Hilary Knight, Kendall Coyne Schofield, Megan Bozek, Julie Chu, and Lee Stecklein.

When the Boyntons realized how underfunded the USA's national women's program was, they began chipping in financially. First, they founded the Sochi Family Fund to help pay travel costs for the families of Team USA players who would otherwise not be able to see their daughters and sisters play. The Boyntons, with their kids in tow, were at the 2014 gold medal game that ended in heartbreak for the USA and for their family, which had grown to love the players who frequented their home.

Three years later, with another Olympic year approaching, those same American players threatened to boycott the 2017 Women's World Championships unless USA Hockey committed to pay equity: they would sit out the tournament if USA Hockey would not pay them the same as the men's team. "In 2017 it was what was super moving . . . everybody said, 'No, I won't play for you, you need to start treating this as women's rights, you need to start giving us what we deserve'," recalls Lisa Brown-Miller. "We weren't really in that position in between 1990 and 1998, but the Olympics laid the groundwork. Once '98 passed, we saw the need to set a minimum expectation. And now those women got wiser and realized the inequities that were really taking place. So they challenged them."

Under pressure from their women's program leader, Reagan Carey, USA Hockey agreed. But paying women equitably left USA Hockey short on funds, so the Boyntons stepped up again, contributing their own money to make up the shortfall. "They had them over a barrel," JoJo Boynton explains.

Team USA went on to win gold in Pyeongchang. Not long after, JoJo Boynton found herself sitting in a café with players Kendall Coyne Schofield and Hilary Knight. The Boyntons had been approached about becoming minority owners of a team in the NWHL and, after reviewing the league's finances, operations and future plans, saw it as another opportunity to help. Sitting in that cafe, Coyne Schofield and Knight, who were boycotting the league, told her to avoid it at all costs. "We did a ton of due diligence. We learned about those who walked out, we learned about the conditions and all that," says JoJo Boynton. "I sat with Kendall and Hilary in a café and asked them about it. Pretty much everyone said, 'Don't touch it, it's toxic, it will blow up, don't touch it.'"

Boynton left that meeting believing she could help bring members of the PWHPA and NWHL together and finally realize her dream of creating a professional league for women's hockey players where they were compensated fairly, enjoyed benefits and played in conditions that matched those of men. "We did a lot of contemplating about 'don't touch it,' but our gamble was, 'We know these players so well.' We peeked under the tent and saw that things were pretty skeletal. Any time we had conversations about the NWHL, we found ourselves at the table at more than just a team-ownership level, more at the league level, investor-level stuff. We thought we could have more of an impact by going in and rolling up our sleeves and doing our work."

And so they did. Not only did the Boyntons take a minority ownership in the Boston Pride, they took over the Metropolitan Riveters, pledged to launch Canadian teams in Toronto and Montreal, and joined the board of the league. They believed the relationships they'd formed in 2014 and 2017 would allow them to mend the chasm that had formed in the women's hockey world. "We bet, we now know naïvely so, that we could get these guys to the table," says JoJo.

"That was our critical miscalculation," her husband chimes in. He chaired the NWHL, then the PHF. "We assumed that, based on the relationships and trust we thought we had with those US players—we knew the two women who were leading the PWHPA charge on the US side—we had nothing but goodwill there, and we wanted the same thing. We wanted to see women's hockey on a pedestal getting the same level of respect and love and fandom that men's hockey has. We said, 'Well they may not be willing to come over today, but let's get in there, let's improve things, and then let's see if we can't bring them back into the league.'"

The Boyntons were told that the PWHPA would not consider merging until things improved, so they set about reshaping the NWHL, rebranding it to the PHF to remove the gender marker. "We changed the name, changed the commissioner, changed the investors, a wholesale cleanout. We felt then they could see it was us, not the people prior who they'd reached this toxic boiling point with. Every calculation was, 'This is what we've got to do to bring all women's hockey players into one professional league.'"

The PWHPA was playing their Dream Gap Tour and working with consultants and advisors like Billie Jean King and her wife, Ilana Kloss, to plan and find investors for their league. "We spent three-and-a-half years trying to get at the table with these guys, and all the while improve what we had just gotten into," explains JoJo Boynton. The two sides met many times between 2019 and 2022, sometimes publicly, sometimes in secret, often with the NHL involved.

The PHF increased its salary cap to $750,000 in 2022–23, and announced they'd be doubling that cap to $1.5 million per team in 2023–24. The league also brought in health care and benefits for all players. Following these announcements, the PWHPA and PHF met one last time. The players in the PWHPA, represented by Jayna Hefford, recognized the progress the PHF was making, but didn't want to return to something that needed fixing. "There was small progress in areas within the PHF, but do you just go there and take your little wins and hope that over time you get there? Or do you flip this thing upside down and say, 'We've got to find a better way, we've gotta do it better, we've gotta set a standard?'" The players were convinced that the incremental approach had failed. Jayna Hefford recalls their mantra: We're not going to pass this problem on to the next generation. It was a new league or bust.

"It was really the efforts of the PWHPA and those players that I think helped define what this professionalism was that we were all seeking and talking about," said Hefford. "We had to do some deep work to understand our aspirations—what it meant and what would need to be true for that professionalism to exist. I think all of those moments were important; they were steppingstones to getting to this. With each one, we sort of learned a bit more about where we're trying to go and how we're going to get there."

It was clear that the PWHPA and PHF were not going to get there together. And there was no way they could do it apart. The NHL was clear that it would not take sides. Sponsors and media corporations split their resources or avoided women's hockey altogether. Fans chose sides, creating villains and heroes. Eventually, many of the players did the same, and the friction slowed progress for everyone.

"We ate ourselves from the inside," says JoJo Boynton. "It wasn't working because of us. So much of it was because of our own little ecosystem; it meant it was going to hold everybody back."

Both sides eventually found common ground, not in each other, but in a new investor. In May 2022, the PWHPA announced it had secured a partnership with BJK Enterprises, owned by Billie Jean King, and the Mark Walter Group, owners of MLB's Los Angeles Dodgers, the WNBA's Los Angeles Sparks, and the Premier League's Chelsea FC.

The following spring, I received a text message informing me that the PHF would be "merging" with the PWHPA to form the long-awaited single professional women's hockey league in North America. Unbeknownst to the PWHPA, the PHF had begun negotiating with the same group in November 2022. Those discussions had continued into the new year but delays had forced the PHF to begin planning for the 2023–24 season, signing contracts with dozens of players.

My phone rang again on June 29—a deal had been signed. The press release included quotes from members of both the PWHPA and PHF but the words "unification" or "merger" had been deleted from the initial draft created by the PHF. In a move reminiscent of the CWHL's announcement in 2019, the players, coaches, staff, and general managers of the PHF were blindsided—more than one hundred women, many of whom had just signed lucrative six-figure deals, learned that the PHF had been acquired by the Mark Walter Group. Their contracts had been voided.

The acquisition sent shockwaves across the hockey world. For many, it felt like a revisiting of history, watching leagues fold and rise. But this was it, the final chance to launch a league that would stand the test of time and feature the best players on the planet under one roof. *The Hockey News* reported reactions from all stakeholders.

"I have always believed that professional sports should bring the highest levels of performance and organization, and this new league will have the backing and resources it needs to represent the very best of women's hockey," said Mark Walter, who at the time of the acquisition had a net worth estimated to be $5.9 billion. "This is an extraordinary opportunity to advance women's sports," said Billie Jean King, who would sit on the PWHL's board. "I have no doubt that this league can capture the imagination of fans and a new generation of players."

For the Boyntons, it was the end of a passion project, but one they recognized as necessary. "This is another step forward for the women who play professional hockey and the girls who dream of it every day," JoJo Boynton said. "The PHF has been a game-changer and catalyst for growth in the women's professional game. Today's announcement builds on this foundation, represents a shared vision for one new league, and reaffirms our belief that collective and collaborative leadership is in the best interest of women's professional hockey."

For Jayna Hefford, the merger brought a renewal of hope, even though the deal had been negotiated behind the backs of those in the PWHPA. "This new league will be unlike anything we have seen in women's hockey," said Hefford. "I am inspired by this generation of players who are redefining the sport. We will create dreams and opportunities for girls and women around the world for decades to come."[2]

It was the end of competition within the sport, and the beginning of competition for the sport. Days after the acquisition, members of the PWHPA voted to ratify a collective bargaining agreement, the first signed by players and a league before play had begun. Even though the agreement, which would last for eight years, did not cover members of the PHF, graduating NCAA players, or pros from Europe and Asia who would join the league, members of the PHF quickly communicated their solidarity.

"Today, all women's hockey players are united stronger than ever as we enter this new era," said the PHF's leadership committee. "We look to depart from the divisive narrative that too often plagued the many great achievements across professional women's hockey, and become unified as we collectively create hockey's future. As we embark on another league formation, we bring the power and the infrastructure we fought to build. We are hugely excited to see a unified league that will house all of the best athletes that hockey has to offer and aim to build the strongest league that can stand the test of time. The PWHPA was an incredible mirror that asked us to reflect on the changes we desired and fight for them in solidarity, and we will bring that momentum with us."[3]

Five months later, when my alarm pulled me from sleep, I popped out of bed filled with excitement. This time I was heading to Utica, New York, to cover the Professional Women's Hockey League's first centralized preseason. Over the past months, through many trials and tribulations, the PWHL had chosen six markets: Boston, Minnesota, Montreal, New York, Ottawa, and Toronto. Hockey legend Jayna Hefford was chosen to lead the new league, not as a commissioner, but as the senior vice-president of hockey operations. The new PWHL had gone through free agency, held a draft and hired more than a hundred staff. This preseason event was the final step in forming the inaugural rosters.

I had a six-and-a-half-hour drive but it passed in a blink. Walking into Utica, it was all hands on deck. Only three weeks remained before the season began and everyone involved was working tirelessly.

There were still hiccups. On the first night of scheduled practices, Montreal arrived late, missing their practice time. When they came in, superstars of the sport like Marie-Philip Poulin and Ann-Renée Desbiens strode toward their dressing room, followed by carts of equipment. Pushing one of them was the team's general manager, Danièle Sauvageau, who had been Canada's head coach at the 2002 Olympics, leading Team Canada to their first gold medal. I couldn't imagine a National Hockey League general manager ever helping in this way. But Sauvageau, wearing thick-rimmed glasses and a look of determination, pushed a cart that appeared twice her size with ease. It seemed representative of Sauvageau's life in women's hockey, and the lives of many other women, who saw any job to be done and took the lead, pushing forward, working together for a common purpose.

•

When I read back over the multiple drafts of this chapter, it's clear that everyone involved wanted the same thing: a single professional women's hockey league that would take care of its athletes, treating them as professionals equivalent to their men's hockey counterparts. The PWHPA and the PHF were running on parallel tracks toward the identical destination. The PWHPA believed a radical approach was necessary; the PHF thought incrementalism would be more effective.

In piecing together this history, it's important to note that this type of division and struggle, failing leagues, unsustainable business models, and unsuccessful attempts at new ventures, is not unique to women's sport. The NHL was founded in 1917, following the collapse of the National Hockey Association (NHA). The NHA had been formed to compete with the Canadian Hockey Association, an off-shoot of the collapsed Eastern Canadian Hockey Association. And those leagues were in direct competition with the Pacific Coast Hockey Association (PCHA), which eventually merged with the Western Canada Hockey League.

The NHL's most notable battle was the one it waged with the World Hockey Association from 1971 to 1979. Like the PHF in its final seasons, the WHA coaxed top players with higher salaries, successfully attracting sixty-seven members of the NHL for its inaugural 1972–73 season. Also like the PHF, the WHA focused on attracting European talent. The NHL and WHA pushed each other to evolve—the WHA introduced free agency and overtime, both NHL staples today. Eventually, financial realities forced a merger and, in 1979, the WHA and NHL came to an agreement that brought the Quebec Nordiques, Edmonton Oilers, Winnipeg Jets, and Hartford Whalers into the NHL.

Throughout the process, both the NHL and WHA received criticism, had fans and detractors, celebrated successes and weathered failures. Unlike women's professional hockey, however, there was no discussion that a failed league signaled a lack of public interest. Today, when an NHL team relocates, few question the overall viability of professional men's hockey.

In discussing this portion of women's hockey history, I often agreed with JoJo Boynton, who viewed the rivalry as cannibalistic. I don't believe that anymore. As with any ecosystem, there were predators and parasites, but these were not the players or organizers. They were the introduction of ringette, the misogyny of the IIHF, the obstinacy of Hockey Canada and USA Hockey, the naming of the Lipstick Tournament and Canada's pink jerseys. Men spent a century fostering an environment that ensured hockey was a game for men and men alone.

I have come to believe that everyone involved in women's hockey was a protagonist in the symbiotic process essential to successful ecosystems. The entire women's hockey world benefited from the CWHL, NWHL, PWHPA, PHF and the many leagues that came before them. All of them played integral roles in forming a collaborative future. Every woman who played in those leagues kept the dream alive until the pieces fell into place. When one improved, the other fought to catch up and do better. When one demanded more, the other showed they could get there first. Eventually the bar was raised, and the athletes got to the finish line at the same moment.

While, as Jayna Hefford points out, "All of those experiences were part of getting to today," justifying each failure and success as necessary for progress ignores the intersectional challenges faced by women of color, members of the LGBTQ+ community, and women from different socioeconomic backgrounds. According to Leavitt and Adams, "Women's elite sport experiences are shaped by many forms of discrimination and oppression based on gender, race, ethnicity, sexuality, and class that are often actively erased through narratives of progress and achievements that get storied and retold."[4] While progress has been made, the PWHL and leagues across the globe still have many gaps. Salaries remain light years behind men's, media coverage has lagged behind, power imbalances and gatekeepers remain, and non-conforming women, who do not fit society's narrow definition of femininity or who do not identify as cisgender, face risks of exclusion.

There remain significant gaps in the experience of young women compared to men in hockey. Rules continue to differ, a prime indicator of ongoing paternalism. According to the IIHF's rule book, women at all levels of competition are required to "wear a full-face protection (full-visor, or cage facial protection)," a regulation that only applied to men's U-18 or minor players. Within Hockey Canada, the same was long true for neck guards: "The wearing of a BNQ-certified throat protector is required for players registered in minor and female hockey . . . goaltenders in minor or female hockey who wear an attachment to the mask or helmet designed to protect the throat, must still wear a BNQ-certified throat protector." As scholar Taylor McKee points out, "This is a blatantly infantilizing policy that equates women with children."[5]

The rules in the IIHF differed slightly, only recommending neck protection for women at the senior level until 2023. In 2023, following the death of American player Adam Johnson from a skate laceration to his neck, the IIHF mandated neck protection for all levels of international competition, for men and women.

Despite acknowledging that "women's hockey is not just an important long-term investment. It's also an untapped market that is well-positioned to pay off,"[6] gaps also still remain in the availability of international competition for women. Other world governing bodies, including FIFA (soccer) and FIBA (basketball), feature identical competitions for men and women. The IIHF holds a World Junior Championships for men annually but no such competition exists for women. Men's competitions include the U-18 World Championships, U-20 World Junior Championships, and senior national events. Women's hockey jumps directly from the U-18 tournament to the senior national level with nothing in between.

In a 2023 interview with IIHF Council Member Zsuzsanna Kolbenheyer, she told me the organization has "had a lot of discussions about (a World Junior) already, it's already on the table. Of course it's not easy to create a new category, it's also money questions, because it would mean a new championship structure. On the other hand, we also know this has to come some day. Maybe not next year, but in the near future. We are talking about it."

It's never been difficult for the IIHF and other governing bodies to accommodate men's hockey. During the peak of the COVID-19 pandemic, the

IIHF canceled the women's U-18 World Championship, but the men's U-20 World Juniors were supported and run by the IIHF.

"This is not a gender issue, this is a COVID-19 issue," IIHF president Luc Tardif claimed in 2021. "Is there an economic incentive to host the men's World Championship and World Juniors every year no matter what? Absolutely. But people misunderstand that this is because we favor men's hockey over women's, which is completely false. The revenue generated from these two events enables our federation to survive and support the operation of all other IIHF World Championship events. So if I have to make every effort to host a specific tournament to ensure the survival of other events, then it is my responsibility as IIHF President to do this."

The first men's world championship was held in 1920, seventy years prior to a women's tournament, an event men sanctioned only after women had organized the unofficial 1987 championship in the face of staunch opposition. Even after 1990, the women's world championships did not become an annual event until after the 1998 Nagano Olympics. Still, Tardif maintained that the IIHF's "commitment to women's hockey is longstanding, legitimate, and substantial."[7]

Women have been relentlessly pursuing the puck for over one hundred years. As any player knows, that path is never linear. You take the puck onto your stick, and for those moments, you control the way forward, the pace of play, and the fate of the game while your opponent tries to stop you. You either fail or you catch your target. There is hope that today's incarnation will finally stick. Media are providing blanket coverage to women's hockey at all levels, rules are changing, and barriers to access are slowly being chipped away.

•

With the inaugural PWHL season underway, I sat down at a table at the Weston Golf and Country Club in Toronto. To my left was Olympic gold medalist Sami Jo Small. To my right was Graeme Rouston, owner of *The Hockey News* and board member of the old CWHL. One seat over was Lisa-Marie Breton who, along with Small, had founded the CWHL. At the next table was Angela James; another Hockey Hall of Fame inductee, Danielle Goyette, was at the table beside her. The room was filled with trailblazing women including Fran Rider, longtime CWHL commissioner Brenda

Andress, Hockey Hall of Famer Geraldine Heaney, a dozen athletes competing in the PWHL's inaugural season and many more from the now-defunct PHF. We were all there to celebrate the PHF's Toronto Six, winners of the final Isobel Cup, and to present players with their championship rings. It was the closing of one chapter and the beginning of another.

Near the end of the evening, one speaker reminded us all that, "a house divided against itself cannot stand." I drove home thinking about that moment, and how I wished Marian Coveny were there. I also felt satisfied knowing the history discussed that evening, albeit a small portion of the history of women in hockey, was being kept alive, to be shared to another generation.

Two months earlier, on New Year's Day 2024, I was eagerly waiting for the puck to drop at Mattamy Athletic Centre in Toronto for the inaugural game of the Professional Women's Hockey League. It was my fortieth birthday and this felt like an incredible gift. Women of all ages across the globe were watching as fans poured in, some holding signs that read "finally." Toronto had sold out all twelve of their home games weeks before the season began and the stands were full. The following day, Ottawa would break the all-time attendance record for a women's professional hockey game; days after that, Minnesota broke the record again. In the coming months, those records would all be smashed again.

On this day, the referee blew the whistle, bringing the teams to center ice. Lining up in the face-off circle, Toronto's Blayre Turnbull stepped to the dot to face New York's Alex Carpenter. There was a brief pause as the officials and teams readied themselves; a pulse of electricity flowed through the arena. It was happening, at last. In the crowd, fans swung towels as Turnbull and Carpenter leaned in for the face-off. The referee extended her hand, holding a puck emblazoned with a PWHL logo. The crowd took a collective breath as she released it. The crack of the puck was audible as skates cut the ice and players called to each other. With the puck on their sticks, a new generation of women were carrying the game forward.

Remember the Past, Illuminate the Future
AFTERWORD BY SAMI JO SMALL

I recently had the honor of hosting the ring ceremony to commemorate the Isobel Cup Championship won by the PHF's Toronto Six. As the president of this women's professional hockey club, it filled me with immense pride and warmth to preside over such a significant event. However, amidst the jubilation, there lingered a bittersweet sentiment, for this ceremony marked the conclusion of yet another chapter in the annals of women's hockey. It was a chapter adorned with the visionary efforts of builders and pioneers who relentlessly pushed boundaries and crafted enduring legacies for all who have been touched by the sport.

The ceremony unfolded as a poignant reflection of our collective journey—a celebration of resilience, camaraderie, and unwavering dedication that has defined elite women's hockey in North America. It wasn't just about the championship title; it was a tribute to the rich tapestry of history woven by the stalwarts of the game. From every corner of the greater Toronto area and beyond, luminaries of the sport converged, their presence a testament to the enduring legacy they've sculpted through tireless effort and sacrifice.

The evening transported us back to the illustrious days of the Central Ontario Women's Hockey League (COWHL), where pioneers carved paths of courage and breakthroughs across Ontario and Quebec. Their determination laid the groundwork for the remarkable evolution that followed, and we owe them a profound debt of gratitude for paving the way and smashing countless glass ceilings. Women like Cathy Phillips, Geraldine Heaney, and Angela James balanced work, training, and competition to create a foundation for the future.

As I was finishing up my degree in mechanical engineering from Stanford University, I was fortunate to represent Canada at the very first Olympic Women's Ice Hockey tournament, winning a silver medal. I learned how so many made this happen, led by the voices of Fran Rider of the

Ontario Women's Hockey Association and Hazel McCallion, the mayor of Mississauga, amongst others.

The torch of progress was passed to the original National Women's Hockey League (NWHL), under the visionary stewardship of Commissioner Susan Fennell. With each passing season, the NWHL, which I had the honor of playing in with the Brampton Thunder, blossomed into a beacon of progress, transcending boundaries and captivating hearts with its electrifying brand of hockey. Through resilience and unity, players, coaches, and supporters dared to dream beyond convention, laying the foundation for women's professional hockey.

There were a lot of huge steps made by the NWHL including a nearly fifty-game schedule with playoffs, television deals, bigger arenas, international stars, and locations right across the country. Players moved from across North America to play in this league, including future Hall of Famers like Cammi Granato and Hayley Wickenheiser. Sponsorship dollars increased, and players were expected to be professional athletes.

All Canadian National Team athletes played in this league, as well as most of the American team. It was the training ground for selection to the World Championships and Olympics Games. It was during my time in the NWHL that I was selected to represent Canada, winning my first World Championship in 1999, later helping Canada to five World Championships and two Olympic Gold Medals in 2002 and 2006.

Playing for the national team was incredible, but my "real" teams were the ones I played with all season. My club teams were my sanctuary, my teammates that I trained alongside on a daily basis, rode the long bus trips with. They became like family. This is why these professional leagues were so important to all of us.

As the evening at the ring gala progressed, we celebrated the people who had made these leagues and achievements possible; all those who coached, managed, and played, as well as those that sat on boards, and supported and sponsored the league. So many had a part to play. In the chronicles of women's hockey history, 2007 stands as another pivotal chapter, with the emergence of the Canadian Women's Hockey League (CWHL), which further solidified the sport's legacy, uniting talent from across the globe and captivating fans with thrilling competition and championship triumphs. As one of the CWHL's co-founding players, I spent ten seasons in the league playing for one team that went by many different names. Initially, the Toronto Aeros and then the Mississauga Aeros in the NWHL, we became the Mississauga Hockey Club. We rebranded as the Toronto Hockey Club and eventually, the Toronto Furies. It was a league in which superstars such as Marie-Philip Poulin, Caroline Ouellette, Kim St-Pierre, Hilary Knight, Jennifer Botterill, Vicky Sunohara and Cherie Piper played alongside peers that pushed them to be better every day.

As the league evolved, so did its impact and reach. From humble beginnings in makeshift offices to the grandeur of televised broadcasts, the league was a testament to the power of collective action and community spirit. Amidst uncertainty, players forged ahead, rallying under the banner of solidarity to establish a league that transcended mere competition. The CWHL was a beacon of excellence that united talent from across the globe. With each passing season, the league blossomed, expanding its reach and redefining the landscape of professional women's hockey.

Brenda Andress presided over the CWHL as its commissioner for more than a decade, increasing its operating budget from $350,000 in Year One to $3.5 million at the end. For the first time, the league paid for all travel, ice rentals, uniforms, and equipment costs. The former Governor General of Canada, Adrienne Clarkson, had a cup commissioned for the Champion of club hockey in North America, and eventually the CWHL merged with the Western Women's Hockey League to compete for the Clarkson Cup.

As we reflected on the journey that brought us to our 2023 Isobel Cup Championship, all of us in that room extended our deepest gratitude to those who paved the way. We thanked all the players whose sacrifices fueled our dreams, the staff whose tireless dedication ensured our success, and the fans whose unwavering support breathed life into our endeavors.

During the CWHL era, a new league emerged, naming itself the same as our previous league, the National Women's Hockey League (NWHL). Eventually, it rebranded as the Premier Hockey Federation (PHF). Formed by Dani Rylan in March 2015 with four original American franchises, it became the first professional women's hockey league to pay its players salaries. In 2017, with the closure of the CWHL, the NWHL continued to grow, (despite a boycott by some players forming their own association) and explored Canadian expansion. In 2020, thanks to the leadership of Johanna and John Boynton, the Toronto Six were born.

I became President in 2022, just as the salary cap was raised from US$750,000 to US$1.5 million. The Toronto Six captivated Toronto fans, sneaking through the playoffs and winning the Isobel Cup Championship in overtime, in Tempe, Arizona, watched live on national television. At our ring ceremony, we celebrated this chapter in women's hockey. As I called up my colleague, Angela James, the General Manager of the Six, to help me hand out the rings, jubilation for all friendships made, the strides taken, permeated the room. But it was touched with sadness because the presentation of the rings coincided with the culmination of the PHF. Future plans that would no longer include us. As each previous league had ended, the feelings had been the same: no closure, no chance to say goodbye, no chance to share the lessons learned with the next generation. But on that night, at the ring ceremony, we tried to accomplish all of that on behalf of so many. It was a bookend to celebrate all that was and all that will be.

We ceremoniously passed the torch to the Toronto franchise in the Professional Women's Hockey League (PWHL), celebrating all the good that has come early in its existence. A huge influx of money had led to sold-out crowds, crazy excitement, and more interest than has ever been shown in women's hockey.

All of us in the room leave our future in the hands of the PWHL, so proud of our roles, as we now simply watch on TV and pack the arenas. The future of women's professional hockey is bright thanks to all the hard work of so many that were in that room.

All of us in women's hockey are the caretakers of this incredible history. Let's remember it and dig deeper to unveil the stories and lessons from our shared past so that we may illuminate the future together.

Acknowledgments

Many of the women profiled here, including Isobel Stanley, Hilda Ranscombe, and Albertine Lapensée, passed away without ever seeing where this game would go. They fought discrimination, misogyny, and inequity, and I am grateful for the opportunity to celebrate their lives, achievements, and impact, not only in sport but in society.

In particular, the story of Marian "Mern" Coveny was paramount to this project. Our common hometown, passion for hockey, and my ignorance of her considerable contributions to the game inspired me to continue researching and uncovering other individuals and teams without whom no history of hockey would be complete.

To the girls' hockey players I've coached, this is your story too. You brought back my love for this game and opened my eyes to the inequities of all shapes and sizes that still exist in the sport today.

I would like to thank Tidewater Press for their continued commitment to me as a writer, but more importantly to telling diverse stories. I'd also like to acknowledge *The Hockey News* for giving me space to follow my passion, and space in print and online to showcase the growth of women's hockey. Thank you also to Corwin Dickson for her original cover illustration.

Thank you to the following individuals who generously contributed their oral histories and recollections to this project. In alphabetic order, they are: Deb Adkins, Line Baun Danielsen, Bev Beaver, Laura Bennion, Kristina Bergstrand, Justine Blainey, Johanna Boynton, John Boynton, Lisa Brown-Miller, Shirley Cameron, Adrienne Clarkson, Marian Coveny, Cindy Curley, Kelly Dyer, Kim Eisenreid, Jayne Gilhuly, Cammi Granato, Grace Harvey, Geraldine Heaney, Jayna Hefford, Jackie Hughes, Angela James, Zsuzsanna Kolbenheyer, Heather Kramble, Deb Maybury, Hazel McCallion, Dawn McGuire, Margot Page, Cathy Phillips, Cheryl Pounder, Fran Rider, Sharon Sanderson, Tamae Satsu, Sami Jo Small, Vicky Sunohara, Estey Ticknor, and Pat White.

About the Author

Ian Kennedy manages *The Hockey News'* women's hockey coverage, and writes about women's hockey, social issues, and the global growth of the game. A journalist with a passion for sport and storytelling, he has contributed feature articles to newspapers and publications that range from *The Globe and Mail* and *Toronto Star* to *The Guardian* and *Yahoo Sports*. A resident of Erie Beach, Ontario, he is also the author of *On Account of Darkness: Shining Light on Race and Sport*.

Endnotes

Chapter 1: Lady-in-Waiting

1. Syers, E. (Edgar) and Mrs. Madge Syers, *The Book of Winter Sports* (London: E. Arnold, 1908). Pg. 69
2. Syers and Syers. Pg. 74
3. Hall, M. Ann, *Immodest & Sensational: 150 Years of Canadian Women in Sport* (Toronto, Ont: James Lorimer Pub, 2008). Pg. 8
4. Ascroft, Sheila, "Skating Through Woods on a Snowy Evening," *Ottawa Outdoors Magazine,* December 1, 2015.
5. Byng, Evelyn Moreton, Viscountess, *Up the Stream of Time* (Toronto: Macmillan, 1945). Pg. 139
6. Byng. Pg. 140-141
7. "NHL Lady Byng Memorial Trophy Winners | NHL.Com," May 30, 2024, https://www.nhl.com/news/nhl-lady-byng-memorial-trophy-winners-complete-list-287910994.
8. Kalbfleisch, John, "From the Archives: Lord Stanley's Cup Had an Inauspicious Debut," *The Gazette*, February 7, 2017.
9. Kalbfleisch.
10. McFarlane, Brian, *Proud Past, Bright Future: One Hundred Years of Canadian Women's Hockey* (Toronto: Stoddart, 1994). Pg 8
11. Taylor, Rhonda Leeman, "A Glorious Game: The History of Women's Hockey | Women's Hockey Life," September 11, 2019, https://womenshockeylife.com/womens-hockey-history/.
12. "Ice Hockey," *Buffalo Courier Express*, January 7, 1894.
13. "A Fad with Women," *North Loup Loyalist*, April 28, 1898.
14. McFarlane, *Proud Past, Bright Future*. Pg. 14-15
15. Alma Mater Society of Queen's University, "Sports," *Queen's College Journal* 22, no. 8 (February 16, 1895).
16. Hall, *Immodest & Sensational*.
17. "The New Woman AWheel," *San Francisco Call*, July 29, 1895.
18. "Women's Sports History," National Women's History Museum, August 4, 2016, https://www.womenshistory.org/articles/womens-sports-history.
19. Hardy, Stephen and Andrew C. Holman, *Hockey: A Global History, Sport and Society* (Urbana Chicago Springfield: University of Illinois Press, 2018). Pg. 251

Chapter 2: A League of Their Own

1. "League of Women Ballplayers | Baseball Hall of Fame," accessed April 23, 2024, https://baseballhall.org/discover-more/stories/baseball-history/league-of-women-ballplayers.
2. Hall, *Immodest & Sensational*. Pg 35
3. "Ladies' Teams in Readiness," *Ottawa Citizen*, February 23, 1916.
4. "Queen of the Ice -Eva Catherine Buels | Beechwood," October 19, 2023, https://beechwoodottawa.ca/en/blog/queen-ice-eva-catherine-buels.
5. "Miss Lapensee Gone To New York Says Z. Runions," *The Montreal Star*, June 23, 1917.
6. "Girls Ready for Hockey," *Times Union*, November 27, 1916.
7. "Miss Lapensee Is a Real Hockey Player," *The Ottawa Journal*, March 6, 1916.
8. Yaccato, Bruce, "Puck Pioneers Captivate a City," *The Gazette*, January 4, 2014.
9. "Miss Lapensee Is a Real Hockey Player."
10. Holman, Andrew C., "Stops and Starts: Ideology, Commercialism and the Fall of American Women's Hockey in the 1920s," *History Faculty Publications*, no. Paper 5 (January 2005): Pg. 330–41.
11. Holman.
12.Menke, Frank G., "Indoor Ice Skating Season Opening Shows This Sport Is Much in Favor," *The Herald Statesman*, October 28, 1916.

13. "Mrs. T.A. Howard Would Teach Hockey to Girls of Brooklyn," *The Brooklyn Daily Eagle*, February 8, 1917.
14. "Girls' Hockey Tonight," *The Pittsburgh Post*, January 14, 1917.
15. Lyman-Phillips, Amy, "Girls of the Snow," *The Buffalo Commercial*, March 8, 1917.
16. Deachman, Bruce, "Ottawa's 'Queen of the Ice' Popularized Women's Hockey a Century Ago," *Ottawa Citizen*, accessed April 23, 2024, https://ottawacitizen.com/sports/local-sports/queen-of-the-ice-popularized-womens-hockey-a-century-ago.
17. "Miss Lapensee Again Showed That She Is Wonderful Player," *The Ottawa Journal*, March 11, 1916.
18. "Miss Lapensee Is a Young Lady, Says Cornwall," *The Montreal Star*, February 12, 1916.
19. "Miss Lapensee Is a Young Lady, Says Cornwall."
20. "Lady In the Iron Mask for Next Cornwall Game," *The Montreal Star*, February 12, 1916.
21. "Miss Lapensee Is a Young Lady, Says Cornwall."
22. "Miss Lapensee Gone To New York Says Z. Runions."
23. "Miss Lapensee Gone To New York Says Z. Runions."
24. "Girls Ready for Hockey."
25. Hall, *Immodest & Sensational*. Pg. 32–33
26. "Ladies' Puck Squads Ready for Campaign," *The Edmonton Bulletin*, November 23, 1932.
27. "Calgary Byngs Beat Vancouver at Banff 1 To 0," *The Calgary Albertan*, February 2, 1922.
28. Podnieks, Andrew, "IIHF -Women Made History 100 Years Ago," IIHF International Ice Hockey Federation, February 21, 2021, https://www.iihf.com/en/news/24545/women_made_history_100_years_ago.
29. Green, B.E., "Amazons Win Hockey Trophy," *The Province*, February 6, 1922.
30. "Fernie Gives Royal Welcome to Its Team," *Calgary Herald*, March 12, 1923.
31. Adams, Carly, "Troubling Bodies: 'The Canadian Girl,' the Ice Rink, and the Banff Winter Carnival," *Journal of Canadian Studies* 48, no. 3 (2014): Pg. 200–220.
32. Holman.
33. Gershon, Livia "A Century Ago, Women Played Ice Hockey," *JSTOR Daily*, January 2, 2020, https://daily.jstor.org/a-century-ago-women-played-ice-hockey/.
34. Holman.
35. Adams, Carly and Julie Stevens, "Change and Grassroots Movement: Reconceptualising Women's Hockey Governance in Canada," *International Journal of Sport Management and Marketing* 2, no. 4 (May 23, 2007): 350.
36. Holman, "Stops and Starts: Ideology, Commercialism and the Fall of American Women's Hockey in the 1920s."
37. Adams, Carly, "Organizing Hockey for Women: The Ladies Ontario Hockey Association and the Fight for Legitimacy, 1922-1940," *Coast to Coast: Hockey in Canada to the Second World War* (University of Toronto Press, 2009), Pg. 132–59.
38. Adams.
39. Yaccato, "Puck Pioneers Captivate a City."

Chapter 3: No Man's Land

1. Quoted in a scrapbook created by Betty Barnes, Hilda and Nellie Ranscombe's niece, and Dave Menary, reporter for the *Cambridge Times* as part of the Hockey Hall of Fame nomination package, 1999. Hockey Hall of Fame archives, Toronto, Ontario.
2. Thornton, Barbara, "Hasn't Lost Her Touch," *Windsor Star*, February 10, 1968.
3. Gibb, Alexandrine, "Pats Ladies Win Game in Montreal," *Toronto Daily Star*, March 23, 1929.
4. Gibb, Alexandrine, "No Man's Land of Sport," *Toronto Daily Star*, April 12, 1935.
5. Adams, "Organizing Hockey for Women: The Ladies Ontario Hockey Association and the Fight for Legitimacy, 1922-1940."
6. Letter from Mary McGuire to Betty Barnes, 15 February 1999, *Ranscombe Scrapbook*, Hockey Hall of Fame Archives, Toronto, Ontario
7. "Fe Fi Fo Fum," *Galt Evening Reporter*, March 6, 1931.
8. Gibb, Alexandrine, "No Man's Land of Sport," *Toronto Daily Star*, March 2, 1938.
9. Cook, Myrtle, "In the Women's Sportlight," *The Montreal Star*, December 7, 1933.
10. "Dominion Hockey Final for Ladies," *The Montreal Star*, April 14, 1933.
11. "Edmonton Has Advanced in Girls' Hockey," *The Calgary Albertan*, December 3, 1932.
12. "Rivulettes Lose Out 3-2," *Star-Phoenix*, March 20, 1933.
13. "Preston Rivulettes," Cambridge Sports Hall of Fame (blog), accessed July 31, 2024, http://cambridgeshf.com/inductee/preston-rivulettes/.
14. "Summerside Crystal Sisters -Team-Hockey," PEI Sports Hall of Fame (blog), January 24, 2022, https://peisportshalloffame.ca/summerside-crystal-sisters-team-hockey/.
15. "Ladies Win from Sterner Sex After a Hard Struggle," *Charlottetown Guardian*, January 6, 1930.

16. "All-Star Team Chosen," *The Gazette*, August 3, 1934.

17. "Noted Crystal Sisters Will Play Here," *The Montreal Star*, March 13, 1934.

18. "Maroons In Draw with Crystal Six," *The Montreal Star*, March 20, 1934.

19. "Minutes of the 38th Ontario Hockey Association Meeting," OHA Papers (Library and Archives Canada, November 19, 1927), M2308.

20. "Ladies' Hockey Bars Firm Crests," *The Montreal Star*, December 15, 1933.

21. Cook, Myrtle, "In the Women's Sportlight," *The Montreal Star*, April 22, 1937.

22. "Come On, Vic.!," *The Sun*, August 11, 1925.

23. "French Team Defeated at Birmingham Rink," *Birmingham Gazette*, February 23, 1932.

24. Frison-Rochie, Roger, "En Hockey Les Parisiennes Battent L'Equipe Locale," *Le Petit Dauphinois*, January 30, 1932.

25. "Spartan Girls Play Ice-Hockey," *The Daily Telegraph*, March 29, 1935.

26. Associated Press, "Eveleth Claims Only Girls' Hockey Team," *The Albert Lea Tribune*, February 20, 1933.

27. Cook, Myrtle, "In the Women's Sportlight," *The Montreal Star*, December 5, 1939.

28. Canadian Press, "Toronto Girls Lead Royals," *The Montreal Star*, December 7, 1939.

29. Adams, "Organizing Hockey for Women: The Ladies Ontario Hockey Association and the Fight for Legitimacy, 1922-1940."

30. Hall, *Immodest & Sensational*. Pg. 43

31. Rosenfeld, Fanny, "Girls Are in Sports for Good," *Chatelaine*, July 1933.

32. Stephen Hardy and Andrew C. Holman, *Hockey: A Global History, Sport and Society* (Urbana Chicago Springfield: University of Illinois Press, 2018).Pg. 416

33. Cook, Myrtle, "In the Women's Sportlight," *The Montreal Star*, February 5, 1940.

34. Hardy and Holman. Pg. 417

35. Hardy and Holman. Pg. 539

36. Quoted in a scrapbook created by Betty Barnes, Hilda and Nellie Ranscombe's niece, and Dave Menary, reporter for the *Cambridge Times* as part of the Hockey Hall of Fame nomination package, 1999. Hockey Hall of Fame archives, Toronto, Ontario.

37. Adams, Carly, "'Queens of the Ice Lanes': The Preston Rivulettes and Women's Hockey in Canada, 1931–1940," *Sport History Review* 39 (2008): 1–29.

Chapter 4: Put a Ring on It

1. Young, Iris Marion, *Throwing like a Girl and Other Essays in Feminist Philosophy and Social Theory* (Bloomington: Indiana University Press, 1990). Pg. 154

2. McKinley. Pg. 187

3. Varpalotai, Aniko, "Sport, Leisure and the Adolescent Girl: Single Sex vs. Co-Ed?," *Canadian Woman Studies/Les Cahiers de La Femme*, September 1, 1995, https://cws.journals.yorku.ca/index.php/cws/article/view/9360. Pg. 32-33

4. Etue, Elizabeth and Megan K. Williams, *On the Edge : Women Making Hockey History* (Toronto: Second Story Press, 1996), http://archive.org/details/onedgewomenmakin0000etue. Pg. 116

5. Varpalotai, "Sport, Leisure and the Adolescent Girl."

6. Hardy and Holman, *Hockey*. Pg. 543-544

7. Reid, Patrick Alexander, "The First Women's World Ice Hockey Championship and the Emergence of the Routine of Women's Elite Hockey" (University of Alberta, 2018), https://era.library.ualberta.ca/items/1b1deaa9-0c37-4529-88e3-51dc8b568a32/view/7b39b1e0-fd11-4893-a057-240fa83a8557/Reid_Patrick_A_2018March29_PhD.pdf. Pg 23

8. Lajoie, Ron, "From a Tiny Target to a Ringette Star," *Edmonton Journal*, April 9, 1983.

9. Cowley, Norm, "Olympic Dream Tough to Top," *Edmonton Journal*, December 11, 1997.

10. Lajoie, Ron, "From a Tiny Target to a Ringette Star."

11. Cowley, Norm, "Olympic Dream Tough to Top."

12. Cowley, Norm.

13. MacKinnon, John, "Diduck Stars in Juggling Act," *Ottawa Citizen*, March 18, 1990.

14. Strojek, Sylvia, "Ringette, Hockey in Battle," *Edmonton Journal*, February 23, 1995.

Chapter 5: Applying Concealer

1. Canadian Press, "Boy-Sterous Rink Star Real Gal-Lant," *Windsor Star*, March 8, 1956.

2. Smith, Stephen, "We Didn't Have the Heart to Tell Him," Puckstruck (blog), March 9, 2021, https://puckstruck.com/2021/03/09/we-didnt-have-the-heart-to-tell-him/.

3. Canadian Press.

4. Canadian Press, "Hockey Star Is a Girl!," *Vancouver News-Herald*, March 9, 1956.
5. Canadian Press, "Habs Have Toronto Rooter in Young Abigail Hoffman," *Ottawa Citizen*, April 2, 1956.
6. Canadian Press, "Ban Girls in Peewee Hockey," *The Kingston Whig-Standard*, April 10, 1958.
7. Beddoes, Dick, "Hoffman's Hockey Hoax," *Vancouver Sun*, August 4, 1962.
8. Canadian Press, "Ban Girl Wrestlers," *Ottawa Journal*, April 4, 1959.
9. Bell, Richard C., "A History of Women in Sport Prior to Title IX," *The Sport Journal*, March 14, 2008.
10. Gordon, Alison, "New Challenge for Abby," *Toronto Star*, August 8, 1981.

Chapter 6: Be My Sweetheart

1. O'Flynn, Gary, "Brainstorm Works Out; Gal's Hockey Rebounds.," *Windsor Star*, February 18, 1967.
2. Botosan, Mary, "Hockey's Appeal for Women Evident at Area Tourney," *Windsor Star*, November 2, 1967.
3. Botosan, Mary.
4. "Wallaceburg Tournament Features Women's Hockey," *Windsor Star*, February 17, 1975

Chapter 7: Power Plays

1. Hohler, Bob, "Carl Gray, Founder of Prestigious Assabet Hockey Valley Hockey Program Comes under Fire for Treatment of Players," *The Boston Globe*, April 5, 2020.
2. Hohler, Bob.

Chapter 8: Changing on the Fly

1. Brake, Deborah "The Struggle for Sex Equality in Sport and the Theory Behind Title IX," *University of Michigan Journal of Law Reform* 34 (2001), https://scholarship.law.pitt.edu/fac_articles/2.
2. Gray, Carl, "Olympic Dreams Forged at Famed Assabet Valley Girl's Hockey Program," Radio, February 14, 2018, https://www.wbur.org/news/2018/02/14/assabet-valley-girls-hockey.
3. English, Bella, "Rink Leader," *The Boston Globe*, March 14, 2001.
4. Lerch, Bruce, "Assabet Girls Set Standard on Ice," *Boston Herald*, April 16, 2012, https://www.bostonherald.com/2012/04/16/assabet-girls-set-standard-on-ice/.
5. Hohler, Bob, "Treatment Questioned," *The Boston Globe*, April 5, 2020.
6. Hohler, Bob, "Carl Gray, Founder of Prestigious Assabet Hockey Valley Hockey Program Comes under Fire for Treatment of Players," *The Boston Globe*, April 5, 2020.
7. Beaton, Rod, "Delaware Bobcats Aiming for Top in Women's Hockey," *The Morning News*, November 2, 1978.
8. Finocchiaro, Ray, "Goalie Skirts Another Male Frontier," *The News Journal*, March 22, 1974.
9. Lewis, Chuck, "Sylvia Wasylyk Sets High Goal for Rappa," *The News Journal*, February 15, 1975.
10. Finocchiaro, Ray, "Goalie Skirts Another Male Frontier."
11. Lewis, Chuck, "Sylvia Wasylyk Sets High Goal for Rappa."
12. Miller, Beth, "Bobcats Eye Women's Hockey Title," *The News Journal*, October 2, 1979.
13. Canadian Press, "OMHA Rules Girl Ineligible," *The Sault Star*, January 21, 1978.
14. Associated Press, "Ontario Hockey Rule Bars Girl Goaltender," *The Montreal Star*, January 23, 1978.
15. Granger, Bill, "Tender Goalie, 9, Nettled by Ouster," *St. Louis Post-Dispatch*, January 25, 1978.
16. Allen, Karen, "Girl Goalie Ousted from Silver Stick," *The Times Herald*, January 22, 1978.
17. Associated Press, "Another Slap Shot Aimed at Michele," *The Times Herald*, February 10, 1978.
18. Associated Press, "'Friendship' Is Unfriendly," *The Times Herald*, February 10, 1978.
19. Carpenter, Ross, "LEGENDS | Women's Hockey," Legends of Australian Ice, accessed August 28, 2024, https://icelegendsaustralia.com/1stIceChampions-whockey.html.
20. Jacub, George, "More Suspensions as Girl Plays," *Winnipeg Sun*, February 18, 1981.
21. Jacub, George.
22. Canadian Press, "Women's Hockey Council Approved," *Ottawa Citizen*, May 26, 1981.

Chapter 9: Fran's Got a Plan

1. "13. Hazel McCallion," 150 Stories | 150 Récits (blog), February 15, 2017, https://arts.lgontario.ca/canada150/hazel-mccallion/.
2. Cook, Myrtle, "In the Women's Sportlight," *The Montreal Star*, January 12, 1940.
3. Kalchman, Lois, "Canuck Women Hammer Swiss," *Toronto Star*, April 22, 1987.
4. Nugent-Bowman, Daniel, "Why Fran Rider Belongs in the Hockey Hall of Fame: 'She's a True

Pioneer,'" *The Athletic*, accessed June 23, 2024, https://www.nytimes.com/athletic/3217700/2022/03/31/fran-rider-hockey-hall-of-fame/.
5. Nugent-Bowman, Daniel.

Chapter 10: Hockey Nation

1. Hardy and Holman, *Hockey*. Pg. 545, 547
2. "Girls Teams Play a Fast Game on Ice," *The Australian Women's Weekly*, June 25, 1949.
3. Stevens, Julie, "Thirty Years of 'Going Global': Women's International Hockey, Cultural Diplomacy, and the Pursuit of Excellence," in *Hockey: Challenging Canada's Game Au-Delà Du Sport National*, ed. Ellison, Jenny and Anderson, Jennifer (University of Ottawa Press, 2018).
4. "En Pionjär Med 14 SM-Guld – Old School Hockey Kristina 'Krickan' Bergstrand," *Hockey Sverige*, accessed June 25, 2024, https://hockeysverige.se/2018/03/25/en-pionjar-med-14-sm-guld-old-school-hockey-kristina-krickan-bergstrand.
5. K. Gilenstam, S. Karp, and K. Henriksson-Larsén, "Gender in Ice Hockey: Women in a Male Territory," *Scandinavian Journal of Medicine & Science in Sports* 18, no. 2 (2008): 235–49, https://doi.org/10.1111/j.1600-0838.2007.00665.x.
6. "En Pionjär Med 14 SM-Guld – Old School Hockey Kristina 'Krickan' Bergstrand."
7. Kalchman, Lois, "Salming Delights Swedes," *Toronto Star*, 1987.
8. "Tamae Satsu: The Road to Hero," May 28, 2013, https://blog.skoda-hockey.com/post/51561758516/tamae-satsu-the-road-to-hero.
9. Kalchman, Lois, "Hockey's Big Among Women in Japan Firms," *Toronto Star*, 1987.
10. "En Pionjär Med 14 SM-Guld – Old School Hockey Kristina 'Krickan' Bergstrand."
11. Stevens, Julie, "Thirty Years of 'Going Global': Women's International Hockey, Cultural Diplomacy, and the Pursuit of Excellence." Pg. 150

Chapter 11: Playing Like Girls

1. Davidson, James, "Women's Hockey Intent on Escaping Obscurity," *The Globe and Mail*, March 26, 1990.
2. Barnes, Dan, "Game On," *The Gazette*, December 23, 2023.

Chapter 12: Faceoff

1. Canadian Press, "Girl's Right to Hockey Defended," *Red Deer Advocate*, December 3, 1977.
2. Canadian Press, "Toronto Girl Loses Hockey Battle, but War Will Continue," *Windsor Star*, September 26, 1985.
3. Canadian Press.
4. Kelly, Doug, "Barred Last Week, Four Area Girls Will Now Play on Boys' Hockey Teams," *Ottawa Citizen*, October 30, 1985.
5. Babad, Michael, "Blainey Fights for 'Other Little Girls' to Get Chance at Boys' Hockey," *Ottawa Citizen*, September 20, 1985.
6. Canadian Press, "Ontario Attacks Sports Sexism," *Regina Leader-Post*, July 26, 1985.
7. Canadian Press, "Most Women Too Weak for Hockey, MD Tells Human Rights Hearing," *The Kingston Whig-Standard*, August 26, 1987.
8. Canadian Press, "Blainey's Fight for Rights Poses Risk to Girls Hockey, Says Association Boss," *Ottawa Citizen*, June 12, 1987.
9. Canadian Press, "Girl Shoots, Scores Place in Boys' Hockey," *Times Colonist*, December 5, 1987.
10. Canadian Press, "Female Athletes Cry Foul," *Red Deer Advocate*, April 27, 1995.
11. Adams and Stevens, "Change and Grassroots Movement." Pg. 353
12. Bohuslawsky, Maria, "Breaking the Sex Barrier," *Ottawa Citizen*, May 3, 1992.
13. "Hockey Arena Exiles Girls to Washroom so AAA Boys Can Have Their Change Room," CTV News, December 18, 2017, https://www.ctvnews.ca/canada/hockey-arena-exiles-girls-to-washroom-so-aaa-boys-can-have-their-change-room-1.3726238.
14. Hayley Wickenheiser [@wick_22], "Really People? This Is the Crap I Was Dealing with in 1985. It's 2018!! Just Make It Right. Period! https://T.Co/BTO4S7kANZ," Tweet, Twitter, December 19, 2017, https://x.com/wick_22/status/943184840035201024.

Chapter 13: Powerful in Pink

1. Stevens, Julie, "Thirty Years of 'Going Global': Women's International Hockey, Cultural Diplomacy, and the Pursuit of Excellence."

2. Reid, Patrick Alexander, "The First Women's World Ice Hockey Championship and the Emergence of the Routine of Women's Elite Hockey."
3. MacGregor, Roy, "Fast-Growing Women's Game Has Become 'the Pinnacle of Hockey,'" *The Globe and Mail*, March 12, 2013.
4. Canadian Press, "Pink Power Rules Rink at Tourney," *Edmonton Journal*, March 22, 1990.
5. Scanlan, W., "Women's World Championship: We Win!; Canada Beats Early Jitters to Crush US in Front of 8,724," *Ottawa Citizen*, March 26, 1990.

Chapter 14: Red Line

1. Weaving, Charlene and Samuel Roberts, "Checking In: An Analysis of the (Lack of) Body Checking in Women's Ice Hockey," *Research Quarterly for Exercise and Sport* 83, no. 3 (September 1, 2012): 470–78, https://doi.org/10.1080/02701367.2012.10599882.
2. Reid, Patrick Alexander, "The First Women's World Ice Hockey Championship and the Emergence of the Routine of Women's Elite Hockey." Pg.77
3. Reid, Patrick Alexander. Pg. 83
4. Reid, Patrick Alexander. Pg. 85
5. Bishop, Rachel, "No Coward Plays Hockey," Electronic Thesis and Dissertation Repository, September 26, 2019, https://ir.lib.uwo.ca/etd/6575. Pg. 71
6. K. Gilenstam, S. Karp, and K. Henriksson-Larsén, "Gender in Ice Hockey: Women in a Male Territory," Scandinavian Journal of Medicine & Science in Sports 18, no. 2 (2008): 235–49, https://doi.org/10.1111/j.1600-0838.2007.00665.x.
7. Brophy, Mike, "No-Hit, Perfect Game," *The Hockey News*, April 15, 1994.
8. Wyshynski, Greg, "Check, Please: Swedish Women's League OKs Hits," ESPN.com, May 20, 2022, https://www.espn.com/olympics/hockey/story/_/id/33951467/swedish-women-hockey-league-ok-body-checking-2022-23-season.
9. Adams, Alex, "PWHL's Physicality Is How the Players Want to Play the Game," *The Hockey News*, January 8, 2024, https://thehockeynews.com/womens/pwhl/pwhls-physicality-is-how-the-players-want-to-play-the-game.

Chapter 15: Don't Tell Me What I Can't Do

1. "Sports Equipment Makes Unveil Designs for Women," *Chicago Tribune*, August 18, 1996, https://www.chicagotribune.com/1996/08/18/sports-equipment-makers-unveil-designs-for-women/.

Chapter 16: Power Forward

1. Brake, "The Struggle for Sex Equality in Sport and the Theory Behind Title IX."
2. Branch, John, "They Called It 'Improper' to Have Women in the Olympics. But She Persisted," *The New York Times*, July 10, 2024, sec. Sports, https://www.nytimes.com/2024/07/10/olympics-women milliat.html.
3. Branch.
4. Cook, Myrtle, "In the Women's Sportlight," *The Montreal Star*, October 19, 1932.
5. Cook, Myrtle. December 17, 1934.
6. Cook, Myrtle. April 6, 1935.
7. "Women's Hockey Growth Is Traced." *The Gazette*. May 21, 1935.
8. Cook, Myrtle. January 28, 1937.
9. Beaton, Rod, "Delaware Bobcats Aiming for Top in Women's Hockey."
10. Allen, Kevin and Jeremy Roenick, S*tar-Spangled Hockey: Celebrating 75 Years of USA Hockey* (Chicago, Ill.: USA Hockey: Triumph Books, 2011). Pg. 330
11. "Twenty-Eight 1998 Nagano Hopefuls on Hand to Open Canadian Women's Olympic Team Training Program," accessed July 6, 2024, https://www.hockeycanada.ca/en-ca/news/1997-nr-087-en
12. Rutherford, Kristina, "A Player Before Her Time," *Sportsnet*, accessed July 7, 2024, https://www.sportsnet.ca/hockey/nhl/isnt-wayne-gretzky-womens-hockey-better-known/
13. Adams, Alan, "'Great One' Angela James Gunning for Olympic Glory | The Hockey News Archive," accessed July 7, 2024, https://archive.thehockeynews.com/issue/613646/616101?t=%E2%80%98Great%20One%E2%80%99 20Angela%20James%20gunning%20for%20Olympic%20glory.
14. Campbell, Ken, "Changing of Guard | The Hockey News Archive," accessed July 7, 2024, https://archive.thehockeynews.com/issue/613694/595414?t=Changing%20of%20guard.
15. Rutherford, Kristina, "A Player Before Her Time."
16. McKenzie, Alex I. and Janelle Joseph, "Whitewashed and Blacked Out: Counter-Narratives as an Analytical Framework for Studies of Ice Hockey in Canada," *Human Kinetics Journal*, April 21, 2023, https://journals.humankinetics.com/view/journals/ssj/40/2/article-p144.xml.

17. Sadler, Emily, "Black History Month: The Lasting Impact of Angela James," accessed July 7, 2024, https://www.sportsnet.ca/hockey/nhl/black-history-month-lasting-impact-angela-james/

18. "Fall and Rise of Sunohara | *The Hockey News* Archive," accessed July 7, 2024, https://archive.thehockeynews.com/issue/613667/574129?t=Fall%20and%20rise%20of%20Sunchara.

Chapter 17: Man Advantage

1. Brumm, Leonard, "Marquette Iron Rangers: Karen Koch," July 14, 2011, https://web.archive.org/web/20110714041722/http://www.marquetteironrangers.com/kar.htm.

2. Murphy, Mike, "Origins: The Story of Karen Koch, the First Woman to Be Paid to Play," *The Ice Garden,* June 30, 2017, https://www.theicegarden.com/womens-hockey-history-origins-pioneer-karen-koch-marquette-iron-rangers-goalie-ushl-pro-paid-to-play/.

3. Canadian Press, "Girl Goalie Is Sought by Elgins," *Niagara Falls Review*, October 7, 1970.

4. Canadian Press, "Rule Keep Getting in Way for Karen Koch and Hockey," *Brantford Expositor*, September 28, 1971.

5. Crerar, Jim, "Girl Goalie Challenges Hockey's 'Boys Only' Rule," *Toronto Star*, October 3, 1970.

6. Zurkowsky, Herb, "Mais Oui, Manon! A Hockey First | *The Hockey News* Archive," accessed July 8, 2024, https://archive.thehockeynews.com/issue/611996/555229?t=Mais%20oui,%20Manon!%20A%20hockey%20first.

7. McKenzie, Bob, "Rheaume Tryout More than a Stunt | *The Hockey News* Archive," accessed July 8, 2024, https://archive.thehockeynews.com/issue/612025/533213?t=Rheaume%20tryout%20more%20than%20a%20stunt.

8. Habib, Marlene, "Women's Sports Leaders Concerned Rheaume May Be Hindering Cause," *Vancouver Sun*, September 25, 1993.

9. Etue, Elizabeth and Megan K. Williams, *On the Edge*. Pg. 33

10. TIG Staff, "Her Own Person: Talk about Female Athletes, Not Their Male Relatives," *The Ice Garden*, September 14, 2018, https://www.theicegarden.com/leave-their-family-out-of-it-cwhl-nwhl-olympics-international/.

11. Theberge, Nancy, "Playing with the Boys: Manon Rheaume, Women's Hockey, and the Struggle for Legitimacy," *Canadian Woman Studies/Les Cahiers de La Femme*, September 1, 1995, https://cws.journals.yorku.ca/index.php/cws/article/view/9361.

12. McFarlane, Bruce, "Pioneer Female Goalie Out to Prove She Belongs | *The Hockey News* Archive," accessed July 8, 2024, https://archive.thehockeynews.com/issue/613778/657475?t=Pioneer%20female%20goalie%20out%20to%20prove%20she%20belongs.

13. Canadian Press, "It's No Longer a Boys' League," *The Hamilton Spectator*, January 23, 2002.

14. Fowler, Annie, "She's Breaking the Ice," *Tri-City Herald*, August 30, 2002

15. Campbell, Ken, "Canada's Wickenheiser First Woman to Try Flyer | *The Hockey News* Archive," accessed July 8, 2024, https://archive.thehockeynews.com/issue/613714/600985?t=Canada%E2%80%99s%20Wickenheiser%2 0first%20woman%20to%20try%20Flyer.

16. Spencer, Donna, "Looking to Be the Best," *Regina Leader-Post*, November 5, 2002.

17. Adams, Alan, "Women Welcome in Sweden," *The Hockey News*, January 31, 2003.

18. Editorial Staff, "Fasel's Paternalism Disservice to Women | *The Hockey News* Archive," accessed July 8, 2024, https://archive.thehockeynews.com/issue/613941/715439?t=Fasel%E2%80%99s%20paternalism%20disservice%20to%20women.

19. Doyle, Matt, "Sister, Brother Hit Ice as Teammates," *Tulsa World*, January 28, 2005.

20. Overall, Michael, "Publicity Is Just Icing on the Cake," *Tulsa World*, January 27, 2005.

21. Doyle, Matt, "Making Her Mark," *Tulsa World*, January 29, 2005.

22. Brophy, Mike, "Rugged Ruggiero Makes Her Point | *The Hockey News* Archive," accessed July 8, 2024, https://archive.thehockeynews.com/issue/614028/736478?t=Rugged%20Ruggiero%20makes%20her%20 point.

23. "Battle of the Sexes Tennis Match | Billie Jean King," Billie Jean King Enterprises, accessed June 22, 2024, https://www.billiejeanking.com/battle-of-the-sexes/.

Chapter 18: Bench Strength

1. St. James, Helen, "How Marguerite Norris, Colleen Howe and Marian Ilitch Shaped Detroit Red Wings," *Detroit Free Press,* February 27, 2022.

2. Allen and Roenick, *Star-Spangled Hockey*.

3. Aykroyd, Lucas, "Growing Up Granato: An American Legend Recalls," April 3, 2007, https://www.hockeycanada.ca/en-ca/news/2007-wwc-033-en.

4. Hersh, Philip, "A Deep Cut for Granato," *Chicago Tribune*, September 12, 2005.

5. Proteau, Adam, "IIHF President Fasel's Defense of Women's Olympic Hockey a Welcome Sight," *The Hockey News*, February 18, 2014, https://thehockeynews.com/news/iihf-president-fasels-defense-of-womens-olympic-hockey-a-welcome-sight.
6. Stevens, Julie. Pg 147
7. Spencer, Donna, "Canada's MacLeod Lends Hockey Expertise to Japanese Women for Sochi 2014," *The Globe and Mail*, February 16, 2013, https://www.theglobeandmail.com/sports/hockey/canadas-macleod-lends-hockey-expertise-to-japanese-women-for-sochi-2014/article8773348/.
8. Brady, Rachel, "With a Former Canadian Star Helping Out, Japan Dreams Big," *The Globe and Mail*, March 11, 2013, https://www.theglobeandmail.com/sports/hockey/with-a-former-canadian-star-helping-out-japan-dreams-big/article9652592/.
9. Long, Wendy, "Vancouver Woman Axes into College Hockey Scene," *Vancouver Sun*, November 22, 1991.
10. Depner, Wolf, "Blue Line. Red Cross," *The Ubyssey*, March 3, 1998.
11. Depner, Wolf.
12. Berenyi, Valerie, "Exercising for Two No Longer Taboo," *The Edmonton Journal*, April 11, 2011.
13. Jurevicz, Chris, "A Life in Love with Hockey," accessed July 11, 2024, https://www.hockeycanada.ca/en-ca/news/2021-iwd-bennion-lives-a-life-in-love-with-hockey.

Chapter 19: Breakaways

1. Rutherford, Kristina, "Questions, Frustration Remain in Wake of CWHL's Decision to Fold," Sportsnet, March 31, 2019, https://www.sportsnet.ca/hockey/nhl/questions-frustration-remain-wake-cwhls-decision-fold/.
2. Editorial Staff, "PHF Releases Official Statement On New League," *The Hockey News*, June 30, 2023, https://thehockeynews.com/womens/pwhl/phf-releases-official-statement-on-new-league.
3. Kennedy, Ian, "'United Stronger'-PHF Players Release Statement," *The Hockey News*, July 2, 2023, https://thehockeynews.com/womens/pwhl/united-stronger-phf-players-release-statement.
4. Leavitt, Stacey and Carly Adams, "Troubling the Road to the NWHL and Professional Women's Hockey," in *The Professionalisation of Women's Sport: Issues and Debates* (Emerald Publishing Limited, 2021), https://www.perlego.com/book/2419628/the-professionalisation-of-womens-sport-issues-and-debates-pdf.
5. McKee, Taylor, "Rewriting the Rule Books: Ensuring Gender Equity in Canadian Hockey," The Conversation, June 22, 2022, http://theconversation.com/rewriting-the-rule-books-ensuring-gender-equity-in-canadian-hockey-183901.
6. Aykroyd, Lucas, "IIHF -What's next for the Women's Game?," IIHF International Ice Hockey Federation, February 27, 2022, https://www.iihf.com/en/events/2022/olympic-w/news/32242/what_s_next_for_the_women_s_game.
7. Steiss, Adam, "IIHF -Addressing Tournament Cancellations," IIHF International Ice Hockey Federation, December 29, 2021, https://www.iihf.com/en/news/31418/addressing_tournament_cancellations.

Sources

Adams, Carly. "Organizing Hockey for Women: The Ladies Ontario Hockey Association and the Fight for Legitimacy, 1922-1940." In *Coast to Coast: Hockey in Canada to the Second World War*, 132–59. University of Toronto Press, 2009.

Adams, Carly, "'Queens of the Ice Lanes': The Preston Rivulettes and Women's Hockey in Canada, 1931–1940," *Sport History Review* 39 (2008): 1–29

Adams, Carly, "Troubling Bodies: 'The Canadian Girl,' the Ice Rink, and the Banff Winter Carnival," *Journal of Canadian Studies* 48, no. 3 (2014): Pg. 200–220.

Adams, Carly and Julie Stevens, "Change and Grassroots Movement: Reconceptualising Women's Hockey Governance in Canada," *International Journal of Sport Management and Marketing* 2, no. 4 (May 23, 2007)

Allen, Kevin and Jeremy Roenick, *Star-Spangled Hockey: Celebrating 75 Years of USA Hockey* (Chicago, Ill.: USA Hockey: Triumph Books, 2011).

Bell, Richard C., "A History of Women in Sport Prior to Title IX," *The Sport Journal*, March 14, 2008.

Bishop, Rachel, "No Coward Plays Hockey," Electronic Thesis and Dissertation Repository, September 26, 2019, https://ir.lib.uwo.ca/etd/6575.

Brake, Deborah "The Struggle for Sex Equality in Sport and the Theory Behind Title IX," *University of Michigan Journal of Law Reform* 34 (2001), https://scholarship.law.pitt.edu/fac_articles/2.

Byng, Evelyn Moreton, Viscountess. *Up the Stream of Time.* Toronto: Macmillan, 1945.

Carpenter, Ross. "LEGENDS | Women's Hockey." Legends of Australian Ice. Accessed August 28, 2024. https://icelegendsaustralia.com/1stIceChampions-whockey.html.

Etue, Elizabeth and Megan K. Williams, *On the Edge : Women Making Hockey History* (Toronto: Second Story Press, 1996), http://archive.org/details/onedgewomenmakin0000etue.

Gershon, Livia "A Century Ago, Women Played Ice Hockey," *JSTOR Daily*, January 2, 2020, https://daily.jstor.org/a-century-ago-women-played-ice-hockey/.

K. Gilenstam, S. Karp, and K. Henriksson-Larsén, "Gender in Ice Hockey: Women in a Male Territory," *Scandinavian Journal of Medicine & Science in Sports* 18, no. 2 (2008): 235–49, https://doi.org/10.1111/j.1600-0838.2007.00665.x.

Hall, M. Ann, *Immodest & Sensational: 150 Years of Canadian Women in Sport* (Toronto, Ont: James Lorimer Pub, 2008)

Hardy, Stephen, and Andrew C. Holman. *Hockey: A Global History.* Sport and Society. Urbana Chicago Springfield: University of Illinois Press, 2018.

Holman, Andrew C. "Stops and Starts: Ideology, Commercialism and the Fall of American Women's Hockey in the 1920s." *History Faculty Publications*, no. Paper 5 (January 2005): 330–41.

Leavitt, Stacey and Carly Adams, "Troubling the Road to the NWHL and Professional Women's Hockey," in *The Professionalisation of Women's Sport: Issues and Debates* (Emerald Publishing Limited, 2021), https://www.perlego.com/book/2419628/the-professionalisation-of-womens-sport-issues-and-debates-pdf.

McFarlane, Brian, *Proud Past, Bright Future: One Hundred Years of Canadian Women's Hockey* (Toronto: Stoddart, 1994)

McKee, Taylor, "Rewriting the Rule Books: Ensuring Gender Equity in Canadian Hockey," The Conversation, June 22, 2022, http://theconversation.com/rewriting-the-rule-books-ensuring-gender-equity-in-canadian-hockey-183901.

"Minutes of the 38th Ontario Hockey Association Meeting." OHA Papers. Library and Archives Canada, November 19, 1927. M2308.

National Women's History Museum. "Women's Sports History," August 4, 2016. https://www.womenshistory.org/articles/womens-sports-history.

PEI Sports Hall of Fame. "Summerside Crystal Sisters -Team -Hockey," January 24, 2022. https://peisportshalloffame.ca/summerside-crystal-sisters-team-hockey/.

Reid, Patrick Alexander. "The First Women's World Ice Hockey Championship and the Emergence of the Routine of Women's Elite Hockey." University of Alberta, 2018. https://era.library.ualberta.ca/items/1b1deaa9-0c37-4529-88e3-51dc8b568a32/view/7b39b1e0-fd11-4893-a057-240fa83a8557/Reid_Patrick_A_2018March29_PhD.pdf.

Stevens, Julie. "Thirty Years of 'Going Global': Women's International Hockey, Cultural Diplomacy, and the Pursuit of Excellence." In *Hockey: Challenging Canada's Game Au-Delà Du Sport National*, edited by Ellison, Jenny and Anderson, Jennifer. University of Ottawa Press, 2018.

Syers, E. (Edgar), and Mrs Madge Syers. *The Book of Winter Sports*. London: E. Arnold, 1908. http://archive.org/details/bookofwinterspor00syer.

Taylor, Rhonda Leeman, "A Glorious Game: The History of Women's Hockey | Women's Hockey Life," September 11, 2019, https://womenshockeylife.com/womens-hockey-history/.

Theberge, Nancy, "Playing with the Boys: Manon Rheaume, Women's Hockey, and the Struggle for Legitimacy," *Canadian Woman Studies/Les Cahiers de La Femme*, September 1, 1995,

Varpalotai, Aniko. "Sport, Leisure and the Adolescent Girl: Single Sex vs. Co-Ed?" *Canadian Woman Studies/Les Cahiers de La Femme*, September 1, 1995. https://cws.journals.yorku.ca/index.php/cws/article/view/9360.

Weaving, Charlene, and Samuel Roberts. "Checking In: An Analysis of the (Lack of) Body Checking in Women's Ice Hockey." *Research Quarterly for Exercise and Sport* 83, no. 3 (September 1, 2012): 470–78. https://doi.org/10.1080/02701367.2012.10599882.

Young, Iris Marion, *Throwing like a Girl and Other Essays in Feminist Philosophy and Social Theory* (Bloomington: Indiana University Press, 1990).

Index

Want more little-known hockey stories?

Meet . . .

- Boomer Harding, the first Black player in the International Amateur Hockey League
- The Chin brothers, a trio of talented players who gave Paul Henderson his start
- Eddie Wright, the first Black coach in NCAA hockey history
- Herb and Mel Wakabayashi, who left their Canadian town to become stars in Japan
- Shirley Huff, an Indigenous athlete who used hockey to break barriers

In *On Account of Darkness: Shining Light on Race and Sport*, Ian Kennedy combines tales of personal triumph with sports history and social commentary to examine systemic racism and ambivalent attitudes that persist to this day.

"*On Account of Darkness* is a book we can all learn from. Overcoming obstacles such as racism as well as prejudice from different minorities. These are the truths that need to be heard across the globe."
    BRIGETTE LACQUETTE, Indigenous hockey player and Olympian

Available from booksellers everywhere or from the publisher, tidewaterpress.ca